À vos marques!

A Communicative Grammar Worktext with Written and Oral Practice

Phil Turk

Geneviève García Vandaele

National Textbook Company
a division of NTC/CONTEMPORARY PUBLISHING GROUP
Lincolnwood, Illinois USA

Acknowledgments

As with *Action Grammaire!,* this book owes much to the Bradford on Avon–
Sully-sur-Loire sister cities association. Our thanks to our many friends in both
towns and in their sister cities association, who have given us their support
and encouragement, and who may, unwittingly, have lent their names to some
of the "characters" in this book. Our thanks also to Liz Gibson, for reading
the manuscript and offering some valuable suggestions, and to other teachers
in the Bradford on Avon and Sully-sur-Loire areas for their valuable input.
Thanks also to Brenda Turk for her customary support and help with
proofreading.

ISBN: 0-658-00120-5

This edition first published 2001 by National Textbook Company,
a division of NTC/Contemporary Publishing Group, Inc.,
4255 West Touhy Avenue,
Lincolnwood (Chicago), Illinois 60712-1975 U.S.A.
©1998 by Phil Turk and Geneviève García Vandaele

00 01 02 03 04 05 06 07 08 09 VHG 0 9 8 7 6 5 4 3 2 1

Contents

Introduction

To the teacher

À vos marques! is an organized method of presenting, reviewing, and practicing French grammar for high school students. Each of the main chapters is divided into three sections: *À vos marques!* explains the grammar point clearly in simple English and provides examples, advice, and cautions; *Prêts?* offers reinforcement exercises on each point; and *Partez!* provides a variety of oral and/or written activities in which the particular grammar point occurs naturally. To the extent possible, the exercises and activities in the *Prêts?* and *Partez!* sections are designed to supplement and enrich material presented in most basal textbooks.

Although the grammar explanation comes first in each regular chapter, it is expected that students will have encountered most of the grammar points already in their basal textbooks and that this worktext will be used for consolidation, review, and reference. The *Prêts?* section contains traditional exercises, such as fill-in-the blanks, to practice the principal grammar points covered in the chapter. The *Partez!* section contains communicative activities for independent, but guided, application of the grammar. These activities are suitable for oral or written practice for independent, pair, or group work. The exercises are informally graded in difficulty with a ✪ denoting those that require a higher level of ability.

The last two chapters cover topics that are often challenging for students: negative expressions and the present subjunctive.

To the student

This worktext is called *À vos marques!* because
it helps get you ready to communicate in French
by learning and practicing the elements of French
grammar. Contrary to popular belief, learning
grammar can be fun, which is a good thing, because
grammar is the foundation for understanding how
a language works. You've probably had plenty of
practice in speaking, reading, listening, and maybe writing; but you may still be a little shaky
on some of the verb tenses, prepositions, adjective agreements, and other points of grammar.
This book is designed to help you understand and use the building blocks of French.

Each chapter in *À vos marques!* is divided into three sections, representing "Ready! Set! Go!"
at the start of the race. First, you'll find the section *À vos marques!,* in which each grammar
point is explained in simple English and is backed up with plenty of examples. Then you'll
see the first activity section, *Prêts?,* with exercises that help strengthen and reinforce your
understanding and get you ready to use the language on your own. The second activity section
is *Partez!* with role-play activities, conversation starters, a few games, and some "real-life"
writing situations. In these activities, you and your classmates apply what you have learned—
and build your confidence as well—in your race to become proficient in French.

People and Things
nouns

 *À vos marques!*

What is a noun?

A noun tells you what something is or who someone is. It can be a person, an animal, a thing, a country, an idea: Jean-Pierre, a girl, a boy, a teacher, a dog, a pen, a book, rain, France, pollution, a moment, etc.

Gender

One of the main differences between French and English nouns is that in French **every** noun, whether it is alive or not, is either **masculine** or **feminine.** So, for example, *un livre* "book," *un verre* "glass," *un bus* "bus" are masculine, and *une table* "table," *une glace* "ice cream," *une tasse* "cup" are feminine. You can see that the indefinite article (the word meaning "a" or "an") changes according to which gender the noun is. In fact, this is so important, you should learn each new noun with either *un/une* or the definite article *le/la* (= "the").

People and animals

■ Male people and common male animals are usually masculine: *un homme* "man," *un garçon* "boy," *un boulanger* "baker (male)," *un conducteur* "driver (male)," *un taureau* "bull," *un chat* "cat (male)."

■ Female people and common female animals are usually feminine: *une femme* "woman," *une fille* "girl," *une boulangère* "baker (female)," *une conductrice* "driver (female)," *une vache* "cow," *une chatte* "cat (female)."

⊙|⊙ Attention!

> Grammatical **gender** doesn't always correspond to the actual **sex** of
> the person or animal in question. For example, some professions where
> the noun doesn't change form are grammatically masculine: ***un** professeur*
> "teacher (male or female)," ***un** médecin* "doctor (male or female)."
> On the other hand, ***une** personne* "person (male or female)," ***une** vedette*
> "star of stage or screen" are always feminine. The same thing happens
> with the majority of animals: ***un** éléphant*, ***un** singe* "monkey," ***une** girafe*.

Mainly masculine

The following nouns are masculine:

- Days, months, and seasons: *le lundi, un janvier très froid, un été chaud.*

- Weights and measures: *un kilo, un kilogramme, un demi-litre, un kilomètre.*

- Languages: *le français, l'allemand.*

- Trees: *un arbre, un pommier, un poirier.*

- Most nouns ending in:

  -age: un voyage, un garage, quel âge avez-vous? **NOT** *une cage, une page, une plage*

  -eau: un château, un gâteau. **NOT** *l'eau, la peau* "skin"

As a general guide, nouns ending in a **consonant** (*c, f, l, m, n, r, s, t, x, z*) tend to be masculine, though some are feminine: *une clef, une main, une souris.*

The following nouns ending in *-e* that you are likely to need are also masculine: *un centre, un dictionnaire, un échange, un groupe, un incendie, un lycée, un musée, un nombre, un rôle, un service, un siècle, un signe, un verbe, un vocabulaire.*

Mainly feminine

The following nouns are feminine:

- Nouns ending in *-ion: une destination, une invitation, la pollution, la télévision* (most correspond to English words also ending in "-ion," especially "-ation," "-ution"). **NOT** *un avion* "plane," *un camion* "truck."

- Nouns ending in *-té: l'électricité, une nationalité, une université, la vérité* "truth" (most correspond to English words ending in *-ty*).

- Many words ending in *-e,* including:

  Continents, countries, and rivers: *l'Europe, la France, la Seine, la Loire;*

  Fruits and vegetables: *une pomme, une cerise, une carotte;*

  Shops ending in *-erie* or *-ie: une boulangerie, une crêperie, une pharmacie;*

Nouns ending in *-te* or *-tte: une cravate, une omelette;*

School subjects ending in *-ie: la géographie, la biologie;* also *l'histoire, les maths (mathématiques).*

Conseil!

There are thousands of nouns ending in *-e* in French, and the tendency is for them to be feminine. However, there are quite a lot which are masculine: so always check in a dictionary if in doubt!

Making nouns plural

When you have more than one of a noun, it is plural.

Regular plurals

The usual way to make a noun plural in French is to write an *-s* on the end:

train	*trains*	train/s
chaussure	*chaussures*	shoe/s
avion	*avions*	plane/s
élève	*élèves*	student/s
chemise	*chemises*	shirt/s
magasin	*magasins*	shop/s

Ojo Attention!

However, since you don't usually sound the last consonant(s) of a word, this *-s* usually makes no difference to the pronunciation of the word. Therefore you have to listen for or say **something else** which indicates that the noun is plural. This is usually indicated by a changing *le/la/l'* to *les,* or *un/une* to *des,* or by a number:

le train	***les** trains*
la chaussure	***les** chaussures*
l'avion	***les** avions*
un élève	***des** élèves*
une chemise	***des** chemises*
un magasin	***trois** magasins*

Practice these examples and note how it is the **beginning, and not the end,** of the spoken phrase that tells you it is plural!

This also happens with the demonstratives *ce/cette/ces* (see Chapter 6) and the possessives *mon/ma/mes,* etc. (see Chapter 7).

Plurals that don't behave: irregular plurals

■ Nouns ending in *-s, -x, -z* don't add anything in the plural:

un bus	*des bus*	bus/es
un choix	*deux choix*	choice/s
le nez	*les nez*	nose/s

■ Nouns ending in *-eau, -au* and most ending in *-eu* add *-x:*

un gâteau	*des gâteaux*	cake/s
un cadeau	*des cadeaux*	gift/s, present/s
un tuyau	*des tuyaux*	pipe/s
un feu	*des feux*	fire/s
un jeu	*des jeux*	game/s

But **NOT** *pneu/pneus* tire/s

■ Some nouns ending in *-ou,* but not all, add *-x:*

le bijou	*les bijoux*	jewel/s
le chou	*les choux*	cabbage/s
le chou-fleur	*les choux-fleurs*	cauliflower/s
le genou	*les genoux*	knee/s

But:

le clou	*les clous*	nail/s
le trou	*les trous*	hole/s

■ Most nouns ending in *-al* change to *-aux:*

un journal	*des journaux*	newspaper/s
un animal	*des animaux*	animal/s
un cheval	*des chevaux*	horse/s

■ One noun is totally irregular:

un œil	*des yeux*	eye/s

Prêts?

▶1 Casse-tête touristique

Voici une liste de 20 noms trouvés dans un dépliant touristique. Classez-les en deux groupes: masculin et féminin, en mettant *le, la, l'* ou *les* devant ces noms. Essayez de le faire d'abord sans dictionnaire!

Here's a list of 20 nouns you might find in a tourist brochure. Put them into two groups: masculine and feminine, and put *le, la, l',* or *les* before them as appropriate. Try to do it without a dictionary first!

1. _____ tourisme		11. _____ piscine
2. _____ pension		12. _____ promenade
3. _____ voiture		13. _____ automne
4. _____ circulation		14. _____ avion
5. _____ hôtel		15. _____ cadeau
6. _____ voyage		16. _____ pique-nique
7. _____ station-service		17. _____ kilomètre
8. _____ musée		18. _____ boisson
9. _____ garage		19. _____ réception
10. _____ bagages		20. _____ plage

▶2 Quel est l'intrus?

Dans chacune de ces listes de cinq mots, il y a un intrus **à cause de son genre.**
Écrivez l'intrus.

In each of these lists of five words there is one that doesn't belong **because of its gender.**
Write the word that doesn't belong.

1. fromage, garage, page, visage, péage _____

2. château, gâteau, tableau, cadeau, eau _____

3. camion, question, manifestation, exposition, profession _____

4. poupée, musée, soirée, entrée, année _____

5. poire, cerise, pommier, fraise, framboise _____

6. carotte, salade, concombre, tomate, pomme de terre _____

7. église, gare, place, rue, passage clouté _____

8. sécurité, nationalité, marché, santé, amitié _____

▶ **3 Les courses**

Votre correspondant en France vous écrit, en décrivant les courses qu'il fait pour sa mère. Mais il a de grands problèmes avec les terminaisons des noms! Corrigez-les-lui! (Il y en a quinze.)

Your pen pal in France writes to you, describing the shopping he does for his mom. But he has big problems with his noun endings! Correct them for him! (There are 15.)

Ce matin je suis allé acheter trois baguette fraîches, six croissant et les journal du dimanche, mail il n'y avait pas de tarte aux fruit, alors j'ai pris des gâteau au chocolat. Et puis je suis allé dans le magasin de jouet pour acheter des cadeau pour mes parent et des poupée avec des longs cheveu pour ma cousine Sophie. Demain je vais chez le marchand de légume pour acheter des carotte, des chou verts et des laitue.

1. _____	9. _____
2. _____	10. _____
3. _____	11. _____
4. _____	12. _____
5. _____	13. _____
6. _____	14. _____
7. _____	15. _____
8. _____	

Partez!

▶ **4 En classe**

La classe est divisée en deux équipes. Chaque élève doit nommer quelque chose qu'il/elle voit, avec *un/une* ou *le/la*. Si le genre est correct, il/elle gagne un point.

Divide the class into two teams. Each student has to name something he or she can see, with *un/une* or *le/la*. If the gender is correct, he or she gains a point.

▶ **5 Au grand magasin**

a. Chaque élève doit dire ce qu'il/elle a acheté au grand magasin, mais les articles doivent alterner entre masculin et féminin.

Each student has to say what he or she bought in the department store, but the articles must alternate between masculine and feminine.

Exemple:

Élève 1:   Moi, j'ai acheté un ballon.
Élève 2:   Et moi, une raquette.
Élève 3:   Et moi, un maillot de bain.
Élève 4:   J'ai acheté des chaussures.

b. Essayer de répéter tout ce que les autres élèves ont acheté.

Try repeating all that the students before have bought.

Exemple:

Nous avons acheté un ballon; nous avons acheté un ballon et une raquette, etc.

▶ **6** Cours de géographie

Regardez une carte d'Europe, de préférence en français. Prenez note des noms des pays principaux (cherchez-les dans un dictionnaire si votre carte est en anglais). Quels sont les pays européens qui sont masculins? (Il y en a très peu!) Écrivez les noms ici.

Look at a map of Europe, preferably in French. Jot down the names of the main countries (look them up in a dictionary if your map is in English). Which European countries are masculine? (There aren't many!) Write the names here.

_____

_____

_____

_____

▶ **7** Vous vous préparez pour aller en France

La semaine prochaine vous allez chez votre correspondant(e) en France. Vous aurez besoin de vêtements et d'articles de toilette, et aussi de choses à offrir à sa famille. Faites une liste des choses dont vous aurez besoin en indiquant combien il en faudra.

Next week you are going to stay with your French pen pal. You'll need clothes, toilet articles, and also gifts for his or her family. Make a list of articles and how many you will need.

Exemple:

cinq chemises, deux shorts, deux paquets de thé, etc.

_____

_____

_____

_____

2 "A," "The," and "Some"
articles and expressions of quantity

À vos marques!

What is an article?

"Article" is the name given to the words for:

1. "A/an" = **indefinite** article: a house, an orange. It's called "indefinite" because it doesn't refer to a particular house or orange.

2. "The" = **definite** article: the house, the orange. It's called "definite" because you know which house or orange you are talking about.

3. "Some/any" = the **partitive** article, because it only refers to "some" or "part" of what you are talking about: **some** houses (not **all** houses), give me **some** orange (not **all** of it), or **some** oranges (not **all** of them).

The definite article: *le/la/l'/les*

The French for "the" is:

■ *Le* for a masculine singular noun: *le lait* "**the** milk," *le frère* "**the** brother."

■ *La* for a feminine singular noun: *la glace* "**the** ice cream," *la sœur* "**the** sister."

■ *L'* for a masculine or feminine singular noun beginning with a vowel or *h* (in most cases): *l'arrêt* "**the** stop," *l'église* "**the** church," *l'homme* "**the** man," *l'heure* "**the** time."

■ *Les* for all plural nouns: *les frères* "**the** brothers," *les sœurs* "**the** sisters," *les glaces* "**the** ice creams." The *-s* is pronounced *-z* before a vowel or an *h: les‿arrêts* "**the** stops," *les‿églises* "**the** churches," *les‿hommes* "**the** men."

Ojo Attention!

1. Remember that it is the sound of the article that shows that the noun is plural: you don't sound the -*s* or -*x* on the end of the noun!

2. There are a few nouns beginning with *h* where you both say and write *le/la* in full: *le haricot* "bean," *la haie* "hedge." You do not pronounce the -*s* of *les* in the plural: *les haricots, les haies.* Learn these as you meet them—there are not many!

3. This article always combines with *à* ("to," "at") and *de* ("of," "from") as follows:

    à + *le* = *au* (*au cinéma* "**to/at the** cinema," *au centre-ville* "downtown")
    à + *les* = *aux* (*aux portes* "**to/at the** doors," *aux femmes* "**to the** women")

    But *à l'* and *à la* are not affected.

    de + *le* = *du* (*la porte du salon* "the door **of the** living room")
    de + *les* = *des* (*les portes des maisons* "the doors **of the** houses")

    But *de l'* and *de la* are not affected.

    This is also the form of the partitive article (see below).

How do you use the definite article?

You use it as in English, but remember also to use it:

■ With the names of countries and languages, except after *en:*

La France est plus grande que l'Angleterre.	**France** is bigger than **England.**
Nous allons en Allemagne.	We're going **to Germany.**
Nous avons des dépliants en allemand.	We've got some leaflets **in German.**

■ When you talk about things in general:

Les routes françaises sont larges.	French roads are wide.
Je n'aime pas le poisson.	I don't like fish.

■ When you **talk about** or **do something** to a part of the body:

Je me suis brûlé la main.	I burned **my** hand.
Il faut ouvrir la bouche.	You must open **your** mouth.
Elle a les yeux bleus.	She has blue eyes.

■ Meaning "per" with measures:

Les pommes sont à 11 francs le kilo.	Apples are 11 francs **a/per** kilo.

The indefinite article: *un/une/des*

The French for "a/an" is:

- *Un* before a masculine singular noun: ***un** paquet* "**a** packet," ***un** garçon* "**a** boy." The *-n* is pronounced when the noun begins with a vowel or *h-*: *un‿arrêt* "a stop," *un‿homme* "a man" (**not** in *un haricot*—see the Attention! box on p. 9).

- *Une* before a feminine singular noun: ***une** bouteille* "**a** bottle," ***une** fille* "**a** girl."

- Before a plural noun, *des* "some" is used. This is a form of the partitive article, which is explained fully in a subsequent section.

How do you use the indefinite article?

You use the indefinite article roughly as in English, except that:

- You don't use it with professions and occupations after *être* "to be" and *devenir* "to become":

*Mon oncle **est ingénieur**,*	My uncle **is an** engineer,
*mais son fils **est devenu professeur**.*	but his son **became a** teacher.

  However, you use *un(e)* if there is an adjective describing the occupation:

*Alexandre Eiffel était **un** ingénieur **célèbre**.*	Alexandre Eiffel was **a famous** engineer.

- It usually becomes *de* after a negative verb. Compare:

*J'ai acheté **un** cadeau pour ma sœur.*	I've bought **a** present for my sister.
*Je n'ai pas acheté **de** cadeau pour ma sœur.*	I haven't bought **a** present for my sister.

  This also happens with the partitive article: see the following section.

The partitive article: *du / de la / de l' / des*

This article means "some" or "any" and has the following forms:

- Masculine singular—*du*: ***du** sucre* "**some** sugar," ***du** parfum* "**some** perfume."

- Feminine singular—*de la*: ***de la** crème* "**some** cream," ***de la** pluie* "**some** rain."

- Singular before a vowel or *h*—*de l'*: ***de l'***argent* "**some** money," ***de l'***eau* "**some** water."

- Plural—*des*: ***des** enfants* "**some** children," ***des** fraises* "**some** strawberries."

How do you use the partitive article?

It means "some" or "any":

*Avez-vous **du** lait, s'il vous plaît?*	Do you have **any** milk, please?
*Je voudrais aussi **de la** confiture.*	I'd also like **some** jam.
*Tu veux **de l'**omelette?*	Would you like **some** omelette?
*Nous avons vu **des** oiseaux sur le lac.*	We saw **some** birds on the lake.

⊙ⅉⵘ Attention!

1. It is very seldom that a noun can be used in French without some kind of article, and this partitive article often has to be used where we would not use any in English.

    *Je vais au supermarché acheter **du** jambon, **des** pommes, **de l'**eau minérale, **du** papier hygiénique, **du** shampooing . . .*
    I'm going to the supermarket to buy ham, apples, mineral water, toilet paper, shampoo . . .

    *Tu aimerais mieux **du** café ou **du** thé?*
    Would you prefer coffee or tea?

2. Like *un/une/des* in the section on the indefinite article above, this article usually becomes simply *de* after a negative verb:

    *Je ne veux pas **de** café.*   I don't want (**any**) coffee.
    *Il n'y a pas **de** trains aujourd'hui.*   There aren't **any** trains today.
    *Je n'ai pas eu **de** problèmes.*   I haven't had **any** problems.

3. You also use the form *de* after most expressions of quantity, such as *combien de?* "how much/many?" *beaucoup de* "much/many, a lot of," *assez de* "enough, quite a lot of," *peu de* "few, not many," *un peu de* "a little, a bit," *trop de* "too much, too many"; and also weights, measures, containers: *un demi-kilo de, une bouteille de, une boîte de,* etc.

    ***Combien de** timbres voulez-vous?*   **How many** stamps do you want?
    *Il y a **trop de** monde ici.*   There are **too many** people here.
    *J'ai **très peu d'**argent.*   I have **very little** money.
    *Je voudrais **une bouteille d'**eau minérale.*   I'd like **a bottle of** mineral water.

    This last rule does not apply after *encore du / de la / des* "more of" and *la plupart de / de la / des* "the majority of," "most of":

    *Est-ce que tu veux **encore de la** salade?*   Do you want **any more** salad?

Prêts?

▶1 Quel travail!

Vous travaillez comme jeune fille / jeune homme au pair dans une famille française. Ils ont laissé une liste des choses à faire. Comme vous n'avez pas très envie de commencer, vous vous amusez à remettre les articles définis *le, la, l', les* dans la liste!

You are working as an au pair in a French family. They have left you a list of things to do. Because you don't much feel like starting, you amuse yourself by putting the definite articles *le, la, l', les* in the list!

sortir **(1)** _____ chien

faire **(2)** _____ vaisselle

passer **(3)** _____ aspirateur

faire **(4)** _____ courses

acheter **(5)** _____ journal

nettoyer **(6)** _____ cage des canaris

appeler **(7)** _____ garagiste

repasser **(8)** _____ chemises

aller voir **(9)** _____ voisine

aller chercher **(10)** _____ enfants au CES

préparer **(11)** _____ dîner

▶2 L'anniversaire

Votre correspondant français est maintenant chez vous aux États-Unis. Son père lui écrit, mais il a omis tous les articles dans sa lettre. Ajoutez-les!

Your pen pal is staying with you in the United States. His father writes to him, but he has left all the articles out of his letter. Put them in!

Ma chère Antoinette,

Aujourd'hui je suis libre et seul, et c'est pourquoi j'ai décidé de t'envoyer (1) _____ lettre. J'ai oublié d'y mettre tous (2) _____ articles pour faire un petit exercice de français pour ton ami(e).

Comme tu sais, hier c'était (3) _____ anniversaire de ta mère et je lui ai fait (4) _____ surprise. (5) _____ matin j'ai acheté des roses et (6) _____ croissants, j'ai fait (7) _____ café et je lui ai porté (8) _____ petit déjeuner (9) _____ lit. Puis vers sept heures (10) _____ soir, tante Amélie et tonton Jean sont arrivés et lui ont porté (11) _____ cadeaux: (12) _____ parfum, (13) _____ collier et (14) _____ fleurs. Plus tard dans (15) _____ soirée, nous sommes allés (16) _____ restaurant. Quel bonheur! En sortant, ta mère a levé (17) _____ mains (18) _____ visage et a pleuré de joie.

Aujourd'hui, elle fait (19) _____ voyage en Italie pour son travail.

▶**3** Pas grand-chose dans la vallée!

Zaïd est à la montagne avec son frère. Il observe la vallée avec ses jumelles. Il répond négativement aux questions de son frère. Attention à l'article partitif!

Zaïd is in the mountains with his brother. He is looking at the valley through his binoculars. He replies in the negative to his brother's questions. Take care with the partitive articles!

Exemple:

—Tu vois **des** voitures dans la vallée?
—Non, je ne vois pas / il n'y a pas **de** voitures.

1. Tu vois des usines?

   _____

2. Tu vois des gens dans les rues du village?

   _____

3. Est-ce qu'il y a des magasins?

   _____

→

4. Est-ce que tu vois de la fumée sortir des cheminées?

_____

5. Il y a un bar?

_____

6. Il y a beaucoup de maisons?

_____

7. Est-ce qu'il y a de la neige dans la vallée?

_____

8. Est-ce que tu vois des animaux dans cette vallée?

_____

Partez!

▶4 Le jour français du collège

Vous préparez votre collège pour un Jour français, et vous faites des étiquettes pour les salles, les meubles, etc.—pour tout ce qui est visible! Écrivez l'article défini devant chaque nom.

You are preparing your school for a French Day, and you are writing the labels for the rooms, furniture, etc.—for everything that's visible! Write the definite article in front of each noun.

Exemples:

le rétroprojecteur, la salle de français, les toilettes des garçons

_____

_____

_____

_____

▶5 Au magasin d'alimentation du camping

Vous et vos amis achetez des articles à manger avant de faire du camping. Chaque personne achète trois choses. Écrivez la liste ici.

You and your friends are buying food before going camping. Each person buys three things. Write the list below.

Exemple:

J'achète du pain, de la saucisse et des carottes.

_____

_____

_____

_____

▶**6** J'en ai beaucoup!

Dites si vous avez *beaucoup de, assez de, peu de* ou *pas de*—des choses suivantes.

Say whether you've got lots of, quite a lot of, not a lot of, or none of the following things.

Exemple:

J'ai beaucoup d'amis, mais je n'ai pas d'argent.

| argent | amis | livres | CD | jeux vidéo | cassettes | posters | vêtements |

Continuez avec d'autres objets de votre choix.

Continue with some other items of your choice.

_____

_____

_____

_____

_____

_____

_____

_____

_____

3 What Are They Like?
adjectives

Ā vos marques!

What is an adjective?

An adjective is a word that describes a noun: a **green** dress, an **old** man, the bread is **fresh.**

Making adjectives "agree"

In French you have to change the ending of adjectives according to the gender (masculine/feminine) and number (singular/plural) of the noun(s) they describe.

"Regular" adjectives

The form you are given in a dictionary is the masculine singular, for example, *vert* "green." To form the masculine plural you add *-s: verts.* To make the feminine singular you add *-e: verte,* and to make the feminine plural you add *-es: vertes.*

Singular		Plural	
Masculine	**Feminine**	**Masculine**	**Feminine**
un pull vert a **green** sweater	*une chemise verte* a **green** shirt	*deux pulls verts* two **green** sweaters	*deux chemises vertes* two **green** shirts

You don't add -s for masculine plural if the adjective ends in -s or -x:

Singular		Plural	
Masculine	**Feminine**	**Masculine**	**Feminine**
un film anglais an **English** movie	*un enfant heureux* a **happy** child	*des films anglais* **English** movies	*des enfants heureux* **happy** children

And you don't add -e for the feminine if the adjective ends in -e already:

Masculine	**Feminine**
un sac jaune a **yellow** bag	*une jupe jaune* a **yellow** skirt

"Irregular" adjectives

Some adjectives do not follow the above pattern:

- Adjectives ending in -al form their masculine plural in -aux: *national/nationaux, principal/principaux;* the feminine is not affected: *nationale(s).*

le sport national	the **national** sport
les sports nationaux	the **national** sports

- Adjectives ending in -el and -en double the consonant to -elle(s) and -enne(s): *naturel(s)/naturelle(s), sensationnel(s)/sensationnelle(s); italien(s)/italienne(s):*

C'est une vedette italienne sensationnelle!	She's a fantastic Italian film star!

- Adjectives ending in -eux do not add -s in the masculine plural, and form their feminine in -euse(s):

Masculine		**Feminine**		
Singular	**Plural**	**Singular**	**Plural**	
heureux *joyeux*	*heureux* *joyeux*	*heureuse* *joyeuse*	*heureuses* *joyeuses*	happy joyful

*Marie-Françoise était très **heureuse**.*   Marie-Françoise was very **happy.**

Conseil!

The following common adjectives are best learned individually:

bas	*basse*	low
épais	*épaisse*	thick
gros	*grosse*	large, fat
neuf	*neuve*	new
cher	*chère*	dear; also expensive
fier	*fière*	proud
blanc	*blanche*	white
sec	*sèche*	dry
frais	*fraîche*	fresh
bon	*bonne*	good
complet	*complète*	complete, full
inquiet	*inquiète*	worried, anxious
secret	*secrète*	secret
favori	*favorite*	favorite
long	*longue*	long
doux	*douce*	soft, gentle

*J'ai acheté une chemise **neuve**. Elle est **blanche**—ma couleur **favorite**!*
I've bought a **new** shirt. It's **white**—my **favorite** color!

■ In addition, the following adjectives have irregular forms plus a special masculine singular form before a vowel or *h*:

beau (bel)	*beaux*	*belle*	*belles*	beautiful
nouveau (nouvel)	*nouveaux*	*nouvelle*	*nouvelles*	new
fou (fol)	*fous*	*folle*	*folles*	crazy, silly
vieux (vieil)	*vieux*	*vieille*	*vieilles*	old

*C'est un **bel** enfant!*	He's a **beautiful** child!
*C'est un **vieil homme** maintenant et sa femme est **vieille** aussi.*	He's an **old** man now, and his wife is **old** as well.

■ Abbreviated adjectives don't agree: *super, sensass, extra, sympa:*

*Elsa et Muriel sont deux filles très **sympa**.*	Elsa and Muriel are two very **pleasant** girls.

Materials

There are few adjectives to describe the material something is made of, so you use *de* + the material (you might also find *en* instead of *de*):

une table de bois	a wooden table
un chemisier de soie	a silk blouse
une montre en plastique	a plastic watch
un sac en cuir	a leather handbag

The position of adjectives

Adjectives after the noun

Adjectives nearly always come **after** the noun they describe, as in nearly all the examples so far.

However, some very common ones usually come **before**: *bon* "good," *beau/belle* "beautiful," *grand* "big," *gros* "fat," *haut* "tall," *joli* "pretty," *long* "long," *mauvais* "bad," *meilleur* "better," *nouveau/nouvelle* "new," *petit* "small, little," *vieux/vieille* "old":

un bon repas	a good meal
une belle fille	a beautiful/pretty girl
une grande omelette	a large omelette
un haut bâtiment	a tall building
un joli village	a pretty village
un petit enfant	a small child
une vieille dame	an old lady

Adjectives after *être, devenir,* and *sembler*

The adjective still has to agree with the noun it describes, even if it is separated from it by a verb such as *être* "to be," *devenir* "to become," or *sembler* "to seem":

Juliette *était* **ravie** *de ses cadeaux.*	**Juliette** was **delighted** with her gifts.
La terre *est devenue* **sèche.**	**The land** became **dry.**
Les enfants *semblent* **fatigués.**	**The children** seem **tired.**

"Determiner" adjectives

"Determiner" adjectives are words like "this," "that" (demonstratives, see Chapter 6), "my," "your," and so forth (possessives, see Chapter 7), and the following words, which are adjectives. Note the need to agree where stated:

■ *Chaque* "each, every" (always singular, so no changes needed):

chaque *fille et* **chaque** *garçon*	**each** girl and **each** boy

There is also a pronoun form *chacun/chacune* "each one":

Chacun** de ses **garçons** et **chacune** de ces **filles.	**Each one** of these **boys** and **each one** of these **girls.**

■ *Tout, toute, tous, toutes* "all":

***Tous** les trains vont à Paris.*	**All** the trains go to Paris.
*J'ai mangé **toute** la tarte!*	I've eaten **all** the tart / the **whole** tart!

Note also: *tout* as a pronoun means "everything":

*Nous avons **tout** vu.*	We've seen **everything.**

Tout le monde means "everybody" and takes a singular verb:

***Tout le monde** est arrivé.*	**Everybody** has arrived.

■ *Un tel, une telle* (singular), *de tels, de telles* (plural) "such a, such":

*Je ne crois pas **une telle** histoire!*	I don't believe **such a** story!
*Je ne crois pas **de telles** choses!*	I don't believe **such** things!

■ *Plusieurs* "several" (always plural, no different feminine form):

*Ils ont **plusieurs** enfants.*	They have **several** children.

■ *Quelques* "some, a few" (mainly used in the plural):

*J'ai apporté **quelques** vidéos.*	I've brought **a few** videos.

■ *Autre, autres* "other," *d'autres* "any other":

*Je voudrais essayer l'**autre** robe.*	I'd like to try on the **other** dress.
*Où sont les **autres** enfants?*	Where are the **other** children?
*Avez-vous **d'autres** chaussures brunes?*	Have you **any other** brown shoes?

Prêts?

▶1 Au gîte

Vous avez passé quinze jours dans un gîte rural en France. À votre départ, on vous demande de remplir un questionnaire pour donner votre avis sur le gîte. Vous le complétez, en choisissant le seul adjectif de la ligne qui s'accorde avec le nom qu'il décrit!

You've spent 2 weeks in a country cottage in France. When you leave, you are asked to fill out a questionnaire giving your opinion on the cottage. You complete it, choosing the only adjective that agrees with the noun it describes!

Chambres:	☐ bons	☐ mauvaise	☐ excellentes
Lits:	☐ mauvaises	☐ confortables	☐ bon
Cuisine:	☐ agréable	☐ très petit	☐ mauvaises
Meubles:	☐ joli	☐ confortables	☐ neuve
Ambiance:	☐ joyeuse	☐ tristes	☐ bon
Paysage:	☐ ennuyeuse	☐ jolis	☐ beau
Jeux pour les enfants:	☐ bien faits	☐ dangereuse	☐ intéressant
Parking:	☐ faciles	☐ difficiles	☐ super

▶**2 À l'école**

Votre sœur visite une école en France pour une dizaine de jours et elle vous écrit en français pour parler de son expérience. Faites accorder ses adjectifs!

Your sister is visiting a school in France for about ten days, and she writes to you in French to talk about her experience. She forgets to make her adjectives agree, so you do it for her!

L'école de ma correspondante est sensationnel **(1)** _____.

Les profs sont très amusant **(2)** _____. Avec Mme Aubriot, la prof

d'EPS (PE), on fait des exercices intéressant **(3)** _____. Mlle Fronsac,

la prof d'anglais, est très vieux **(4)** _____ mais elle est sympa

(5) _____ et ses cours sont très vivant **(6)** _____.

Bien sûr, j'ai de gros **(7)** _____ difficultés en français. La grammaire

français **(8)** _____ me semble difficile **(9)** _____.

Ce que j'adore, c'est la cantine. La nourriture est très bon **(10)** _____

et abondant **(11)** _____. La viande est frais **(12)** _____,

et les crudités sont délicieux **(13)** _____. Les desserts sont sensass

(14) _____. En un mot, je suis heureux **(15)** _____.

C'est une nouveau **(16)** _____ expérience et les écoles français

(17) _____ me semblent incroyable **(18)** _____.

▶3 Les cris du marché

Voici les cris des vendeurs au marché aux puces. Pour chaque groupe de deux cris, seul l'un des cris est correct. Choisissez le bon cri.

Here are the shouts of the vendors at the flea market. For each pair only one is correct: choose the right one.

1. **a.** Achetez cette longue robe rouge!
    b. Achetez cette rouge robe longue!

2. **a.** Venez voir ce grand lit confortable!
    b. Venez voir ce confortable grand lit!

3. **a.** Approchez! Admirez ce magique robot petit!
    b. Approchez! Admirez ce petit robot magique!

4. **a.** Approchez! Approchez!! Écoutez cette ancienne musique jolie!
    b. Approchez! Approchez!! Écoutez cette jolie musique ancienne!

5. **a.** Venez admirer ces grandes parlantes poupées!
    b. Venez admirer ces grandes poupées parlantes!

6. **a.** Venez acheter ces vieux bijoux magnifiques!
    b. Venez acheter ces vieux magnifiques bijoux!

7. **a.** Regardez cette belle chaise en bois!
    b. Regardez cette belle en bois chaise!

▶4 La famille de Romain

Voici quelques détails sur la famille de Romain. Complétez les phrases, en choisissant un des mots de la case. Utilisez chaque mot une fois seulement!

Here are some details about Romain's family. Complete the sentences by choosing one of the words from the box. Use each word once only!

Romain a deux frères. Simon habite à la maison. Son **(1)** _____ frère,

Bruno, est à l'université. Il a aussi **(2)** _____ cousins. **(3)** _____

ses cousins habitent près d'ici. Il va sans dire (*It goes without saying*), alors, qu'il a aussi

(4) _____ oncles et tantes. **(5)** _____ jour il voit au moins un

de ses cousins à l'école. Je n'ai jamais vu **(6)** _____ famille!

quelques	une telle	autre	chaque	plusieurs	tous

Partez!

▶5 Quelques portraits

Vous pouvez faire cet exercice oralement ou par écrit.

You can do this exercise orally or in writing.

a. Le père de votre correspondant(e) va vous chercher à l'aéroport, mais il ne vous connaît pas. Décrivez vous-même.

Your pen pal's father is coming to meet you at the airport, but he doesn't know you. Describe yourself.

_____

_____

_____

_____

b. Votre correspondant(e) va rencontrer un(e) de vos camarades de classe, qu'il/elle ne connaît pas. Décrivez-le/la.

Your pen pal is going to meet one of your classmates he or she doesn't know. Describe your classmate.

_____

_____

_____

_____

⭐6 Encore les cris du marché

Imaginez encore des cris des vendeurs du marché comme dans l'exercice 3.

Imagine some more market cries like those in exercise 3.

_____

_____

_____

_____

▶**7** À quoi est-ce que je pense?

Un(e) élève doit penser à un objet qui se trouve dans votre salle de classe. Les autres doivent lui poser des questions contenant au moins un adjectif. L'élève ne doit utiliser que "oui" et "non" dans ses réponses. Celui qui devine l'objet correctement pense à un autre objet, et ainsi de suite. Vous pouvez écrire vos phrases ci-dessous.

One student thinks of an object in your classroom. The others have to ask him or her questions containing at least one adjective. The student may only use *oui* or *non* in his or her replies. The one who gets the correct answer thinks of the next object. You can write your questions below.

Exemple:

—Cet objet, est-ce qu'il est grand?   —Oui.
—Il est long?   —Oui.
—Il est en bois?   —Oui.
—C'est la table du prof?   —Oui, c'est la table du prof.

_____

_____

_____

_____

_____

_____

How Do They Do That?
adverbs

À vos marques!

What is an adverb?

You already know that adjectives describe or tell you more about nouns. Adverbs tell you more about verbs, adjectives, and other adverbs.

Adverbs can be single words or groups (phrases), or they can be formed from adjectives.

Adverbs in their own right

Adverbs of time, indicating **when?** or **how often?**

maintenant	now	*souvent*	often
hier	yesterday	*toujours*	always
aujourd'hui	today	*tous les jours*	every day
demain	tomorrow	*quelquefois*	sometimes
demain après-midi	tomorrow afternoon		

Adverbs of place, indicating **where?**

ici	here	*partout*	everywhere
là	there	*dans la rue*	in the street

Adverbs of degree, indicating **how?**

très	very	*trop*	too
assez	quite	*si/tellement*	so
peu	not very		

Aujourd'hui nous allons voir le château et demain nous allons à la plage.
Today we're going to see the castle and **tomorrow** we're going to the beach.

Ces chaussures étaient trop chères. Pourquoi étaient-elles si chères?
Those shoes were **too** expensive. Why were they **so** expensive?

Adverbs formed from adjectives, ending in *-ment*

In English we can convert many adjectives to adverbs by simply adding **-ly,** possibly with
a minor spelling adjustment: "frequent" becomes "frequent**ly**," "pretty" becomes "pretti**ly**."
It is similar in French. To convert an adjective to an adverb, **make the adjective feminine
and add *-ment*:**

Masculine	Feminine		Adverb	
heureux	*heureuse*	happy	*heureuse**ment***	happi**ly**
parfait	*parfaite*	perfect	*parfaite**ment***	perfect**ly**
sévère	*sévère*	severe	*sévère**ment***	severe**ly**

¡Ojo Attention!

1. Adjectives ending in *-ant* or *-ent* (except *lent/lentement*) form
   adverbs ending in *-amment* or *-emment*:

fréquent	frequent	*fréqu**emment***	frequently
évident	evident, obvious	*évid**emment***	evidently, obviously
courant	fluent	*cour**amment***	fluently

2. The following also do not quite follow the regular pattern:

vrai	real, true	***vraiment***	really, truly
absolu	absolute	*absol**ument***	absolutely
énorme	enormous	*énorm**ément***	enormously
précis	precise	*précis**ément***	precisely
bon	good	***bien***	well
meilleur	better	***mieux***	better (see Chapter 5)

The position of adverbs

When an adverb is used to describe the action of a verb, it usually comes as close as possible to that verb:

*Est-ce que vous lisez **souvent** ce journal?*   Do you read this paper **often**?
*Michèle parle **très couramment** l'anglais.*   Michèle speaks English **very fluently.**

Prêts?

▶ 1 Comment dire la même chose

Quelquefois on peut utiliser un adverbe qui termine avec *-ment* ou une expression qui signifie la même chose. Faites correspondre les expressions de la colonne A et de la colonne B qui ont le même sens. Écrivez la lettre correcte.

Sometimes you can use an adverb ending in *-ment* or another word or phrase to mean the same thing. Match the phrases in column A with the adverbs in column B. Write the correct letter.

	A		B
_____	**1.** tout à coup	**a.**	particulièrement
_____	**2.** vite	**b.**	silencieusement
_____	**3.** surtout	**c.**	approximativement
_____	**4.** souvent	**d.**	soudainement
_____	**5.** sans bruit	**e.**	immédiatement
_____	**6.** peu à peu	**f.**	fréquemment
_____	**7.** avec soin	**g.**	excessivement
_____	**8.** trop	**h.**	rapidement
_____	**9.** à peu près	**i.**	graduellement
_____	**10.** tout de suite	**j.**	prudemment (*carefully*)

▶ 2 Un sondage

Marc fait un sondage sur les habitudes de vie des jeunes Français pour le journal de son école. Que répondent les élèves? Choisissez l'adverbe qui correspond au dessin.

Marc is conducting a survey about the lives of young French people for his school newspaper. What do the students reply? Choose the adverb which corresponds to the drawing.

1.

2.

3.

4.

5.

6.

17 Lundi	ZZZ	22h	24 Lundi	ZZZ	22h
18 mardi	ZZZ	22h	25 mardi	ZZZ	22h
19 mercredi	ZZZ	24h	26 mercredi	ZZZ	21:30h
20 Jeudi	ZZZ	22h	27 Jeudi	ZZZ	22h
21 Vendredi	ZZZ	22h	28 Vendredi	ZZZ	01:30h
22 Samedi	ZZZ	24h	29 Samedi	ZZZ	22h
23 dimanche	ZZZ	22h	30 dimanche	ZZZ	22h

1. Aimes-tu l'école? toujours—quelquefois—jamais

_____

2. Comment travailles-tu? lentement—moyennement (*moderately*) vite—rapidement

_____

3. Fais-tu du sport? peu—beaucoup—modérément (*a fair amount*)

_____

4. Comment joues-tu au tennis? bien—moyennement—mal

_____

5. Comment manges-tu? beaucoup—peu—modérément

_____

6. Te couches-tu tard? rarement—souvent—quelquefois

_____

⭐3 Promenade à vélo

Vous vous promenez à vélo dans une ville française et vous demandez votre chemin. Complétez les réponses avec les adverbes contenus dans la case.

You are going for a bike ride in a French town and you ask for directions. Complete the answers with the adverbs in the box.

—Excusez-moi, comment va-t-on à la poste, s'il vous plaît?

—Oh! Vous pouvez y aller **(1)** _____ en traversant le parc, mais roulez

   (2) _____. Il y a des enfants qui jouent dans le parc.

—Où sont-ils? Je ne les vois pas.

—**(3)** _____, mais faites attention **(4)** _____ autour

   de la camionnette du marchand de glaces.

—Est-ce que je peux aller à la poste en passant par la ville?

—Oui, mais plus **(5)** _____. Il y a des voitures qui roulent

   (6) _____; et puis, c'est **(7)** _____ un problème

   de garer son vélo; mais dans le parc, on se gare plus **(8)** _____.

—Je vous remercie, monsieur.

—De rien! Je vous félicite! Vous parlez français très **(9)** _____!

surtout	partout	dangereusement	vraiment	facilement	directement
couramment	prudemment	difficilement			

Partez!

▶4 **Ne regardez pas!**

a. Sans regarder ni les explications ni les exercices ci-dessus ni le dictionnaire, faites une liste de tous les adverbes que vous savez qui terminent en *-ment*. Qui a fait la liste la plus longue?

Without looking at the explanations or the exercise above or the dictionary, make a list of all the adverbs that you can think of ending in *-ment*. Who has made the longest list?

_____

_____

_____

_____

_____

_____

_____

b. Maintenant cherchez d'autres mots ou expressions qui veulent dire la même chose, comme dans l'exercice 1.

Now look for other words or phrases with the same meanings, as in exercise 1.

_____

_____

_____

_____

_____

_____

_____

⭐5 Un Français curieux

Travail par deux. L'un imagine les questions qu'un(e) Français(e) pourrait poser concernant les États-Unis et les Américaines, et l'autre y répond par un adverbe. Changez fréquemment de rôle! Écrivez vos questions et vos réponses ci-dessous.

In pairs. One student imagines the questions that a French person might ask about the U.S. and Americans, and the other replies with an adverb. Change roles frequently. Write your questions and your answers below.

Exemples:

—Comment joue-t-on au football américain aux États-Unis?
—Bien!

—Comment conduit-on?
—Prudemment (*carefully*)!

—Quand prend-on un petit déjeuner américain?
—Quelquefois, le dimanche.

_____

_____

_____

_____

_____

_____

_____

_____

5 "Good," "Better," "Best"

comparatives and superlatives

![A vos marques!]

À vos marques!

Comparatives

What is a comparative?

You use a comparative to compare things, people, actions, and so forth. There are three ways of making comparisons. You can say that something is:

- **easi**er (or *more* **easy**) than something else,
- *less* **easy,** or
- *as* **easy** or *not as* **easy.**

You can do the same thing in French.

More . . . (than)

In French, to say that something is **easier/more easy,** or that someone is **happier/more happy,** you use *plus* + adjective. **"Than"** is *que.*

*Le français est **plus facile que** les maths.*	French is **easier than** math.
*Marcelle est **plus heureuse que** Françoise.*	Marcelle is **happier than** Françoise.
*Je voudrais une tasse **plus grande,** s'il vous plaît.*	I'd like a **bigger** cup, please.

You can compare adverbs in exactly the same way:

*Jean-Pierre travaille **plus rapidement** que moi.*	Jean-Pierre works **faster than** I do.
*Mais Céline travaille **plus lentement.***	But Céline works **more slowly.**

ojo Attention!

The only time you do not use *plus* is with **meilleur** and **mieux,** both of which mean **"better."** Study the difference very carefully.

Meilleur is to *bon* (**adjectives**) as *mieux* is to *bien* (**adverbs**):

*un **bon** repas*	a **good** meal
*un **meilleur** repas*	a **better** meal

*Tu joues **bien**.*	You're playing **well.**
*Tu joues **mieux**.*	You're playing **better.**

In other words, use *meilleur* with a **noun,** and *mieux* with a **verb**!

You will also come across *pire,* meaning **"worse"**:

*Ici, c'est **pire**.*	Here, it's **worse.**

Less . . . (than)

To say that something is **less . . . (than),** you use *moins . . . (que).*

*Le français est **moins facile que** les maths.*	French is **less easy than** math.
*Je voudrais une tasse **moins grande,** s'il vous plaît.*	I'd like a **less large** cup, please.
*Moi, je travaille **moins rapidement que** Jean-Pierre.*	I work **less fast than** Jean-Pierre.

As . . . as, not so . . . as

To say that something is **"as . . . as"** or **"not so . . . as,"** you use *aussi . . . que,* or *ne . . . pas aussi . . . que.*

*Le français est **aussi facile que** les maths.*	French is **as easy as** math.
*Le français **n'est pas aussi facile que** les maths.*	French **is not as easy as** math.
*Tu parles anglais **aussi bien que** moi.*	You speak English **as well as** I do.
*Je **ne parle pas** français **aussi bien que** toi.*	**I don't speak** French **as well as** you.

Superlatives

What is a superlative?

A superlative is when you talk about "the easi**est,**" "the **best,**" "the **most** interesting," or "the **least** exciting."

"The easiest, the most easy"

You say this in French by using *le / la / les plus* + adjective:

*La matière **la plus facile** c'est le français.*	The **easiest** subject is French.
*Le train **le plus rapide** part à onze heures.*	The **fastest** train leaves at 11:00.
*Mes deux frères sont les enfants **les plus méchants** de la classe.*	My two brothers are the **naughtiest** children in the class.
*Sauvigny est **le plus joli** village de la région.*	Sauvigny is the **prettiest** village in the area.

o|o Attention!

1. When the adjective comes after the noun (in most cases), you repeat *le/la/les* to correspond with the gender of the noun.

2. The superlative is always followed by *de* when you talk about "the naughtiest **in** the class" *les plus méchants **de** la classe,* "the prettiest **in** the area" *le plus joli **de** la région,* and so forth.

3. With an adverb you use *le plus* + adverb:

*Jean-Pierre travaille **le plus rapidement**.*	Jean-Pierre works **fastest** (the most quickly).

o|o Attention!

"Best" is:

■ *Le meilleur* (agreeing as necessary) + noun:

*Ce sont **les meilleures cerises** du marché.*	These are the **best cherries** in the market.

■ Verb + *le mieux* (*le* doesn't change):

*C'est Catherine qui **parle** anglais **le mieux**.*	It's Catherine who **speaks** English **best**.

"The least easy/easily"

You can get a "negative" superlative by using *le / la / les moins* + adjective or *le moins* + adverb:

*La physique c'est la matière **la moins facile**.*	Physics is **the least easy** subject.
*C'est Roger qui parle anglais **le moins bien**.*	Roger speaks English **the least well**.

Prêts?

▶ 1 On fait des comparaisons

Dites à vos camarades ce que vous pensez de ces activités ou des ces aliments en utilisant *plus . . . que, moins . . . que, aussi . . . que* et les adjectifs entre parenthèses. Attention à l'accord *est/sont* et des adjectifs! Écrivez vos réponses ci-dessous.

Tell your classmates what you think of these activities or foods using *plus . . . que, moins . . . que, aussi . . . que* and the adjectives in parentheses. Watch out for the need for singular or plural *est/sont* and the agreement of the adjectives! Write your answers below.

Exemples:

Le rugby est plus dangereux que le hand (*handball*).
Les boums sont moins agréables que le cinéma.
La cuisine n'est pas aussi fatigante que la vaisselle.

1. le foot—le rugby—le tennis—le hand (intéressant—amusant—dangereux)

   _____

   _____

2. les boums—le cinéma—le concert (agréable—amusant—cher)

   _____

   _____

3. les maths—le dessin—l'EPS (*PE*) (facile—difficile—instructif)

   _____

   _____

4. la vaisselle—la cuisine—les courses (ennuyeux—amusant—fatigant [*tiring*])

   _____

   _____

5. l'hôtel—le camping—le gîte rural (*country cottage*) (intéressant—facile—cher)

   _____

   _____

6. la pizza—la salade—la crème caramel (bon—sucré—sain)

   _____

   _____

▶2 Testez vos connaissances de géographie

Répondez en faisant une phrase complète. Faites attention aux accords!

Reply using a complete sentence. Be careful with agreement!

Exemple:

Quel est le plus petit pays du monde? (le Vatican—le Liechtenstein—l'Albanie)
Le plus petit pays du monde, c'est le Vatican.

1. Quel est le plus long fleuve de France? (le Rhône—la Seine—la Loire)

   _____

2. Quelle est la montagne la plus haute du monde? (le Ben Nevis—le Mont Blanc—l'Everest)

   _____

3. Quel est le pays le plus peuplé (*populated*) du monde? (l'Inde—la Chine—la France)

   _____

4. Quelle est la ville la plus peuplée de France? (Lyon—Marseille—Paris)

   _____

5. Quel est le pays d'Europe où le nombre de divorces est le moins important (*in this sense, lowest*)? (l'Irlande—l'Italie—l'Espagne)

   _____

6. Quel est la frontière la plus longue du monde? (la frontière Canada–États-Unis—la frontière Chine–Russie—la frontière France–Belgique)

   _____

Partez!

▶3 Comparé(e) avec moi . . .

Décrivez quelqu'un (de votre classe ou un personnage bien connu), en le comparant à vous sans le nommer. La classe devine de qui vous parlez. Écrivez vos phrases ci-dessous.

Describe someone (in your class or a well-known personality), comparing him or her to you, but without saying who. The class guesses who you are talking about. Write your sentences below.

Exemple:

Il/elle est plus grand(e) que moi. Il/elle est meilleur(e) en maths que moi. Il/elle n'est pas aussi mince que moi.

_____

_____

_____

_____

⭐4 Ce n'est pas vrai!

Travail par deux. En utilisant des comparatifs et des superlatifs, l'un joue le rôle de votre correspondant(e) français(e), l'autre, c'est vous! Votre correspondant(e) vous fait des observations *incorrectes* sur votre région des États-Unis. Vous devez le/la corriger. Écrivez vos phrases ci-dessous.

Pair work. Using comparatives and superlatives, one plays the role of your pen pal in France, and you play yourself. Your pen pal makes statements about your area of the U.S. which are *wrong*. You have to correct him or her. Write your sentences below.

Exemple:

pour la région de Chicago (adaptez les endroits à votre propre région):
for the Chicago area (adapt the places to your own area):

—Chicago est plus grand que Los Angeles, non?
—Non, Los Angeles est plus grand que Chicago / Chicago n'est pas aussi grand que
    Los Angeles.
—Le Festival de Blues à Chicago est le festival de blues le moins populaire parmi les jeunes,
    non?
—Non, Le Festival de Blues à Chicago est le festival de blues le plus populaire de la région.

_____

_____

_____

_____

_____

_____

_____

_____

_____

_____

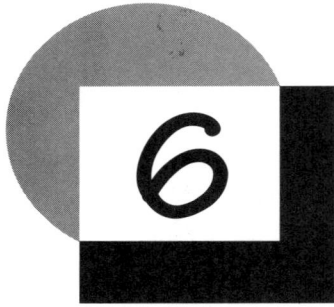

6 Pointing Things Out
demonstratives

What are demonstratives?

These are words you use when you want to point out ("demonstrate") something or somebody by saying "this (one)" or "that (one)." There are three types in French, so read carefully the following explanations to help you sort them out!

Ce (cet), cette, ces

This is the demonstrative adjective, which must always be followed by a noun. It agrees like any other adjective, and can mean "this" or "that":

ce vélo, ces vélos	**this/that** bike, **these/those** bikes
cette voiture, ces voitures	**this/that** car, **these/those** cars

Attention!

1. There is a special masculine singular form before a vowel or silent *h:*

cet autobus	this/that bus
cet homme	this/that man

2. If (and *only* if) you need to make it crystal clear that what you are pointing out is **this** (here, by me) or **that** (there, by you, or over there), you put **-ci** (short for *ici*) on the end of the noun for **this,** and **-là** on the end for **that:**

   *Donnez-moi un kilo de **ces** pommes de terre-**là** et un demi-kilo de **ces** carottes-**ci.***
   Give me a kilo of **those** potatoes and half a kilo of **these** carrots.

> *Je voudrais **ce** gâteau-**ci** et **cette** baguette-**là.***
> I'd like **this** cake and **that** baguette.

Ceci and *cela (ça)*

These are the words for "this" and "that" when pointing or referring to something without naming it:

*Et avec **ceci**?*	(literally) And with **this**? (This is what shopkeepers often say when they ask if you want "anything else.")
*Je n'aime pas **ça**.*	I don't like **that**, I don't like it (another common expression).
***Cela** me fâche.*	**That** makes me angry.

Ça is the shortened form of *cela* and is used frequently in spoken French.

In all of the above examples, "this/that" does not refer to a particular named noun.

Celui-ci, celui-là

These forms, the demonstrative pronoun, mean "this/that one," "these/those ones," and refer to a specific noun. There are four forms, masculine and feminine, singular and plural, so you have to choose the right one for the noun you are referring to. The form must end in *-ci* or *-là,* depending on whether it means "this" or "that."

	Masculine	Feminine	
Singular	*celui-ci/là*	*celle-ci/là*	this/that one
Plural	*ceux-ci/là*	*celles-ci/là*	these/those ones

*Tu aimes ce **pull**-ci? Oui, mais je préfère **celui-là**.*
Do you like this **sweater**? Yes, but I prefer **that one** (= the sweater—masculine).

*Que de **chemises**! J'aime bien **celle-là**.*
What a lot of **shirts**! I do like **that one** (= the shirt—feminine)!

*Je vais acheter des **sandwichs**. **Ceux-là** sont combien, s'il vous plaît?*
I'm going to buy some **sandwiches**. How much are **those** (= sandwiches—masculine), please?

*Voilà les **chaussures**. **Celles-ci** sont moins chères que **celles-là**.*

There are the **shoes. These** (= the shoes—feminine) are not as expensive as **those** (= shoes—feminine).

Conseil!

In all of the above examples, the demonstrative agrees with the noun it represents.

Prêts?

▶1 On vous invite à un buffet

Votre ami Cédric vous invite à une fête pour son anniversaire, et sa mère a préparé un bon buffet. Choisissez la forme correcte de *ce/cet/cette/ces*. Mettez un ✗ pour indiquer la réponse correcte.

Your friend Cédric invites you to his birthday party, and his mom has prepared a nice buffet. Choose the correct form of *ce/cet/cette/ces*. Put an ✗ in the box to indicate the correct answer.

1. Tu veux _____ pâté de canard?

   ☐ cet

   ☐ cette

   ☐ ce

2. Non, merci, je préfère _____ belle terrine (*terrine, a sort of pâté*) de porc!

   ☐ ce

   ☐ cette

   ☐ ces

3. Tu prends un peu de _____ salade verte?

   ☐ cet

   ☐ ce

   ☐ cette

4. Non, j'aimerais mieux _____ carottes râpées (*grated carrots*).

   ☐ ces

   ☐ ce

   ☐ cet

5. Tu vois _____ beau saumon fumé (*smoked salmon*)? Tu en veux?

   ☐ cette

   ☐ ce

   ☐ ces

★2 Sélection pour l'équipe de hand

Votre correspondant français joue au hand dans une équipe mixte. Complétez la conversation de ses entraîneurs avec un des mots "démonstratifs" de la case.

Your French pen pal plays handball on a mixed team. Complete his trainers' conversation with one of the "demonstrative" words from the box.

—J'aime beaucoup **(1)** _____ garçon. C'est un très bon milieu de terrain (*mid-field*).

—Non, moi, je préfère **(2)** _____. Il est plus tactique.

—Regarde **(3)** _____ fille. Elle joue super bien. Elle pourrait peut-être être goal?

—Non, **(4)** _____ est beaucoup plus rapide. Elle serait mieux.

—Et **(5)** _____ enfant tout timide, il faut l'encourager, le mettre ailier (*winger,*

   on the wing), par exemple.

—Non, **(6)** _____ est ridicule, il a trop peur. Nous voulons des gagneurs (*winners*),

   (7) _____ garçons-**(8)** _____, par exemple.

—Pas d'accord! Ils ne sont pas sérieux! **(9)** _____ le sont beaucoup plus!

—**(10)** _____ es très difficile! Nous ne saurons jamais qui choisir!

ce	cette	cet	cela	celui-ci	celle-ci	ceux-ci	ceci	ces	là

Partez!

▶3 Vous achetez des provisions

Vous faites les courses dans un petit magasin de village (ce n'est pas un supermarché où vous prenez vous-même les produits!). Le marchand / la marchande (votre camarade de classe) vous explique ce qu'il y a.

You are shopping in a small village shop (not a supermarket where you pick up the food yourself!). The shopkeeper (your classmate) will explain what he or she has. Swap roles from time to time.

Exemple:

A. Je voudrais des **pommes,** s'il vous plaît.
B. Oui, monsieur/mademoiselle. Il y a **celles-ci** à huit francs le kilo, et **celles-là** à neuf francs.
A. Je prends un kilo de **celles-là,** s'il vous plaît.
B. Bien. Et avec **ceci**?

Continuez. Vous pouvez acheter des pommes de terre, des carottes, un chou, du lait, du café, une bouteille de limonade, des chips, etc., etc. . . . Écrivez vos phrases ci-dessous.

_____

_____

_____

_____

_____

_____

✪4 On fait du lèche-vitrines

Vous venez de passer des vacances chez votre correspondant(e) français(e). Vous avez dépensé tout votre argent, mais vous faites du lèche-vitrines devant les grands magasins à Paris avant de prendre l'avion pour retourner aux États-Unis. Écrivez vos phrases.

You have just spent your vacation with your French pen pal. You have spent all your money, but you are doing some window shopping in the big Paris stores before catching the plane home. Make up conversations using the demonstratives you have been studying. Write your sentences.

Exemples:

—Oh, j'aime bien **cette chemise-là**! Et **cette jupe-ci**!
—Moi, je voudrais acheter **ces chaussures-là,** ou **celles-ci.**

—Regarde **cette raquette de tennis**! Et **ces skis-là**!
—Moi, je préfère **ceux-là,** et **ces chaussures de ski** sont sensass!

Vous pourriez peut-être voir aussi: une robe, un sac, des chaussettes, une bague (*ring*), un bracelet, une/des boucle(s) d'oreille (*earrings*), une montre, etc.

_____

_____

_____

_____

_____

_____

_____

_____

⭐**5 Toujours quelque chose de meilleur**

Vous vous promenez dans la rue avec votre correspondant(e) français(e), qui indique et décrit les choses qu'il/elle voit. Mais vous voyez toujours quelque chose de meilleur . . .

You are walking along the street with your French pen pal, who points out and describes what he or she sees. But you always see something better . . .

Exemples:

A. Tu vois **cette** belle moto là-bas?
B. Oui, mais **celle-ci** est beaucoup plus belle, et plus grande!
C. Regarde **ces** CD à gauche!
D. Oui, ils ne sont pas mal, mais **ceux-là** à droite sont beaucoup moins chers!

_____

_____

_____

_____

_____

_____

7 Whose Is It?
possessives

À vos marques!

What's a possessive?

A possessive is a word that tells you whom something belongs to: **my** bike, **your** house, **Chantal's** cat, this cake is **yours,** that dog is **Martin's.**

No "apostrophe *s*" (*'s*)

One of the things English learners of French need to get used to is to use *de* every time you want to talk about someone's belongings:

*Le chien **de** Martin*	Martin**'s** dog
*Les frères **de** Chantal*	Chantal**'s** brothers
*La chambre **des** enfants*	The children**'s** room
*Les chaussures **des** élèves*	The students**'** shoes
*Les footballeurs **de** France*	France**'s** soccer players

My, your, his, her: the possessive adjective

The important thing to remember about this is that it agrees masculine/feminine/plural **with the thing you possess:**

Masculine	Feminine	Plural	
mon	*ma*	*mes*	my
ton	*ta*	*tes*	your (belonging to *tu/toi*)
son	*sa*	*ses*	his, her, its
notre	*notre*	*nos*	our
votre	*votre*	*vos*	your (belonging to *vous*)
leur	*leur*	*leurs*	their

mon chien	my dog	*ma* chambre	my room
mes frères	my brothers	*mes* sœurs	my sisters
ton oncle	your uncle	*ta* tante	your aunt
notre fils	our son	*notre* fille	our daughter
nos fils	our sons	*nos* filles	our daughters
votre chemise	your shirt	*vos* chaussures	your shoes
leur maison	their house	*leurs* problèmes	their problems

ojo Attention!

1. *Son/sa/ses* mean "his," "hers," or "its," but changes according to the **thing possessed, not** the possessor: *son vélo* can mean either "his bike" or "her bike," because *vélo* is masculine, and *sa famille* can mean either "his family" or "her family," since *famille* is feminine. The possessor is usually obvious from the context:

*Paul a mis **son vélo** dans le garage.*	Paul put **his bike** in the garage.
*Chantal a mis **son vélo** dans le garage.*	Chantal put **her bike** in the garage.
*Kévin a envoyé une carte postale à **sa famille.***	Kevin sent a postcard to **his family.**
*Claire a envoyé une carte postale à **sa famille.***	Claire sent a postcard to **her family.**
*M. Albaret est allé en Angleterre avec **sa femme.***	Mr. Albaret went to England with **his wife.**
*Mme Albaret est allée en Angleterre avec **son mari.***	Mrs. Albaret went to England with **her husband.**

2. You say *mon, ton,* and *son* before a singular word beginning with a vowel or silent *h,* even if it is feminine:

***mon amie** Michelle*	my (female) friend Michelle
ton école	your school
*Paris et **son histoire***	Paris and its history

Mine, yours, his, hers

That's mine!

When you want to say something **is mine, yours, Jean's,** and so forth, after *être,* you use *à* + a noun or the disjunctive pronoun such as *moi, toi* (see Chapter 9). "Whose" is *à qui?*

*À **qui** est cette jupe? Est-ce qu'elle est **à toi,** Louise? Non, elle est **à Sylvette.***
Whose is this skirt? Is it **yours,** Louise? No, it's **Sylvette's.**

*Cette montre n'est pas **à moi,** elle est **au professeur.***
This watch isn't **mine,** it's **the teacher's.**

Mine's better than yours!

Otherwise you use the **possessive pronoun,** which **agrees** masculine/feminine and singular/plural **with the noun it replaces:**

Masculine		Feminine		
Singular	**Plural**	**Singular**	**Plural**	
le mien	*les miens*	*la mienne*	*les miennes*	mine
le tien	*les tiens*	*la tienne*	*les tiennes*	yours (*tu*)
le sien	*les siens*	*la sienne*	*les siennes*	his, hers, its
le nôtre	*les nôtres*	*la nôtre*	*les nôtres*	ours
le vôtre	*les vôtres*	*la vôtre*	*les vôtres*	yours (*vous*)
le leur	*les leurs*	*la leur*	*les leurs*	theirs

*Ce **sandwich** est à moi. **Le tien** est sur la table.*
This **sandwich** is mine. **Yours** is on the table.
(*Le tien* refers to "sandwich," which is masculine singular.)

*Ta **glace** est plus grande que **la mienne**! Et regarde **la sienne**!*
Your **ice cream** is bigger than **mine**! And look at **his/hers**!
(*La mienne* and *la sienne* are feminine singular and refer to *la glace*. *La sienne* could mean either "his" or "hers," but this would be obvious from the context of the conversation, as you would be pointing to the ice cream or its owner!)

*Voici **les chemises** d'équipe. **Les nôtres** sont bleues et **les leurs** sont vertes.*
Here are the team **shirts. Ours** are blue and **theirs** are green.
(*Les nôtres* and *les leurs* refer to *les chemises*.)

My bike is newer than Marc's!

With a noun, you use the demonstrative pronoun (see Chapter 6):

Masculine		Feminine		
Singular	**Plural**	**Singular**	**Plural**	
celui	*ceux*	*celle*	*celles*	+ *de* + noun

*Mon **vélo** est plus neuf que **celui** de Marc.*   My **bike** is newer than **Marc's.**
*Notre **équipe** est meilleure que **celle** de*   Our **team** is better than **Saumur's.**
  Saumur.

Prêts?

▶1 À chacun ses goûts

Les deux enfants de la famille Migault sont très différents. François aime la musique et Valérie aime le sport. Imaginez à qui appartiennent ces objets, en complétant les phrases ci-dessous selon les exemples.

The two Migault children are very different. François likes music and Valérie likes sports. Imagine whom these objects belong to, completing the sentences below according to the examples.

Exemples:

Ce sont les baskets *de Valérie.*
C'est le violon *de François.*

C'est la raquette **(1)** _____.

C'est le piano **(2)** _____.

Ce sont les CD **(3)** _____.

Ce sont les skis **(4)** _____.

C'est le vélo **(5)** _____.

C'est le billet de concert **(6)** _____.

C'est le lecteur de CD **(7)** _____.

C'est le ballon **(8)** _____.

▶2 Un garçon très étourdi

François est très étourdi. Et parfois il prend les affaires des autres. Lisez sa conversation avec sa sœur et continuez de la même façon.

François is very absent-minded. And sometimes he takes other people's belongings. Read his conversation with his sister and continue in the same way.

Exemple:

—Regarde! Tu as mis le T-shirt de papa!
—Ah, oui! J'ai mis son T-shirt!

—Et tu as mis les lunettes de maman!

—Ah! pardon, j'ai mis **(1)** _____!

—Et tu as mangé la glace de grand-mère!

—Oh! pardon, j'ai mangé **(2)** _____!

—Et tu as pris mes clés!

—Oh, zut! J'ai pris **(3)** _____!

—François, tu as mis les bols des chiens dans le frigo!

—Oh, zut! J'ai mis **(4)** _____ dans le frigo!

—Et tu as mis ta brosse à dents dans le lave-vaisselle!

—Oh, pardon! J'ai mis **(5)** _____ dans le lave-vaisselle!

—Et tu as mis tes chaussures à l'envers!

—Oui, c'est exact j'ai mis **(6)** _____ à l'envers! Je suis un vraie catastrophe!

▶3 Ça devient insupportable!

Valérie continue les réprimandes à son frère. Réagissez comme dans l'exemple.

Valérie continues telling her brother off. React as in the example.

Exemple:

—François! Tu as encore mis les lunettes de maman!
—Oh, oui! Ces lunettes sont à maman!

—Et tu as encore pris le T-shirt de papa!

—Oh, oui, ce T-shirt est **(1)** _____!

—Et tu as encore mangé la glace de grand-mère!

—Oh, oui! Cette glace est **(2)** _____!

—Et tu as jeté mes baskets à la poubelle!

—Oh! Ces baskets sont **(3)** _____!

—Et tu as bu le lait du chat!

—Vraiment! Ce lait est **(4)** _____!

—Et tu as pris les chewing-gums de Sophie!

—Oh! Ces chewing-gums sont **(5)** _____!

—Et tu as ouvert le courrier des voisins!

—Oh! Ce courrier est **(6)** _____!

★4 Antonio préfère le Portugal

Antonio vit en France, mais il préfère le Portugal, où vivent ses grands-parents. Il écrit à son correspondant américain. Dans sa lettre, remplacez les expressions en italique par _le mien, le tien, le sien,_ etc.

Antonio lives in France, but he prefers Portugal, where his grandparents live. He is writing to his American pen pal. In his letter, replace the phrases in italics with _le mien, le tien, le sien,_ and so forth, making it agree as necessary.

Ma maison est belle, mais je préfère vivre au Portugal, dans la maison de ma grand-mère. (_La maison de ma grand-mère_) **(1)** _____ est au bord de la mer avec un grand jardin. En France, nous avons quelques fleurs au jardin, mais (_les fleurs de ma grand-mère_) **(2)** _____ sont plus grosses, plus colorées. Mon grand-père a acheté une planche à voile et nous nous amusons tous les deux. (_Ma planche à voile_) **(3)** _____ est plus petite que (_la planche à voile de mon grand-père_) **(4)** _____, mais elle est plus rapide. Mes parents et moi, nous aimons beaucoup les restaurants portugais. Nous pensons que (_les restaurants des Portugais_) **(5)** _____ sont meilleurs que (_nos restaurants_) **(6)** _____. Bientôt, nous allons nous construire une maison au Portugal. (_La maison de mes grands-parents_) **(7)** _____ est au bord de la mer, mais (_notre maison_) **(8)** _____ sera dans la montagne. J'espère que tu viendras nous y voir avec tes parents!

Partez!

5 C'est le crayon de qui?

Travaillez en groupes. Chaque élève met un objet sur la table. Le chef de groupe prend un des objets et demande: *C'est le crayon de John, Emma, etc.?* Un(e) autre élève répond: *Non, c'est le crayon de Michael/Anne, etc.* ou *Oui, c'est son crayon.* Écrivez vos questions et vos réponses.

Group work. Each student puts an object on the table and the group leader takes one of the objects and asks: *C'est le crayon de John, Emma, etc.?* Another student answers: *Non, c'est le crayon de Michael/Anne, etc.* or *Oui, c'est son crayon.* Write your questions and your answers.

Exemple:

—C'est le crayon de John?
—Non, c'est le crayon de Theresa *or* Oui, c'est son crayon.

_____

_____

_____

_____

_____

_____

_____

_____

6 À qui est cette montre?

C'est le même jeu, mais cette fois le chef de groupe demande, par exemple: *À qui est cette montre?* et on répond: *Elle est à Catherine.*

Same game, but this time the group leader asks, for example: *À qui est cette montre?* and the answer is: *Elle est à Catherine.*

_____

_____

_____

_____

_____

_____

▶**7** Un visiteur interplanétaire

Travail par deux. Vous avez reçu un visiteur d'une autre planète, et vous lui montrez votre école. Il répète vos explications en forme de questions, auxquelles vous devez répondre. Écrivez votre dialogue.

Pair work. You are entertaining a visitor from another planet, and are showing him your school. He repeats your explanations in the form of questions, which you have to answer. Write your dialogue.

Exemples:

—Voici notre salle de classe.
—Ah! C'est notre salle de classe?
—Oui, c'est notre salle de classe!

—Voici mes copines Sophie et Tiphaine.
—Ah! Ce sont tes copines Sophie et Tiphaine?
—Oui, ce sont mes copines Sophie et Tiphaine!

_____

_____

_____

_____

_____

_____

_____

_____

▶8 On fait des comparaisons

Vous comparez vos possessions, votre famille, etc. avec celles de vos camarades.

You compare your possessions, family, and so forth with those of your friends.

Exemples:

—Voici ma montre. Elle est en plastique. Et la tienne?
—La mienne aussi, elle est en plastique.

—Voici mes grands-parents. Ils sont vieux. Et les vôtres?
—Les nôtres aussi sont assez vieux.

_____

_____

_____

_____

_____

_____

_____

_____

You and I, Them and Me

8

personal subject and object pronouns

À vos marques!

What is a pronoun?

A pronoun replaces a noun so that you don't have to keep on repeating it. For example, instead of saying "James suggested that Tracy meet James at 7 o'clock and Tracy agreed," you would usually say: "James suggested that Tracy meet **him** at 7 o'clock, and **she** agreed." "Him" stands for James, and "she" for Tracy. These pronouns are often called "personal pronouns," because (surprise!) they refer to persons.

Subject pronouns

A subject pronoun is one which is the subject of the verb—the doer of the action. They are the ones you see when you look up a verb in a verb chart:

je mange	*nous* mangeons
tu manges	*vous* mangez
il mange	*ils* mangent
elle mange	*elles* mangent
on mange	

je	I	*nous*	we
tu	you (familiar)	*vous*	you (polite and plural)
il	he, it (*m.*)	*ils*	they (*m.* and mixed)
elle	she, it (*f.*)	*elles*	they (*f.*)
on	one		

ojo Attention!

1. *Je* becomes *j'* before a vowel: *j'ai, j'étais,* etc.

2. *Tu* or *vous? Tu* is singular only, and used only when talking to a member of your family, a close friend, a young person of your own age, a child, or a pet. Otherwise use *vous* when talking to one person. If in doubt, use *vous* until you are asked to use *tu*! You use *vous* when talking to more than one person, regardless of who they are.

3. When you invert the verb and subject to make a question, if the verb ends in *-a* or *-e* you need to insert *-t-* before *il, elle, on:*

Que mange-t-il?	What does he eat?
Quand arrive-t-elle?	When does she arrive?
Que dira-t-on?	What will one/they say?

4. *On* means literally "one," but is often the equivalent of "they," "you" in a general sense, or "people":

Qu'est-ce qu'on peut faire?	What can one/we/you do?
On dit que ce n'est pas vrai.	They/people say that it's not true.

Object pronouns

Objects can be "direct" or "indirect."

Direct object pronouns

The direct object is the person or thing that undergoes the action of the verb:

"I bought **the ham.**" "I bought **it.**" "**Ham**" is the direct object, and "**it**" is the pronoun which replaces the noun "ham," also as the direct object.

*J'ai acheté **le jambon.** Je l'ai acheté.*

Some more examples of direct objects:

Monique saw **Mr. Lechat.**	*Monique a vu **M. Lechat.***
Monique saw **him.**	*Monique l'a vu.*
The children broke **the windows.**	*Les enfants ont cassé **les fenêtres.***
The children broke **them.**	*Les enfants **les** ont cassées.*

The direct object pronouns in French are:

me	me	*nous*	us
te	you (familiar)	*vous*	you (polite and plural)
le	him, it (for *m.* noun)	*les*	them (*m.* and *f.*)
la	her, it (for *f.* noun)		

¡OJO! Attention!

1. Object pronouns usually come **before** the verb (but see Commands—Chapter 22).

La glace à la fraise? Je l'adore!	Strawberry ice cream? I love **it.**
*Tu connais ma cousine Françoise? Non, je ne **la** connais pas.*	Do you know my cousin Françoise? No, I don't know **her.**

2. Remember that they come **before** an infinitive and **after** any verb that is linked to it:

*Je vais **les lui** donner.*	I'm going to give **them to him.**
*Je ne veux pas **vous** déranger.*	I don't want to disturb **you.**
*Le médecin va **nous** voir demain.*	The doctor is going to see **us** tomorrow.

3. *Me, te, le, la* become *m', t', l'* before a vowel.

*Je **t'**attends devant le cinéma.*	I'll meet **you** outside the movie theater.
*Nous **l'**avons vu(e) hier.*	We saw **him/her/it** yesterday.

4. In the *passé composé* and other "compound" tenses, it may be necessary to make the past participle agree when the object pronoun comes before it: see Chapter 27 for a full explanation.

*Ces journaux? Je **les** ai déjà lus.*	Those newspapers? I've already read them.

5. The object pronoun *le* is often used in phrases such as *je le sais* "I know," *je le crois* "I think so."

—Il est difficile, ce problème!	"This problem is a difficult one!"
—Oui, je le sais!	"Yes, I know!"

Indirect object pronouns

The indirect object "receives" the direct object, and is frequently used with verbs like "send," "write," "say" to. It is generally associated with the preposition *à* "to."

*J'ai envoyé une carte postale **à mes parents.***
I sent a postcard **to my parents.**
*Je **leur** ai envoyé une carte postale.*
I sent **them** a postcard / I sent a postcard **to them.**
(The postcard is the direct object, and **my parents / them** is the indirect object.)

*Qu'est-ce que la directrice **t'**a dit?*
What did the principal say **to you**?
*Elle **m'**a dit que je suis l'élève parfait(e)!*
She told **me** (said **to me**) that I am the perfect student!

The indirect object pronouns are:

me	to me	*nous*	to us
te	to you (familiar)	*vous*	to you (polite and plural)
lui	to him, to her, to it	*leur*	to them

*Je **vous** téléphonerai demain.*   I'll phone (to) **you** tomorrow.
*Ils **nous** ont offert un si beau cadeau.*   They gave (to) **us** such a beautiful present.
*La serveuse **leur** a apporté l'addition.*   The waitress brought **them** the bill.

Attention!

Sometimes a verb will take an indirect object in French as opposed to a direct object in English, or vice versa:

*Ils **nous** ont demandé cent francs.*   They asked **us** for 100 francs.
Quand ton professeur parle,   When your teacher speaks, you must
  *il faut **lui** obéir!*   obey **him**!
*Regarde cet avion! Regarde-**le**!*   Look **at** that plane! Look **at it**!

You will find a list of these verbs in Chapter 34, page 240.

Direct and indirect objects together

When you have both a direct and an indirect object together, the direct comes first:

*Nous avons écrit **les cartes postales***   We wrote **the postcards to our friends.**
  à nos amis.

*Nous **les leur** avons envoyées.*   We sent **them to them.**

*Didier **m'**a donné **la bague**.*   Didier gave **me the ring.**
*Didier **me l'**a donnée.*   Didier gave **it to me.**

*N'envoie pas **cette lettre à ta mère**!*   Don't send **that letter to your mother**!
*Ne **la lui** envoie pas!*   Don't send **it to her**!

See Chapter 22 for what happens with positive commands (= do!).

Reflexive pronouns

These are the object pronouns you use with reflexive verbs: they can be the direct or indirect object according to the sense:

se laver   to wash (oneself)

*je **me** lave*	*nous **nous** lavons*
*tu **te** laves*	*vous **vous** lavez*
*il **se** lave*	*ils **se** lavent*
*elle **se** lave*	*elles **se** lavent*

You can see that the only pronoun which is different from the ordinary direct/indirect object pronoun is *se,* which means "himself, herself, oneself, themselves" according to the subject of the verb.

You will find further information about these reflexive pronouns in Chapter 30 on reflexive verbs.

Prêts?

▶1 Je connais le sujet

Par quel pronom sujet remplaceriez-vous ces noms ou pronoms?

Which subject pronoun would you use to replace these nouns or pronouns?

le chien **(1)** _____

la machine à laver **(2)** _____

toi et moi **(3)** _____

les fourchettes **(4)** _____

Thomas et Sylvie **(5)** _____

la caissière du supermarché **(6)** _____

ton frère et toi **(7)** _____

les vélos **(8)** _____

▶2 Que donne le serveur?

À l'aide des mots suivants, faites des phrases avec un complément d'objet direct et un complément d'objet indirect. Ensuite remplacez tous les noms par des pronoms.

With the help of the words below, make up sentences with a direct and an indirect object. Then replace all the nouns with pronouns.

Le serveur donne . . .

| un verre d'eau | deux verres à eau | à Annie | l'addition | à Nicolas |

| une bouteille de limonade | aux enfants | deux assiettes propres | à son patron |

| à l'homme d'affaires | aux demoiselles | à Angelique et Caroline |

Exemples:

Le serveur donne | un verre d'eau | à Annie.
Il **le lui** donne.

_____

_____

_____

_____

_____

_____

_____

_____

▶3 Le match de football

Dans ce commentaire d'un match de football entre Doullens et Albert, remplacez les noms en italique par *il, le, la* ou *lui*.

In this commentary between Doullens and Albert, replace the nouns with *il, le, la,* or *lui*.

Santini prend *la balle. Santini* voit Martin. *Santini* passe *la balle à Martin. Martin* prend *la balle* et se dirige vers les buts (*the goal*). Un joueur de l'équipe adverse (*opposing*), Rivière, voit *Martin*. Il rattrape (*to catch up with*) *Martin*, prend *la balle* a son tour et court vers l'autre côté du terrain (*field*). Tous les spectateurs regardent *Rivière*. Ils crient *à Rivière:* "Vas-y, Riri! Un but!" *Rivière* tire et marque *le but*. Bravo Rivière!

_____

_____

_____

_____

_____

_____

_____

_____

_____

_____

▶4 Les trésors de Bernadette

Bernadette, une jeune Française, vous parle de ses trésors. Choisissez le bon pronom.

Bernadette, a young French girl, talks about her treasures. Choose the right pronoun.

Viens! Je vais (te/toi) **(1)** _____ montrer ma collection de timbres et de poupées.

Tu vois toutes ces poupées? Regarde-(les/leur) **(2)** _____ bien. Ils viennent

d'Inde. Mon père me (la/les) **(3)** _____ amène quand il rentre de voyage.

Il (lui/nous) **(4)** _____ aime beaucoup, ma sœur et moi. Il rentre le soir et il vient

(nous/vous) **(5)** _____ voir dans notre chambre. Viens voir sa photo, que j'ai prise

moi-même. Je vais te (la/leur) **(6)** _____ montrer. Il est à cheval. Le cheval s'appelle

Fanfan. Nous irons (lui/le) **(7)** _____ voir demain.

★5 Au bureau du tourisme

Vous êtes dans une petite ville de la vallée de l'Authie dans la Somme et vous prenez quelques renseignements sur la région. Ajoutez le pronom personnel ou d'objet direct qui convient.

You are in a little town in the Authie valley in the Somme and you are gathering some information about the area. Add the appropriate personal/subject or object pronoun.

—Pouvez-**(1)** _____ m'indiquer l'hôtel le meilleur marché de la ville?

—Oui, bien sûr. **(2)** _____ peux **(3)** _____ indiquer où **(4)** _____ se trouve.

    C'est l'hôtel du Lion d'Or, première rue à droite.

→

—Peut-**(5)** _____ visiter l'abbaye de Valloires?

—Oui, **(6)** _____ peut **(7)** _____ visiter de 9h à 18h.

—Et est-ce qu'**(8)** _____ est possible de voir les orgues (_organs_) du XVIIIe siècle?

—Oui, bien sûr, on peut **(9)** _____ voir.

—Y a-t-il un guide?

—Oui, mais il faut **(10)** _____ téléphoner pour prendre rendez-vous (_to make an appointment_); **(11)** _____ pouvez poser toutes sortes de questions. **(12)** _____ aime raconter l'histoire de ces orgues.

—Est-ce qu'il **(13)** _____ laissera jouer?

—Oui, bien sûr, il **(14)** _____ laissera jouer si **(15)** _____ êtes bon organiste, et **(16)** _____ **(17)** _____ montrera tout le mécanisme. C'est une visite très intéressante.

—Faut-il **(18)** _____ payer?

—Non, mais **(19)** _____ sera très heureux si vous **(20)** _____ donnez un pourboire.

—Je **(21)** _____ remercie beaucoup.

Partez!

▶**6** Maman/papa vous harcèle de questions

Travail par deux. L'un joue le rôle de votre mère ou votre père, qui vous harcèle de questions concernant les choses que vous n'avez pas faites. Vous jouez votre propre rôle. Utilisez des pronoms dans vos réponses.

Pair work. One plays the role of your mom or dad, who hassles you about the things you haven't done. You play yourself. Use pronouns in your answers.

Exemples:

—As-tu sorti le chien?
—Non, maman/papa, je le sortirai bientôt!

—As-tu fini tes devoirs?
—Non, maman/papa, je les finirai après.

_____

_____

_____

_____

_____

_____

_____

_____

mettre la table	nettoyer tes chaussures	donner à manger au hamster
laver la vaisselle	passer l'aspirateur	faire ton lit ranger ta chambre

▶7 Tu m'aimes?

Imaginez que vous participez à un feuilleton à la télé. Vous posez à vos camarades des questions qui contiennent *me* ou *nous* comme complément d'objet direct ou indirect. Eux, ils doivent y répondre, en utilisant *te* ou *vous*.

Imagine you are taking part in a TV daytime drama. You ask your classmates questions containing *me* or *nous* as direct or indirect object pronouns. They have to reply using *te* or *vous*.

Exemples:

—Lucie, tu m'aimes?
—Oh, oui, Michel, je t'adore! (Bah, non, Michel, je ne t'aimes pas, je te déteste!)

—Vous nous accompagnez à la piscine?
—Oui, nous vous accompagnons.

(Vous pouvez utiliser: *aimer, adorer, détester, écouter, regarder, accompagner au cinéma, acheter, donner, offrir un cadeau,* etc.)

_____

_____

_____

_____

_____

_____

_____

_____

9 For Me? From You?

personal pronouns: the disjunctive pronoun

À vos marques!

What is a disjunctive pronoun?

A disjunctive pronoun refers to the *moi, toi,* etc., set of "personal" pronouns. Here is the complete list:

moi	I, me	*nous*	we, us,
toi	you (for *tu*)	*vous*	you (polite and plural)
lui	he, him, it (*m.*)	*eux*	they, them (*m.* or mixed)
elle	she, her, it (*f.*)	*elles*	they, them (*f.*)

They are used in the following instances.

For emphasis

In French you can't emphasize the subject pronouns (*je, tu, il,* etc., see Chapter 8) with your voice, so you have to "double up" with one of these pronouns:

***Moi,** je vais en ville.*	**I**'m going to town.
*Et **toi,** qu'est-ce que tu vas faire?*	And what are **you** going to do?
*Est-ce qu'ils restent ici, **eux**?*	Are **they** staying here?

When there is no verb

A disjunctive pronoun is also used when there is no verb in the French sentence and after *c'est:*

—*Qui veut aller en ville? —**Nous!***	"Who wants to go to town?" "**We do!**"
—*Qui? **Moi**? —Oui, **toi!***	"Who? **Me**?" "Yes, **you!**"
*Oui, c'est **lui!***	Yes, it's **him**!

After prepositions

The disjunctive pronoun is used after prepositions, such as *avec* "with," *sans* "without," *contre* "against," *pour* "for," *devant* "in front of," *derrière* "behind," and so forth.

*Tu viens **avec moi**?*	Are you coming **with me**?
*Je n'y vais pas **sans toi**!*	I'm not going there **without you**!
*J'ai un petit cadeau **pour vous**.*	I've got a little present **for you**.
*Tu t'assieds là, **devant elle**.*	You sit there, **in front of her**.

Attention!

This pronoun is also used with *être à* to indicate possession (Chapter 7):

*Ce parapluie est **à nous**!*	That umbrella is **ours**!

In comparisons

*Je suis plus paresseux que **toi**.*	I am lazier than **you**.

Prêts?

▶1 Le bureau des objets trouvés

Dans une école française, on vous demande à qui sont les différents objets trouvés pendant la semaine. Répondez selon le dessin.

In a French school you are asked who owns the various articles lost during the week. Reply according to the drawings.

Exemple:

C'est à qui cette montre? C'est à lui.

1. Et ces chaussures de sport? C'est _____.

2. Et ces cahiers de maths? C'est _____.

→

3. Et ces tenues de sport? C'est _____.

4. C'est à qui ce livre d'anglais? C'est _____.

5. Et ce stylo-plume? C'est _____.

▶2 Le cours de sport

Au cours de sport, le professeur répartit les élèves en groupes selon les activités qu'ils veulent faire. Complétez avec le pronom qui convient.

In PE class, the teacher divides the students into groups according to the activities they want to do. Complete with the appropriate pronouns.

—Qui veut faire du rugby?

—**(1)** _____, je veux en faire!

—Qui veut faire du basket?

—Michèle, **(2)** _____, elle veut en faire!

—Et du foot? Vous voulez en faire, les garçons?

—Oui, **(3)** _____, nous voulons en faire!

—Il reste une place pour le tennis.

—Pierre, **(4)** _____, il veut en faire.

—Et **(5)** _____, Émilie, tu veux faire du ping-pong?

—D'accord.

—Un groupe doit faire du canoë-cayak sur la rivière. Qui veut en faire?

—Cédric et Vincent, **(6)** _____, ils veulent en faire.

⭐3 Le quartier de Bellevue

Au quartier de Bellevue, tout le monde se connaît. Expliquez où habitent les différents personnages, en complétant les phrases.

In the Bellevue district, everyone knows each other. Explain where the various residents live by completing the sentences.

Paul et Claudine, ils sont au premier étage, et Lucie, elle est au-dessus d'(**1**) _____.

Clémentine est au troisième étage et Marielle est dans l'appartement à côté

d'(**2**) _____. Yasmina et Amélie sont au troisième étage aussi et Fabien est

en dessous d'(**3**) _____. Olivier est au deuxième étage à droite, et Lucie est à côté

de (**4**) _____. Julien a l'appartement en face de (**5**) _____. Moi et ma sœur,

nous sommes au premier étage, les jumeaux sont en face de (**6**) _____, et la famille

Bertrand est à côté de (**7**) _____.

Partez!

▶4 C'est à qui?

Un(e) élève prend un objet qui appartient à un(e) autre ou à lui/elle-même et demande "C'est à qui?" Les autres répondent en utilisant les pronoms.

One student takes an article belonging to another or himself or herself and asks *"C'est à qui?"* The others reply using pronouns.

Exemple:

—C'est à qui cette gomme?
—C'est à lui/elle/toi!

_____

_____

_____

_____

_____

_____

▶5 Les intérêts de votre famille

Vous écrivez à votre correspondant(e) au sujet des intérêts des membres de votre famille, en utilisant les pronoms disjonctifs pour souligner chaque personnage.

You are writing to your pen pal about the interests of the members of your family, using disjunctive pronouns to emphasize the persons you are talking about.

Exemples:

Moi, j'aime faire des promenades à vélo. Mon frère, lui, préfère écouter la musique pop toute la journée. Ma mère, elle, passe beaucoup de temps dans le jardin. Et toi, qu'est-ce que tu aimes faire?

_____

_____

_____

_____

_____

▶**6** Ma classe

Décrivez où les élèves de votre classe sont assis, en utilisant les pronoms disjonctifs.

Describe where the members of your class are sitting, using disjunctive pronouns.

Exemple:

Emma est assise à gauche de Sophie. Ben est assis derrière elle. À côté de lui il y a Lucy. Devant eux . . . etc.

_____

_____

_____

_____

▶**7** Mon quartier

Décrivez votre quartier et ses habitants, un peu comme dans l'exercice 3. Utilisez *à côté de, à gauche de, à droite de, en face de, tout près de,* etc., avec des pronoms disjonctifs.

Describe your neighborhood and its residents, as in exercise 3. Use *à côté de, à gauche de, à droite de, en face de, tout près de,* etc., with disjunctive pronouns.

Exemple:

Les Brown habitent à côté de nous, et les Black en face d'eux. M. Green habite tout près de chez eux. Il y a des magasins à gauche de chez lui, etc.

_____

_____

_____

_____

10 "There" and "Some"

y and *en;* order of object pronouns

À vos marques!

Y and *en* are two little words which are normally put together with the personal pronouns (Chapters 8 and 9), because they also come before the verb, and have their place in the word-order chart on page 69.

Y

Y means "there"

*Je suis allée aux Nouvelles Galeries et j'**y** ai acheté des chaussures.*
I went to Nouvelles Galeries and bought some shoes **there.**

*Nous avons passé le week-end au Futuroscope. Nous **y** avons fait beaucoup de choses.*
We spent the weekend at the Futuroscope. We did lots of things **there.**

*On peut **y** dépenser beaucoup d'argent!*
You can spend a lot of money **there**!

Y used as a pronoun

Y is also used as a pronoun to link *à* + a non-living noun:

*Il faut penser **à Noël**! Il faut **y** penser!*
We must think **about Christmas**! We must think **about it**! (*penser à* = to think about)

Il y a

Remember also the phrase *il y a* = "there is, there are." The question form is *y a-t-il?* "is there / are there?", *n'y a-t-il pas?* "isn't there / aren't there?"

*Il y a eu un accident! **Y a-t-il** un médecin ici?*
There has been an accident! **Is there** a doctor here?

Il n'y a pas de pain. Hier, il n'y avait pas de fromage.
There's no bread. Yesterday **there wasn't any** cheese.

En

En basically means "some" or "any" and replaces *de* + a (usually) non-living noun:

*Tu veux **des frites**? —Oui, j'**en** veux bien, s'il te plaît.*
Would you like **some fries**? Yes, I'd like **some,** please.

*Est-ce que tu as **de l'argent**? Non, je n'**en** ai pas.*
Do you have **any money**? No, I don't have **any.**

*Avez-vous vu ce nouveau film? Non, mais j'**en** ai vu des extraits à la télé.*
Have you seen this new movie? No, but I've seen some scenes (**from it**) on TV.

Ojo Attention!

En is needed in many phrases giving quantities, where no equivalent is needed in English:

*Tu as beaucoup de sœurs? —J'**en** ai deux.*
Do you have a lot of sisters? I have two.

*Il y a combien de personnes ici? —Il y **en** a huit.*
How many people are there here? There are eight.

*Combien de pommes de terre voulez-vous? —J'**en** veux deux kilos.*
How many potatoes do you want? I want 2 kilos.

Summary

The position of object pronouns—a summary of this and the two preceding chapters:

Conseil!

You can never use more than two object pronouns together, and they always come in the order of the columns in this table (exception: after positive commands, see Chapter 22).

me te se nous vous	le la les	lui leur	y	en

*Cédric **me l'**a envoyé.*	Cedric sent **it to me.**
*Cédric **m'en** a envoyé.*	Cedric sent **me some.**
*Nous **l'y** avons vu hier.*	We saw **him there** yesterday.
*Est-ce que vous **vous en** allez?*	Are **you** going **away**? (*s'en aller* = to go away)

Prêts?

▶ 1 La liste de courses

Avant d'aller faire les courses avec votre correspondant(e), vous vérifiez ce qu'il vous reste à la maison.

Before going shopping with your pen pal, you check what's left in the house.

Exemple:

Y a-t-il du lait? Oui, il y en a (une bouteille).

1. Y a-t-il des œufs? _____

2. Y a-t-il des fruits? _____

3. Y a-t-il de la salade? _____

4. Y a-t-il du beurre? _____

5. Y a-t-il du fromage? _____

6. Y a-t-il du sucre? _____

7. Y a-t-il du thé? _____

8. Y a-t-il du café? _____

▶**2** Après le pique-nique

Les Dubois viennent de faire un pique-nique. Voici ce qui reste après le repas, quand M. Dubois veut tout remettre dans la voiture.

The Dubois have just had a picnic. This is what is left after the meal, when Mr. Dubois is wanting to put everything back into the car.

Exemple:

Combien de bouteilles de coca voyez-vous?
J'en vois trois.

1. Combien de paquets de chips y a-t-il? _____

2. Combien de morceaux de poulet reste-t-il? _____

3. Combien de tomates trouvez-vous? _____

4. Combien de paquets de biscuits voyez-vous? _____

5. Combien de verres trouvez-vous? Et d'assiettes? _____

6. Combien de fruits reste-t-il? _____

7. Combien de sortes de fromages comptez-vous? _____

▶3 Le voyageur de commerce

Le père de votre correspondant(e) est voyageur de commerce. Il connaît bien la France et vous le questionnez sur ses voyages. Utilisez *y* au lieu des mots en italique dans ses réponses.

Your pen pal's father is a traveling salesperson and knows France very well. You question him about his travels. Use *y* in place of the words in italics in his replies.

Exemple:

—Vous vous arrêtez souvent à Paris?
—Oui! Je m'arrête souvent *à Paris.*
—Oui! Je m'*y* arrête souvent.

1. —Vous connaissez Orléans? —Oui, je dors quelquefois *à Orléans.*

   _____

2. —Vous êtes allé souvent à Lyon? —Oui, je mange souvent *à Lyon.*

   _____

3. —Vous connaissez Marseille? —Oui, je fais souvent des affaires *à Marseille.*

   _____

4. —Et Le Havre? —Oui, je prends le bateau pour l'Angleterre *au Havre.*

   _____

5. —Vous avez visité Bordeaux? —Oui, je reste *à Bordeaux* dans un hôtel Ibis.

   _____

6. —On me dit que vous avez eu un accident à Bayonne. C'est vrai? —Oui, c'est vrai, j'ai eu un accident *à Bayonne* il y a quelques mois.

   _____

▶4 Rêve de vacances

Émilie rêve des vacances. Complétez les phrases par *y* ou *en* selon le cas.

Émilie is dreaming of vacation. Complete the sentences with *y* or *en* as necessary.

Nous partirons de très bonne heure et nous prendrons l'autoroute. Nous nous **(1)** _____

arrêterons pour nous reposer, faire le plein d'essence à la station-service et **(2)** _____ manger

un sandwich ou des glaces. Nous **(3)** _____ mangerons une ou deux puis nous repartirons jusqu'à Biarritz. En arrivant, nous chercherons la maison que nous **(4)** _____ avons louée,

nous **(5)** _____ laisserons nos valises et nous irons à la plage en courant. Nous nous **(6)** _____

baignerons. Nous achèterons des frites et des pizzas et nous **(7)** _____ mangerons beaucoup.

Puis nous nous assiérons sur la terrasse et nous parlerons de nos projets. Nous **(8)** _____

parlerons jusqu'à minuit.

⭐5 Enquête au supermarché

On fait une enquête sur les services du supermarché Super-U. Voici les questions qu'on fait un matin à Mme Lechat. Répondez "Oui" pour elle, en remplaçant les mots en italique par deux pronoms.

They are conducting a survey about the Super-U supermarket. These are the questions Mrs. Lechat is asked one morning. Answer "Yes" for her, replacing the words in italics with two pronouns.

Exemple:

Est-ce que vous faites souvent *vos courses au Super-U?*
Oui, je *les* y fais souvent.

1. Est-ce que vous prenez *notre bus spécial au coin de votre rue* pour venir au Super-U?

_____

2. Est-ce que vous avez vu *la promotion d'aujourd'hui dans le journal?*

_____

3. Est-ce que vous faites *tous vos achats au Super-U?*

_____

4. Est-ce que vous avez présenté *vos bons de promotion* (coupons) *à la caissière?*

_____

5. Est-ce que vous *vous* asseyez quelquefois *dans notre café?*

_____

6. Est-ce que vous avez parlé *au gérant* (manager) *de nos produits?*

_____

7. Est-ce que vous parlerez *à vos voisins de notre excellent service?*

_____

Partez!

▶5 À l'école

Dites ce que vous faites à l'école, en utilisant *y*.

Say what you do at school, using *y*.

Exemple:

Nous y étudions, nous y faisons du sport, etc.

_____

_____

_____

_____

_____

▶6 Des questions de famille

Votre camarade de classe vous demande combien vous avez de tantes, d'oncles, etc.
Vous répondez avec *en*. Écrivez vos questions et vos réponses.

Your partner asks you how many aunts, uncles, and so forth you have. You reply with *en*.
Write your questions and your answers.

Exemples:

Combien de tantes as-tu? J'en ai trois / je n'en ai pas.
Combien de: cousins, oncles, frères, sœurs, grands-parents, ami(e)s, etc.

_____

_____

_____

_____

_____

▶**7** *Il y en a* ou *il n'y en a pas*?

Regardez autour de vous et posez des questions à vos camarades comme ci-dessous.
Ils doivent y répondre comme dans les exemples. Écrivez vos questions et vos réponses.

Look around you and ask your classmates questions like those below. They have to reply
as in the examples. Write your questions and your answers.

Exemples:

—Est-ce qu'il y a des mots français au tableau?
—Ou, il y en a (trois, beaucoup, etc.).

—Est-ce qu'il y a des éléphants roses dans la salle?
—Non, il n'y en a pas!

_____

_____

_____

_____

_____

_____

_____

_____

11 Counting
numbers

À vos marques!

You can't get far without using numbers. You need them for shopping (prices, sizes, quantities, weights and measures), traveling (distances, fares, buying gas, flight numbers), eating (recipes, café and restaurant prices), telling time, giving dates, phone numbers, and so forth, so make sure you learn them well!

Counting: "cardinal" numbers

0	zéro				
1	un	11	onze	21	vingt **et** un
2	deux	12	douze	22	vingt-deux
3	trois	13	treize	23	vingt-trois
4	quatre	14	quatorze	24	vingt-quatre
5	cinq	15	quinze	25	vingt-cinq
6	six	16	seize	26	vingt-six
7	sept	17	dix-sept	27	vingt-sept
8	huit	18	dix-huit	28	vingt-huit
9	neuf	19	dix-neuf	29	vingt-neuf
10	dix	20	vingt		

30–69

30	trente	31	trente **et** un	32	trente-deux	etc.
40	quarante	41	quarante **et** un	42	quarante-deux	etc.
50	cinquante	51	cinquante **et** un	52	cinquante-deux	etc.
60	soixante	61	soixante **et** un	62	soixante-deux	etc.

o|o *Attention!*

Note that 21, 31, 41, 51, 61, and 71 contain **et.**

70–79

There is no separate word for 70: you are saying 60 + 10, 60 + 11 right up to 60 + 19 for 79:

70	**soixante-dix**	75	**soixante-quinze**
71	**soixante et onze**	76	**soixante-seize**
72	**soixante-douze**	77	**soixante-dix-sept**
73	**soixante-treize**	78	**soixante-dix-huit**
74	**soixante-quatorze**	79	**soixante-dix-neuf**

80–99

You repeat this process for 80 to 99 (80 + 10, etc.):

80	quatre-vingts	90	**quatre-vingt-dix**
81	quatre-vingt-un	91	**quatre-vingt-onze**
82	quatre-vingt-deux	92	**quatre-vingt-douze**
83	quatre-vingt-trois	93	**quatre-vingt-treize**
84	quatre-vingt-quatre	94	**quatre-vingt-quatorze**
85	quatre-vingt-cinq	95	**quatre-vingt-quinze**
86	quatre-vingt-six	96	**quatre-vingt-seize**
87	quatre-vingt-sept	97	**quatre-vingt-dix-sept**
88	quatre-vingt-huit	98	**quatre-vingt-dix-huit**
89	quatre-vingt-neuf	99	**quatre-vingt-dix-neuf**

100 and above

100	cent	158	cent cinquante-huit
101	cent un	172	cent soixante-douze
102	cent deux, etc.	199	cent quatre-vingt-dix-neuf
121	cent vingt et un		

200 to 999 work in the same way:

200	deux cents	270	deux cent soixante-dix
300	trois cents	349	trois cent quarante-neuf
400	quatre cents	494	quatre cent quatre-vingt-quatorze
500	cinq cents	535	cinq cent trente-cinq
600	six cents	618	six cent dix-huit
700	sept cents	720	sept cent vingt
800	huit cents	863	huit cent soixante-trois
900	neuf cents	998	neuf cent quatre-vingt-dix-huit

1 000	mille	1 237	mille deux cent trente-sept
2 000	deux mille	2 785	deux mille sept cent quatre-vingt-cinq
15 000	quinze mille	15 003	quinze mille trois
1 000 000	un million		

⊙|⊙ Attention!

1. Review the numbers 60 to 79 and 80 to 99, where you are counting in twenties. Note that in French, phone numbers are stated by number pairs—38 36 54 72—and it is good to be able to distinguish between *soixante-deux* (62) and *soixante-douze* (72).

2. There is no *et* in 81–91 *quatre-vingt-un/quatre-vingt-onze* or between the hundreds and the tens: 112 *cent douze*.

3. You probably won't need to write out numbers in full very much, but in case you do, watch these points: 80 and the hundreds from 200, 300, etc., are spelled with *s*, which is dropped when you add a number: *deux cents* but *deux cent un*.

   Mille (1000) does not take an *s: deux mille.*

4. *Un* at the end of a number—no matter how long—agrees with the gender of the noun:

   *Mille vingt et **un** garçons et mille vingt et **une** filles.*
   1,021 boys and 1,021 girls.

5. In French, thousands are separated with a period:

   2.119 *deux mille cent dix-neuf*   two thousand one hundred and nineteen

6. Conversely, decimals are separated by a comma:

   2,119 *deux virgule cent dix-neuf*   two point one one nine

1st, 2nd, 3rd: "ordinal" numbers

These numbers tell you the order things come in:

1st	premier/première	11th	onzième
2nd	deuxième	12th	douzième
3rd	troisième	20th	vingtième
4th	quatrième	21st	vingt et unième
5th	cinquième	22nd	vingt-deuxième
6th	sixième	60th	soixantième
7th	septième	80th	quatre-vingtième
8th	huitième	99th	quatre-vingt-dix-neuvième
9th	neuvième	1000th	millième
10th	dixième		

This is easy: except for *premier/première* (1st), you simply add *-ième* to the basic (= cardinal) number, removing first any final *-e:*

quatre → quatrième   *onze → onzième*

Note also: *neuf → neuvième*

ojo Attention!

1. These ordinal numbers are adjectives, although only *premier/ première* has a separate feminine form:

   La première rue à gauche.   The first street on the left.

2. *Second(e)* is sometimes used instead of *deuxième:*

   Deux aller-retour à Paris en **seconde.**   Two **2nd-class** round-trips to Paris.
   *Ma sœur est en **seconde.***   My sister is in **10th grade.**

   (There are three grades in French high school: *seconde* [10th grade], *première* [11th grade], and *terminale* [12th grade].)

Collective numbers

You may encounter phrases such as:

une dizaine de	about 10
une douzaine de	a dozen, about 12
une quinzaine de jours	2 weeks
une vingtaine de	about 20
une cinquantaine de	about 50

They are often used to give an approximate number and are always linked to their noun with *de:*

*Il y a **une trentaine d'**enfants dans ma classe.*
There are **about 30** kids in my class.

Fractions

The French use decimals much more frequently than fractions, but you will encounter the following quite often:

½	*un demi*
¼	*un quart*
¾	*trois quarts*

un demi-litre	half a liter
une heure et demie	an hour and a half
trois quarts d'heure	three quarters of an hour

La moitié is used for "half" when referring to one of two halves:

J'ai déjà mangé la moitié de mes sandwichs!
I've already eaten half my sandwiches!

Prêts?

▶**1 Un menu**

Sur le menu du restaurant Louis XIII à Péronne, lisez les prix suivants à haute voix.

From the menu of the Louis XIII restaurant in Péronne, read the following prices aloud.

Entrées	*Potage du jour*	21fr
	Oeufs mayonnaise	18fr
	Hors-d'oeuvre variés	34fr
	Terrine du chef	27fr
Viandes	*Entrecôte grillée*	56fr
	Côte de porc à la provençale	41fr
	Poulet basquaise	69fr
Poissons	*Saumon en sauce avec des champignons*	72fr
Fromages	*Plateau de Fromages*	35fr
Desserts	*Crème caramel*	23fr
	Mousse au chocolat	42fr
Boissons	*Vin de Bordeaux*	95fr
	Vin d'Alsace	78fr
	Eau minérale	15fr
	Coca	17fr
	Café	12fr

▶**2** Résultats des matchs de volley

Les deux équipes de volley de Moreuil et de Montdidier jouent tous les samedis. Lisez les dates et les résultats du mois d'avril.

The two handball teams of Moreuil and Montdidier play every Saturday. Read the dates and scores for the month of April.

Samedi 5 avril	Moreuil 14	Montdidier 21
Samedi 12 avril	Moreuil 23	Montdidier 8
Samedi 19 avril	Moreuil 19	Montdidier 18
Samedi 26 avril	Moreuil 13	Montdidier 13

Quel est le total de points (*points*) de Moreuil? Et de Montdidier? _____

Quelle est la meilleure équipe? _____

Combien de points de plus a-t-elle marqué? _____

▶**3** Problèmes

Trouvez la solution des problèmes suivants. Écrivez vos phrases ci-dessous.

Find the solution to the following problems. Write your sentences below.

1. Votre voiture consomme (*consumes*) cinq litres aux cents kilomètres. Combien de kilomètres faites-vous avec un plein (*full tank*) de quarante litres?

   _____

2. Un train roule à cent vingt kilomètres à l'heure. Combien de temps mettra-t-il pour faire quatre cent vingt kilomètres? S'il part à onze heures le matin, à quelle heure arrivera-t-il?

   _____

3. À la librairie vous achetez deux livres de poche à trente-deux francs et un stylo à quatorze francs. Combien dépensez-vous?

   _____

4. Vous jouez vingt-quatre francs au loto (*lottery*) pendant quatre semaines. La quatrième semaine, vous gagnez quatre-vingt dix-huit francs. Avez-vous gagné ou perdu de l'argent? Combien?

   _____

5. Dans un examen vous avez cent quarante-six réponses justes (*right, correct*) sur deux cents. Quel pourcentage de réponses justes avez-vous?

   _____

▶4 Quelques questions d'ordre

Remettez le bon numéro ordinal dans chaque espace blanc.

Put the right ordinal number in each blank.

1. Thérèse habite au _____ étage.

2. David a gagné le _____ prix.

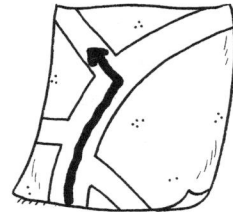

3. Prenez la _____ rue à gauche.

4. Napoléon I est mort au _____ siècle.

5. Cette année j'aurai mon _____ anniversaire.

6. Voici la _____ question de cette exercice!

Partez!

▶ **5** Au restaurant

Travaillez par deux. Vous êtes au restaurant Louis XIII à Péronne comme dans l'exercice 1. Dites ce que vous prenez, avec le prix, et faites l'addition entière. Combien avez-vous payé? Écrivez vos additions ci-dessous.

You're at the restaurant Louis XIII as in exercise 1. Say what you order and add up the whole bill. How much did you pay? Write out your bills below.

_____   _____

_____   _____

_____   _____

_____   _____

_____   _____

_____   _____

_____   _____

▶ **6** Quiz

Savez-vous répondre aux questions suivantes? Écrivez vos réponses.

Can you answer the following questions? Write your answers.

1. Combien de secondes y a-t-il dans une heure? Et d'heures dans un jour? Et de jours dans un an?

_____

2. Combien d'habitants y a-t-il dans votre ville/village?

_____

3. Combien y a-t-il de joueurs dans une équipe de football américain? Et de basket-ball?

_____

4. En quelle année êtes-vous né(e)?

_____

→

5. Quel est votre numéro de téléphone? (Dites les quatre derniers numéros en paires.)

_____

6. Combien y a-t-il d'habitants (à peu près) aux États-Unis? Et en France?

_____

▶7 Apprenons à compter

Continuez.

5, 10, 15 . . . jusqu'à 100
4, 8, 12 . . . jusqu'à 48
3, 6, 9 . . . jusqu'à 42
3, 6, 7, 10, 11 . . . jusqu'à 31
100, 95, 90 . . . jusqu'à 0
50, 46, 42 . . . jusqu'à -2
40, 37, 34 . . . jusqu'à 1

▶8 Jeu de dés

Faites deux ou trois équipes. Chaque équipe a deux dés. Chaque joueur à son tour jette les deux dés, en annonçant tout haut son score et le total courant de l'équipe. La première équipe qui arrive à 100 a gagné.

Make up two or three teams. Each team has dice. Each player in turn throws the dice, and announces aloud his or her score, and the running total of the team. The first team to reach 100 wins.

Puis, on peut aller de 100 à 0, ou de 50 à 0 avec un seul dé, etc.

Then you can go from 100 to 0, or 50 to 0 with only one die, etc.

How Big, How Heavy, How Far?
size, weight, and distance

 **À vos marques!**

Measures

Metric measures are, of course, used in France and other French-speaking countries. The most frequently used are:

Size and distance

un millimètre	a millimeter
un centimètre	a centimeter
un mètre	a meter
un kilomètre	a kilometer

Liquid capacity

un litre	a liter
un demi-litre	half a liter
un centilitre	a centiliter

Weight

un milligramme	a milligram
un gramme	a gram
deux cents grammes	200 grams
cinq cents grammes	500 grams
un kilo	a kilo(gram)

Size

Dimensions

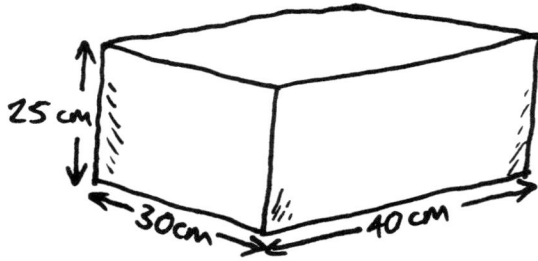

Combien mesure cette boîte?	What are the dimensions of this box?
Combien cette boîte fait-elle de long?	How long is this box?
Combien cette boîte fait-elle de large?	How wide is this box?
Combien cette boîte fait-elle de haut?	How tall is this box?

or

Quelle est la longueur/largeur/hauteur de cette boîte?	What is the length/width/height of this box?
Elle fait/a quarante centimètres de long.	It's 40 cm long.
Elle fait/a trente centimètres de large.	It's 30 cm wide.
Elle fait/a vingt-cinq centimètres de haut.	It's 25 cm tall.
*Elle fait/a 40 cm de long **par** 30 cm de large.*	It's 40 cm long **by** 30 cm wide.

Personal height

Combien mesures-tu/mesurez-vous?	How tall are you?
Je mesure / je fais un mètre soixante-sept.	I'm 1 meter 67.

Weight

Combien pèses-tu/pesez-vous?	What do you weigh?
Je pèse / je fais 57 kilos.	I weigh 57 kilos.
Combien pèse ce paquet?	How much does this package weigh?
Il pèse / il fait 600 grammes.	It weighs 600 grams.

Distance

When you want to say how far away something is, you must use *à:*

Bordeaux est à 565 kilomètres de Paris.	Bordeaux is 565 kilometers from Paris.
Le Syndicat d'Initiative est à deux minutes d'ici.	The Tourist Office is two minutes from here.

Prêts?

▶1 Ça mesure combien?

Donnez les dimensions des objets ci-dessous.

Give the dimensions of the articles below.

Exemple:

Combien mesure votre livre de français?
Il fait vingt-trois centimètres de long par quinze de large.

1. votre trousse à crayons (*pencil case*)

_____

2. votre pupitre

_____

3. le tableau

_____

4. la salle de classe

_____

5. la porte de la salle

_____

6. le bureau du professeur

_____

7. votre professeur

_____

8. vous

_____

▶2 On part en voyage

Lisez à voix haute à quelle distance les villes françaises se trouvent les unes des autres. Puis estimez la durée du voyage en voiture ou par le train. Écrivez vos phrases ci-dessous.

Read aloud how far apart these French towns are from each other. Then estimate the length of the journey by car or train. Write your sentences below.

Exemple:

Amiens est à cent trente-sept kilomètres de Paris. Amiens est à une heure par le train ou à une heure et demie en voiture.

Partez!

▶3 C'est quoi?

Un(e) élève donne les dimensions d'un objet et les autres doivent deviner ce que c'est. Celui qui donne la réponse juste continue. Attention au genre de l'objet: *il* ou *elle*?

One student gives the dimensions of an object and the others have to guess what it is. The one who gives the right answer continues.

Exemples:

Elle mesure/fait deux mètres de haut par un mètre de large.
C'est la fenêtre.

Il fait vingt centimètres de long par quinze de large et il pèse un kilo.
C'est le dictionnaire de français!

▶4 Présentations

Imaginez que vous écrivez à un(e) correspondant(e) français(e). Vous parlez de votre taille, votre poids, ainsi que ceux des membres de votre famille et même ceux de vos animaux!

Imagine that you are writing to a French pen pal. You talk about your height and weight, as well as those of the members of your family and even of your pets!

_____

_____

_____

_____

_____

_____

_____

13 Nine O'clock, April 1
times, dates, and seasons

À vos marques!

Telling time

Quelle heure est-il?	What time is it?
Avez-vous l'heure, s'il vous plaît?	Do you have the time, please?
Il est une heure.	It's one o'clock.

In French, as in English, there are two ways of saying the time: "ten to two" or "one-fifty."

Il est deux heures.

Il est cinq heures.

Il est midi.

Il est minuit.

Il est une heure cinq.

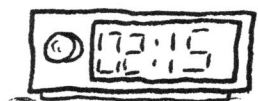

Il est deux heures et quart / il est deux heures quinze.

Il est quatre heures vingt.

Il est six heures et demie / il est six heures trente.

Il est huit heures moins vingt-cinq / il est sept heures trente-cinq.

Il est dix heures moins le quart / il est neuf heures quarante-cinq.

Il est minuit moins dix / il est onze heures cinquante.

ojo Attention!

1. In Europe, the 24-hour clock is used much more than in the U.S. In addition to travel timetables, you will find it used to refer to business hours, mail pick-ups, and so forth, and even in conversation when you need to avoid confusion:

    Heures d'ouverture: 9h à 12h, 14h à 18h
    Open: 9 A.M. to 12 noon, 2 P.M. to 6 P.M.

    Je t'attendrai à 19 heures.
    I'll wait for you at 7 P.M.

    If you don't use the 24-hour clock, you can say *du matin, de l'après-midi, du soir: Je t'attendrai à sept heures du soir.*

2. When writing times in figures, don't forget to put *h* after the hour:

    6h20   6:20

3. "At what time?" is *à quelle heure?* You need *à* in the reply:

    À quelle heure arrive le vol numéro BA345 de Londres?
    At what time does flight BA345 from London arrive?

    Il arrive à 16h33 (à seize heures trente-trois).
    It arrives at 16:33 (at 4:33 P.M.).

4. "About" a certain time is *vers:*

    Il arrive vers quatre heures et demie.
    It arrives about half past four.

5. Note the spelling of *demi(e): demie* after times containing *heure(s)* (*une heure et demie*) but *midi/minuit et demi.*

Days, months, and dates

Les jours de la semaine (Days of the week)

lundi	Monday	*vendredi*	Friday
mardi	Tuesday	*samedi*	Saturday
mercredi	Wednesday	*dimanche*	Sunday
jeudi	Thursday		

¡Ojo! Attention!

1. "On Saturday" is simply *samedi.*

   "On Saturdays," meaning "every Saturday," is **le** *samedi.*

Nous allons au cinéma samedi.	We're going to the movies **on** Saturday.
Ma correspondante arrive jeudi.	My pen pal arrives **on** Thursday.
Beaucoup des magasins sont fermés **le** *lundi.*	A lot of stores are closed **on** Monday**s**.

2. Remember also:

vendredi dernier	last Friday
mardi prochain	next Tuesday
hier	yesterday
avant-hier	the day before yesterday
demain	tomorrow
après-demain	the day after tomorrow
le lendemain	(on) the next day
la semaine dernière/prochaine	last/next week

Les mois de l'année (Months of the year)

janvier	January	*juillet*	July
février	February	*août*	August
mars	March	*septembre*	September
avril	April	*octobre*	October
mai	May	*novembre*	November
juin	June	*décembre*	December

To give a date, except for *le premier* (1st), you simply use the cardinal number. Again, there is no word for "on":

le premier avril	(on) April 1st
le trente et un octobre	(on) October 31st
le jeudi seize mai	(on) Thursday, May 16th

Le groupe de Picquigny arrivera **le** *vendredi 17 mai à 18h.*
The group from Picquigny will arrive **on** Friday, May 17th at 6 P.M.

"In" a month is *en* or *au mois de:*

en / au mois de janvier	in January

Years

You say the whole number for the year: you can't shorten it to "nineteen-ninety-eight" as in English, you must say *dix-neuf cent* or *mille neuf cent*.

1995	*mille neuf cent quatre-vingt-quinze*	2000	*deux mille*
1998	*dix-neuf cent quatre-vingt-dix-huit*	2005	*deux mille cinq*

"In" a year is *en:*

Je suis né(e) en 1984.   I was born in 1984.

As in English, you can omit the hundreds if you know which century you are talking about:

Je suis né(e) en '84.   I was born in '84.

"In" a century is *au:*

En 2001 nous sommes au vingt-et-unième siècle.   In 2001 we are in the 21st century.

Prêts?

▶ 1 Décalage horaire (time difference)

Los Angeles	*New York*	*Londres*	*Paris*

Dites-le de deux façons différentes. Puis, écrivez ce que vous avez dit.

Say it in two different ways. Afterwards, write what you said.

Exemple:

Quelle heure est-il à Paris quand il est 8h30 à New York?
14:30: quatorze heures trente *ou* deux heures et demie de l'après-midi.

1. Quelle heure est-il à Paris quand il est 13h30 à Londres?

   _____

2. Quelle heure est-il à New York quand il est 22h15 à Paris?

   _____

3. Quelle heure est-il à Los Angeles quand il est 14h45 à Londres?

   _____

→

4. Quelle heure est-il à Paris quand il est 8h28 du matin à New York?

   _____

5. Quelle heure est-il à Londres quand il est 12h50 à Paris?

   _____

6. Quelle heure est-il à Los Angeles quand il est 9h35 du soir à New York?

   _____

▶**2** Quel jour sommes-nous (1)?

Écrivez les dates suivantes, ou lisez-les à votre camarade de classe qui écrit ce que vous dites.

Write out the following dates or read them aloud to your partner, who has to write them down. Take turns reading and writing.

Exemple:

12-10 (lundi)
C'est lundi le douze octobre.

1. 07-01 (dimanche)   _____

2. 11-02 (samedi)   _____

3. 09-03 (jeudi)   _____

4. 28-04 (mardi)   _____

5. 31-05 (vendredi)   _____

6. 23-06 (mercredi)   _____

7. 14-07 (samedi)   _____

8. 01-08 (jeudi)   _____

9. 30-09 (lundi)   _____

10. 15-10 (mardi)   _____

11. 03-11 (lundi)   _____

12. 24-12 (dimanche)   _____

Partez!

▶3 Quel jour ça tombe?

Regardez votre calendrier pour cette année et cherchez quel jour tombe chaque événement.

Look at your calendar for this year and find out what day each event falls on.

Exemple:

mon anniversaire
C'est un lundi. C'est lundi le sept janvier.

1. Noël _____

2. le jour de l'An _____

3. la fête du Travail _____

4. le jour de Pâques _____

5. la fête des Mères _____

6. le début des grandes vacances _____

7. votre anniversaire _____

▶4 C'est en quel mois?

Demandez à votre camarade de classe: En quel mois de l'année . . .

Ask your classmate: In which month of the year . . .

a. commence(nt) le printemps, l'été, l'automne, l'hiver, les vacances de Noël, les vacances de Pâques, les grandes vacances?

b. y a-t-il de la neige? des tulipes dans les jardins? des embouteillages sur les routes?

c. fait-il le plus chaud? mange-t-on des crêpes? des glaces? partez-vous en vacances?

▶5 Quel jour sommes-nous (2)?

Travaillez par deux. Demandez-vous l'un à l'autre quel jour nous sommes. Écrivez vos questions et vos réponses.

Work in pairs. Ask each other what date it is, was, and will be. Write your questions and your answers.

Exemples:

Quel jour serons-nous demain?
Nous serons le 31 janvier 2001.

Et dans dix jours?
Nous serons le 10 février.

Et il y a dix jours?
Nous étions le 21 janvier.

_____

_____

_____

_____

_____

_____

"To," "From," "By," "With," "Without"
prepositions

14

À vos marques!

What is a preposition?

A preposition describes a relationship with a noun or pronoun. This may be of **place** (in front of, near, above); in **time** (before, after, until); or some **other relationship** (because of, in spite of). The use of prepositions with verbs is explained in Chapter 33. Here are explanations of some of the common prepositions which have several uses and a list of other prepositions which you will find useful.

Common prepositions

À

> **Conseil!**
>
> Remember that *à* + *le* = *au* and *à* + *les* = *aux*.

■ *À* basically means "to" or "at":

*Jérémie va **à** Amiens.*	Jérémie is going **to** Amiens.
*Il y arrivera **à** huit heures.*	He will arrive there **at** eight o'clock.
*Alors, nous nous retrouverons **au** marché?*	So we'll meet **at the** market?
*Donne ces glaces **aux** enfants.*	Give the ice cream (cones) **to the** children.

■ With a town or village, it also means "in":

*Jérémie habite **à** Picquigny.*	Jérémie lives **in** Picquigny.
*Mais il travaille **à** Amiens.*	But he works **in** Amiens.

■ You use *au/aux* for "to" or "in" countries which are **masculine**—*au Japon* "to/in Japan," *au Portugal* "to/in Portugal," and *aux États-Unis* "to/in the United States." (See *en* for "in" other countries.)

■ You **must** use *à* in French when expressing the distance at which something is situated or the price at which it is being sold:

*Abbeville est située **à** vingt-cinq kilomètres de la côte.*	Abbeville is (**at**) 25 km from the coast.
*Les pommes de terre sont **à** 6 francs le kilo.*	The potatoes are (**at**) 6 francs a kilo.

■ *À* is used with a noun or verb to indicate a use or purpose of an object:

*une tasse **à** café*	a coffee cup
*une machine **à** coudre*	a sewing machine

■ You use *à* with certain modes of travel:

à pied	**on** foot
à vélo/bicyclette	**by** bike
à cheval	**on** horseback

■ You also use *à* to link some verbs to a following infinitive (see Chapter 33) and with some verbs involving taking away (see Chapter 34).

De

De basically means "of" or "from."

Conseil!

Remember that **de** + **le** = **du** and **de** + **les** = **des.**

■ There is no equivalent of 's in French, and you always use *de* with a noun to indicate possession (see also Chapter 7):

*J'ai trouvé le parapluie **de** Madame Piollet.*	I've found **Mrs. Piollet's** umbrella.
*Ce sont les sandwichs **de** Sophie.*	These are **Sophie's** sandwiches.

■ You also use *de* for "of":

*le propriétaire **de** la maison*	the owner **of** the house
*les doigts **de** ma main gauche*	the fingers **of** my left hand
*une tasse **de** café*	a cup **of** coffee (compare *une tasse à café* "a coffee cup" above)

■ Generally you can't use one noun to describe or qualify another in French:

*un match **de** football*	a soccer match
*un concours **de** pêche*	a fishing competition
*le camping **de** Varengeville*	Varengeville campsite

(Use *à* for purpose: see the previous section.)

■ *De* also means "from" in most senses:

*Voici un fax **de** notre patron.*	Here's a fax **from** our boss.
*Delphine vient **de** Toulouse.*	Delphine comes **from** Toulouse.
*Oui, elle est **du** sud.*	Yes, she's **from the** south.

■ It is used between *quelqu'un / quelque chose* "someone / something" and *personne / rien* "no one / nothing" and an adjective:

*quelqu'un **d'**important*	someone important
*personne **d'**important*	no one important
*quelque chose **de** drôle*	something funny
*rien **de** drôle*	nothing funny

■ It is used to join some verbs to a following infinitive (see Chapter 33).

■ It is used to form some "compound" prepositions: *au milieu de* "in the middle of," *autour de* "around" (see the list in the section "Other useful prepositions" on page 100).

Dans and *en*

Both these words mean "in," but are used in different circumstances.

■ *Dans* usually means "physically within" something:

***dans** une boîte*	**in** a box
***dans** la mer*	**in** the sea
***dans** le nord*	**in** the north (and all compass points)
***dans** la Somme*	**in** + all French *départements*
***dans** cinq minutes*	**in** 5 minutes' time, within 5 minutes

■ *En* tends to be used with less physical "containers" and in certain other cases:

***en** 2003*	**in** 2003
***en** janvier*	**in** January (and all months)
***en** été/automne/hiver*	**in** summer/autumn/winter
(but ***au** printemps* "in spring")	
***en** Angleterre*	**in** England (and all **feminine** countries)
***en** anglais*	**in** English (and all languages)
***en** avion, **en** autobus*	**by** plane, **by** bus
***en** vert*	**in** green (and all other colors)

En + a time gives the time taken to perform an action:

*Sylvie a terminé l'examen **en** cinq minutes.*   Sylvie finished the exam **in** 5 minutes.

En + **present participle** (*en arrivant*, etc.): *en* is the only preposition which is not followed by an infinitive. This is fully explained in Chapter 35.

Other useful prepositions

Note that some prepositions can be used in more than one category.

Of place

à côté de	beside, next to	*à côté de notre maison*
à droite de	on/to the right of	*à droite de l'église*
à gauche de	on/to the left of	*à gauche du cinéma*
au bord de	on the edge of	*au bord de la rivière*
au bout de	at the end of	*au bout de la rue*
au centre de	in the center of	*au centre du parc*
*au-dessous de**	underneath, below	*au-dessous des arbres*
*au-dessus de**	above, over the top of	*au-dessus des toits*
au milieu de	in the middle of	*au milieu du lac*
autour de	around	*autour de la table*
chez	at the house of / at _____'s	*chez Christine*, *chez le boulanger*
contre	against	*contre la fenêtre*
derrière	behind	*derrière la porte*
devant	in front of	*devant la classe*
de l'autre côté de	on the other side of	*de l'autre côté de la rue*
en face de	opposite	*en face de l'hôtel de ville*
en haut de	on the top of	*en haut de la tour Eiffel*
entre	between	*entre la gare et la rivière*
jusqu'à	as far as	*jusqu'au pont*
loin de	a long way from, far from	*loin d'ici*
par	through	*allez-y **par** Beauvais*
parmi	among	*parmi les joueurs*
près de	near (to)	*près de la place*
sous	under	*sous le pont*
sur	on	*sur le pont*
vers	toward	*vers le musée*

Of time

à la fin de	at the end of	*à la fin du mois*
après	after	*après le déjeuner*
au bout de	at the end of	*au bout de dix minutes*
avant	before	*avant la guerre*, *avant midi*

depuis	since	*depuis 1997*†
entre	between	*entre dix heures et midi*
jusqu'à	until	*jusqu'à onze heures*
pendant	during, for	*pendant le match, **pendant** un mois*†
vers	toward, about (a time of day)	*vers deux heures*

Other relationships

à cause de	because of‡	*à cause de la neige*
au lieu de	instead of	*au lieu de mon frère*
au sujet de	about, on the subject of	*au sujet des vacances*
avec	with	*avec toi*
malgré	in spite of	*malgré la pluie*
par	by	*fabriquée **par** Renault*
pour	for	*un cadeau **pour** vous*
sans	without	*sans elle*
sauf	except	*sauf le dimanche*
selon	according to	*selon mon prof*
sur	on, about (a subject)	*un livre **sur** Paris*

OJO Attention!

*Be careful when saying *dessus* and *dessous:* they are not pronounced the same and mean the opposite of each other.

†Time spent or to be spent:

  a. If the action is still in progress use **present** tense and *depuis:*

    *Nous **apprenons** le français **depuis** quatre ans.*
    We've been learning French **for** four years (and are still learning it).

  b. If the action is finished or has stopped, use the *passé composé* and *pendant:*

    *Mon frère **a étudié** le français **pendant** cinq ans.*
    My brother **studied** French **for** five years (but he has now stopped).

  c. If the action is projected for the future, use the **future** or *aller* + **infinitive** with *pendant:*

    *Je **vais étudier** (j'**étudierai**) le français à l'université **pendant** quatre ans.*
    I'm going to (**I'll**) **study** French at the university for four years.

‡Don't confuse *à cause de* (because **of**) with *parce que* (because), which is followed by a verb (*parce que nous avons sommeil*)!

Prêts?

▶1 Thomas le chat

Thomas est un chat très agité. Il ne reste au même endroit que quelques minutes.
Où est-il dans chaque dessin?

Thomas is a very restless cat. He stays in one place for only a few minutes. Where is he in each drawing?

1. Il est _____ la table.

2. Il est _____ la table.

3. Il est _____ sa corbeille.

4. Il est _____ la fauteuil et le canapé.

5. Il est _____ les rideaux.

6. Il est _____ le feu.

7. Il est _____ ses amis.

8. Il est _____ la rue.

▶**2** La journée de Georges le chat, frère de Thomas

Voici une journée typique de Georges. Choisissez la bonne préposition à chaque fois.

Here is a typical day in the life of Georges. Choose the right preposition each time.

1. Georges réveille sa maîtresse (avant/après/depuis)

_____ sept heures chaque matin.

2. (Entre/vers/depuis) _____ sept heures et demie, elle lui donne son petit déjeuner de Friskies.

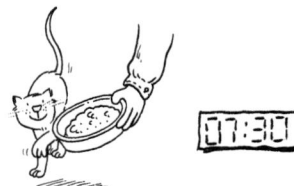

3. (Avant/après/pendant) _____ le petit déjeuner, il se lave.

4. Un peu (avant/vers/après) _____ huit heures, il fait une promenade dans le jardin.

→

5. L'été, il dort au soleil toute la journée,

(à/de/après) _____ 9 heures du matin

(de/entre/jusqu'à) _____ 6 heures

du soir.

6. Sa maîtresse rentre du travail

(vers/jusqu'à/entre) _____ six

heures et quart.

7. Le soir, Georges se couche (sous/dans/sur)

_____ les genoux de sa maîtresse.

8. Il reste là (de/entre/jusqu'à) _____
dix heures, quand il sort.

9. Chaque nuit, (à/de/entre) _____
minuit et six heures du matin, il cherche son
frère Thomas, et se bat avec lui.

10. Et sa maîtresse rêve que Georges dort

(pendant/entre/vers) _____ toute

la nuit!

✪3 Chère maman

Hélène est une Française en stage à San Francisco. Elle vit dans une famille américaine, et après une semaine, elle écrit à sa mère. Malheureusement il y a des erreurs dans les prépositions qu'il faut que vous corrigiez.

Hélène is a French student on a study abroad program in San Francisco. She is staying with an American family, and after a week, writes to her mother. Unfortunately there are some mistakes in the prepositions which you need to correct.

Le salon est très accueillant. Il y a une grande cheminée. Il y a un miroir *au-dessous*

(1) _____ et un canapé *derrière* (2) _____ la cheminée.

La porte *à droite du* (3) _____ canapé mène à la cuisine et la fenêtre *à gauche*

(4) _____ donne sur le jardin. Il y a une jolie table basse *vers*

(5) _____ le canapé et la cheminée et un radiateur *sur* (6) _____

la fenêtre. Comme tu le vois *derrière* (7) _____ la photo que je t'envoie, il y a

deux fauteuils et une table ronde d'où je t'écris *au bord de* (8) _____ la fenêtre.

Tu remarqueras une étagère *dans* (9) _____ de très belles poteries anciennes

au dessous de (10) _____ la porte. Le soir, je regarde la télé, qui est

à droite de (11) _____ la cheminée. Je travaille tous les jours, *selon*

(12) _____ le dimanche, et je suis très fatiguée le soir.

Partez!

▶4 Où est-il?

Un(e) élève prend un objet simple (un crayon, une gomme, etc.) et le cache quelque part dans la salle de classe. Les autres doivent deviner où il est, en employant une préposition dans leur question.

One student takes a simple object (pencil, eraser) and hides it in the classroom. The others have to guess where it is, using a preposition in their questions.

Exemples:

Est-ce qu'il/elle est *derrière* le tableau?
Est-ce qu'il/elle est *dans* ta poche?

▶5 C'est la routine!

Décrivez la journée de votre chat, chien ou autre animal (ou si vous n'en avez pas, de votre frère ou sœur). Utilisez les prépositions, comme dans l'exercice 2.

Describe a typical day for your cat, dog, or other pet (or if you don't have one, your brother or sister's animal). Use prepositions, as in exercise 2.

_____

_____

_____

_____

_____

"The Person Who," "The Thing That"

relative pronouns

15

À vos marques!

What is a relative pronoun?

A relative pronoun is used to attach a clause which gives you more information about a noun or pronoun:

the teacher **who** gave us this homework
the sales associate with **whom** I was talking (**whom** I was talking to)
the one **which** leaves at six o'clock
the purse **that** you found on the bus
the mother **whose** baby was ill

Attention!

Don't confuse **relative** pronouns with the interrogative (= question) pronouns explained in the next chapter. They are often the same words, but are used in different ways. **Relative pronouns don't ask questions!**

Qui "who," "which," "that"

■ *Qui* is used when the "relative" is the subject of the verb, that is, doing the action:

*La femme **qui parle** à ces filles-là est notre professeur de français.*
The woman **who is speaking** to those girls over there is our French teacher.

*Il faut prendre un train **qui s'arrête** à Lille.*
We must catch a train **that stops** at Lille.

*Ceux **qui font** tellement de bruit seront punis!*
Those **who are making** so much noise will be punished!

■ *Qui* is also used to refer to persons and to mean "who(m)" after a preposition:

*Voilà le professeur **avec qui** nous sommes allés en France.*
That's the teacher we went to France **with / with whom** we went to France.

Attention!

You **don't** use *qui* in this way **after** *de* (see the section on *dont* below) or to refer to **things** (see the section on *lequel*, etc., below).

Que "who(m)," "which," "that"

Que is used when the relative is the direct object of the clause, that is, having the action done to it:

*La femme **que** vous voyez là-bas est notre professeur de français.*
The woman **whom/that** you see over there is our French teacher.

You = the subject of "see," so "whom" or "that" referring to the woman is the object.

*Le train **que** nous avons pris s'est arrêté à Lille.*
The train **that** we caught stopped at Lille.
    (We caught; so "**that**" is the object.)

Conseil!

If there is a noun or pronoun subject of the verb, you can't have *qui* because the verb already has a subject (such as *nous* and *vous* in the above examples), so the relative must be *que*.

Dont "whose," "of which," "of whom"

■ "Whose"

*Les gens **dont** je garde le fils le week-end sont très sympa.*
The people **whose** son I watch on the weekend are very nice.

■ *Dont* is used to link *de* to a relative after verbs like *avoir besoin de* "to need," *parler de* "to talk about":

*C'est précisément le livre **dont** j'ai besoin!*
That's exactly the book (**that**) I need!

*On va voir le film **dont** je parlais hier soir?*
Shall we go and see the movie (**that**) I was talking **about** last night?

ojo Attention!

Dont must immediately follow the noun it refers to (its "antecedent").

Lequel, lesquels, laquelle, lesquelles "which," "that," "who"

As you see, *lequel* has four forms and agrees with the noun it refers to (its "antecedent").
It is used to refer to a thing or things, and sometimes people, after a preposition:

*Il faut laver les couteaux **avec lesquels** vous coupez la viande.*
You must wash the knives **with which** you cut the meat / you cut the meat **with.**
  (Agreement is masculine plural with *les couteaux.*)

When you use *à* or *de* + *lequel,* the four forms become:

auquel	auxquels	à laquelle	auxquelles
duquel	desquels	de laquelle	desquelles

*Le bâtiment **à côté duquel** nous sommes garés est le musée.*
The building (**that**) we are parked **next to** is the museum.

ojo Attention!

There are two important differences to notice between French and English
in the use of relatives:

- You can't leave out the relative pronoun in French.

- You can't put prepositions at the end of the clause in French: they must
  always come before the relative.

*la fourchette **avec laquelle** vous mangez . . .*
the fork you are eating **with** . . . (= the fork **with which** you are
  eating . . .)

Ce qui, ce que "what," "that which"

As subject:

ce qui importe le plus . . .   **what** matters most . . .

As direct object:

ce que j'aime mieux . . .   **what** I like best . . .

Celui qui / que "the one which," "the one that"

This refers to a definite noun.

	Masculine	**Feminine**	
Singular	*celui qui/que*	*celle qui/que*	the one who/which/that
Plural	*ceux qui/que*	*celles qui/que*	those who / the ones which / that

As usual, use *qui* for a subject and *que* for a direct object.

*De toutes ces robes, **celle que** j'aime le mieux c'est la jaune.*
Of all these dresses, the **one (that)** I like best is the yellow one.
   (Object, refers to the yellow dress.)

***Ceux qui** ne veulent pas visiter le musée peuvent regarder les magasins.*
Those who don't want to go to the museum can look in the stores.
   (Subject, refers to members of a group.)

Prêts?

▶1 Catherine va faire du babysitting

Catherine va garder le petit Cédric pour la nuit. Elle vient d'arriver chez les Duchêne. Dans sa conversation avec Mme Duchêne, rempliez les espaces blancs à l'aide de *qui* ou *que (qu')*.

Catherine is going to watch little Cédric for the night. She has just arrived at the Duchênes'. In her conversation with Mrs. Duchêne, fill in the blanks with *qui* or *que (qu')*.

—Est-ce que je peux regarder la télé?

—Oui, mais regarde la télé **(1)** _____ est au salon, tu entendras mieux Cédric t'appeler.

   Tu peux aussi regarder toutes les vidéos **(2)** _____ tu vois là ou écouter les CD

   (3) _____ tu verras dans le placard.

—Est-ce que je peux manger le poulet **(4)** _____ est au frigo?

—Oui, et tu peux aussi manger les crêpes **(5)** _____ j'ai faites ce matin.

—Et si Cédric ne veut pas dormir?

—Tu prends un des livres **(6)** _____ tu trouveras sur son étagère et tu lui lis une histoire.

   Celles **(7)** _____ il préfère sont les histoires de pirates.

—Et s'il y a quelqu'un **(8)** _____ téléphone?

—Tu réponds que nous revenons demain.

—Et s'il y a quelqu'un **(9)** _____ sonne à la porte?

—Tu n'ouvres pas et tu lui dis de revenir demain. Tu peux dormir dans la chambre

(10) _____ est ici à droite et utiliser la salle de bains **(11)** _____ se trouve à côté

de la chambre. Tu peux prendre les couvertures **(12)** _____ tu trouveras dans l'armoire

si tu as froid.

▶2 Le début de la saison de football

Le club de football des jeunes de Picquigny reprend ses activités. Voici les instructions du dirigeant le jour de la rentrée. Choisissez le pronom relatif qui convient.

The Picquigny soccer team is resuming its practice sessions. Here are the instructions from the coach on the first day back. Choose the relative pronoun that fits.

1. Vous pouvez utiliser tout le matériel (*equipment*) (qui/que/dont) _____ vous avez besoin.

2. Après l'entraînement (*practice*), rangez les ballons (qui/que/lesquels) _____ vous avez utilisés.

3. Les entraînements ont lieu le jeudi à 18h. Tout jeune (qui/que/dont) _____ ne pourra pas venir doit me téléphoner.

4. Les matchs ont lieu (*to take place*) le samedi à 13h30. Nous vous donnerons la liste des

   matchs (qui/que/lesquels) _____ sont organisés cette saison. Il faut me dire

   s'il y a des matchs (desquels / auxquels / sur lesquels) _____ vous ne pouvez

   pas participer.

5. Les jeunes (dont/que/lesquels) _____ les parents souhaitent (*to wish*) avoir des renseignements peuvent me téléphoner au 03.22.78.06.82.

6. Tout joueur (lequel/que/qui) _____ sera brutal (*rough*) sera exclu (*suspended*).

7. Les entraîneurs (*coaches*) avec (lesquels/que/dont) _____ vous travaillez insistent sur la régularité de l'entraînement pour progresser.

8. Il y a une fête (*celebration*) samedi le 20 septembre (dont / auquelle / à laquelle)

   _____ vous êtes tous invitées.

⭐3 Le stage (*course*) de surf

Vous arrivez à Biarritz pour un stage de surf. On vous présente les lieux. Réécrivez la phrase, en trouvant le pronom relatif qui convient et en le faisant accorder.

You arrive at Biarritz for a surfing course and you are shown around. Rewrite the sentence by finding the appropriate relative pronoun and making it agree.

1.	Voici les moniteurs		vous travaillerez.
2.	Voici les planches (*surfboards*)	avec lequel	vous apprendrez à surfer.
3.	Voici les chambres		vous dormirez.
4.	Voici les jeunes Français	sur lequel	vous partagerez les chambres.
5.	Voici les armoires		vous mettrez vos vêtements.
6.	Voici les cabines	auquel	vous vous doucherez.
7.	Voici le bar		vous prendrez le déjeuner.
8.	Voici le restaurant	dans lequel	vous prendrez le dîner.

1. _____

2. _____

3. _____

4. _____

5. _____

6. _____

7. _____

8. _____

▶4 Le journal de bord

Au stage de surf à Biarritz vous essayez de multiplier les contacts pour améliorer votre français. Vous parlez de ces contacts dans votre journal de bord. Remplacez les noms en italique par *celui/celle/ceux/celles*.

At the surfing course in Biarritz you try to meet new people who can help you improve your French. You list these contacts in your travel journal. Replace the nouns in italics with *celui/celle/ceux/celles*.

Exemple:

J'ai parlé avec *la femme* qui fait la cuisine.
J'ai parlé avec celle qui fait la cuisine.

1. J'ai discuté avec *les filles* qui servent au restaurant.

_____

2. J'ai déjeuné avec *le monsieur* qui nettoie les chambres.

_____

3. J'ai vu *les garçons* qui sont timides et qui ne parlent à personne.

_____

4. *La fille* que j'avais rencontrée le premier jour est venue me parler.

_____

5. *Les garçons* qui travaillent au bar m'ont invité(e) à prendre un verre.

_____

6. *Les touristes* que j'avais vus à la Maison de la Presse sont venus me voir sur la plage.

_____

7. *Les filles belges* que j'ai vues à la piscine vont faire du surf avec moi.

_____

Partez!

▶5 Qu'est-ce que c'est?

Vous faites des descriptions d'objets ordinaires et les autres doivent deviner de quoi vous parlez. Utilisez chaque fois un pronom relatif. Écrivez vos questions et vos réponses.

You describe ordinary objects and your classmates have to guess what you are talking about. Use a relative pronoun each time. Write your questions and your answers.

Exemples:

—C'est un article **que** nous utilisons pour manger la viande et les légumes.
—Une fourchette.

—C'est un article **avec lequel** nous mangeons la soupe ou le dessert.
—Une cuiller.

_____

_____

_____

→

_____

_____

_____

⭐6 "Typiquement" américain

Vous expliquez à des touristes français qui ne connaissent pas du tout les États-Unis quelques éléments de la tradition ou de la nourriture américaines. Utilisez un pronom relatif chaque fois.

You explain to some French tourists who don't know the United States at all some of its traditions or food. Use a relative pronoun each time.

Exemple:

—Qu'est-ce que c'est que les *hash browns*?
—Ce sont des pommes de terre râpées qui sont cuites dans l'huile.

Expliquez aussi: les *cheerleaders,* le *baseball,* le *Thanksgiving dinner,* les *pancakes,* le *fudge,* le *gravy,* etc.

_____

_____

_____

_____

_____

_____

_____

_____

⭐7 Qui est Sylvie? Où est-elle?

Imaginez que votre camarade de classe est nouveau/nouvelle dans votre collège, et que vous lui expliquez qui sont les autres élèves. Il/elle vous pose des questions, et vous lui répondez, en utilisant *celui/celle/ceux/celles* et *qui/que* comme dans l'exemple.

Imagine that your classmate is new to your school and that you are explaining to him or her who the other students are. He or she asks you questions and you reply, using *celui/celle/ceux/ celles* and *qui/que* as in the example.

Exemple:

—Qui est Sylvie?

—C'est *celle qui* est assise à côté de Mélanie, *que* tu connais déjà. C'est *celle qui* a les longs cheveux noirs.

_____

_____

_____

_____

_____

_____

16 Asking Questions
the interrogative

Á vos marques!

What is the interrogative?

"Interrogative" is just the technical word for "question"—as when you interrogate somebody. Questions can be "open," just requiring an answer of "yes" or "no," or be restricted by a specific question word such as "who?" "what?" "when?" "how?" etc.

Open questions

There are several ways of asking questions.

Turn the subject and verb around. (Invert the subject and verb.)

Avez-vous été au Parc Astérix?	**Have you** been to Parc Astérix?
Allez-vous en ville aujourd'hui?	**Are you going** to town today?

Attention!

1. When the subject is a noun, it is stated first, and then the verb is inverted with the corresponding third-person pronoun.

Ton frère va-t-il nous aider?	**Is your brother going** to help us?

2. When a third-person singular verb ends in *-e* or *-a,* a **-t-** is placed between the verb and the subject. The **t** is pronounced with the subject: **arrive-t-il, va-t-il.**

Arrive-t-il aujourd'hui ou demain?	**Does he arrive** today or tomorrow?

Use *est-ce que . . . ?*

You can make any statement into a question by simply adding *est-ce que* at the beginning. This is a very common way of forming a question and has the advantage that you don't have to invert the subject and verb!

Est-ce que vous avez été au Parc Astérix?	**Have you** been to Parc Astérix?
Est-ce que ton frère va nous aider?	**Is your brother going** to help us?
Est-ce qu'il arrive aujourd'hui ou demain?	**Does he arrive** today or tomorrow?

Raise the pitch of your voice

You will sometimes find that French people simply raise the pitch of their voice at the end of a statement to make it into a question. You can't, of course, do this when you are writing. Also note that this is an informal way to ask questions. For more formal situations you will use either inversion or **est-ce que.**

Vous avez été au Parc Astérix?	**Have you been** to Parc Astérix?
Il arrive aujourd'hui ou demain?	**Does he arrive** today or tomorrow?

Interrogative words

> ### Conseil!
> *Est-ce que* can usually be inserted after any question word in order to keep the verb following the subject. However, pay particular attention when using *qui* and *que,* as shown below.

Qui? "who?" "whom?"

As subject:

Qui a pris mon parapluie?	**Who** has taken my umbrella?
Qui est-ce qui a pris mon parapluie?	

As direct object:

Qui as-tu vu au club?	**Whom** did you see at the club?
Qui est-ce que tu as vu au club?	

After a preposition:

Avec qui as-tu joué?	**Whom** did you play **with**?
Avec qui est-ce que tu as joué?	

Que (qu') . . . ? "what . . . ?"

As subject:

Qu'est-ce qui s'est passé?   **What** has happened?
(You can't use *que* by itself here.)

As direct object:

Qu'as-tu vu?
Qu'est-ce que tu as vu?   **What** have you seen?

Quoi? "what?"

You use *quoi?* after prepositions:

Avec quoi l'as-tu fait?
Avec quoi est-ce que tu l'as fait?   **What** did you do it **with**?

And as an emphatic form of "what?":

Il a dit quoi?   He said **what**?

Quel, quelle, quels, quelles? "which?" "what?"

Quel is an adjective and must be used together with a noun, with which it has to agree.
It implies a choice:

Quelles villes allez-vous visiter?   **What towns** are you going to visit?
Quels parfums est-ce que tu préfères?   **Which fragrances** do you prefer?

Lequel, laquelle, lesquels, lesquelles? "which one?" "which ones?"

Lequel is a pronoun which refers to a specific noun. It also implies a choice:

Il y a des glaces à la vanille ou à la fraise. Laquelle est-ce que tu préfères?
There is vanilla or strawberry ice cream. **Which (one)** do you prefer?

Other common question words

Quand?	When?
Où?	Where?
D'où?	Where from?
Comment?	How?
Combien de?	How much, how many?
Pourquoi?	Why?
À quelle heure?	At what time?

Où est-ce que j'ai mis mon parapluie?   **Where** have I put my umbrella?
Comment allez-vous réparer ça?   **How** are you going to repair that?
Pourquoi n'as-tu pas répondu à ma lettre?   **Why** haven't you replied to my letter?

Prêts?

▶ **1** Poisson d'avril

Le 1ᵉʳ avril les élèves aiment jouer des tours à leurs professeurs. Mme Michaut a dû s'absenter de sa classe pendant quelques minutes, et elle y a trouvé une drôle d'ambiance à son retour. Utilisez les expressions de la case pour compléter ses questions.

On April 1 students like to play tricks on their teachers. Mrs. Michaut had to leave her class for a few minutes, and here's the crazy situation she found when she returned. Use the phrases from the box to complete her questions.

1. _____ a dessiné ces poissons au tableau?

2. _____ vous avez fait de mes lunettes?

3. _____ est caché dans l'armoire?

4. _____ je vois sous cette table?

5. _____ a écrit sur ma chaise?

6. _____ vous avez mis dans ce paquet sur mon bureau?

7. Oh! des poissons en chocolat! _____ m'a acheté ces poissons?

8. C'est très gentil à vous! _____ je peux faire pour vous remercier?

9. _____ vous plairait (*to please*)? que je vous raconte une histoire?

| Qui est-ce qui | Qui est-ce que | Qu'est-ce qui | Qu'est-ce que |

▶2 Interrogatoire

Vous allez passer trois mois dans une école française pour améliorer votre français. Le premier jour, tout le monde vous presse de questions, mais ce sont des questions en *est-ce que*. Transformez-les en inversions.

You are going to spend three months in a French school to improve your French. The first day, everyone asks you questions using *est-ce que*. Rewrite their questions using inversion (inverting the subject and the verb).

Exemple:

D'où est-ce que tu viens?
D'où viens-tu?

1. Pourquoi est-ce que tu viens dans notre école?

   _____

2. Où est-ce que tu loges?

   _____

3. Tes parents, qu'est-ce qu'ils font?

   _____

4. Combien de frères et de sœurs est-ce que tu as?

   _____

5. Jusqu'à quelle heure est-ce que tu as le droit (*the right*) de sortir le samedi soir?

   _____

6. Est-ce que tu veux sortir avec nous samedi prochain?

   _____

7. Quel genre de musique est-ce que tu aimes?

   _____

8. Quel sport est-ce que tu pratiques?

   _____

▶3 Au poste de police

En vous promenant, vous avez vu une voiture qui roulait vite et qui a ensuite causé un accident. Voici l'interrogatoire des gendarmes au poste de police. Dans la colonne de droite, cherchez les réponses aux questions des gendarmes.

While out for a walk, you saw a car going fast which then caused an accident. These are the questions the police asked you. Match your answers to them.

_____ 1. Quelle heure était-il quand vous avez vu la voiture qui a causé l'accident?

_____ 2. Que faisiez-vous sur cette route à huit heures du soir?

_____ 3. Combien de personnes y avait-il dans la voiture?

_____ 4. À quelle vitesse roulait-elle?

_____ 5. Avez-vous relevé (*take down*) le numéro d'immatriculation (*registration number*)?

_____ 6. Quelle a été votre réaction quand vous avez vu cette voiture?

_____ 7. Est-ce qu'il y avait d'autres personnes qui marchaient sur la route?

_____ 8. Comment était-il?

a. Oui, un vieux monsieur.

b. Très vite; à environ cent vingt kilomètres à l'heure.

c. Non, je n'ai pas fait attention.

d. Cinq.

e. Il était très vieux et très maigre. Il portait des lunettes, un pantalon gris et une chemise à carreaux (*a checked shirt*).

f. Environ huit heures du soir.

g. Je me promenais.

h. J'ai eu peur. Je me suis dit: cet homme conduit dangereusement.

Partez!

▶4 On fait connaissance?

Imaginez que vous êtes assis(e) à côté d'un garçon / une fille de votre âge à un match de tennis ou de football en France. Vous vous posez des questions pour en savoir plus.

Imagine you are sitting next to a boy/girl of your own age at a tennis or soccer match in France. Ask each other questions in order to learn more. (Use a mixture of *est-ce que*, inverted, and raised-pitch questions).

Exemples:

—Viens-tu souvent voir le tennis / le football?
—Est-ce que tu habites près d'ici?
—Tu es Français(e)?

_____

_____

_____

_____

_____

_____

_____

▶5 Monsieur/Madame le Maire

Imaginez que le maire de votre ville jumelle en France rend visite à votre collège. Il/elle ne parle pas anglais, mail il/elle a invité les élèves de votre cours de français à lui poser des questions au sujet de son travail de maire. Qu'est-ce que vous allez lui demander?

Imagine that the mayor of your French sister city is visiting your school. He or she doesn't speak English, but he or she invites the students in your class to ask him or her questions about his or her job as mayor. What questions will you ask?

Exemples:

—Où est-ce que le maire travaille?
—Depuis combien d'années êtes-vous maire?

Quand vous aurez pensé à une dizaine de questions, vous pourriez y répondre de la part du maire!

_____

_____

_____

_____

_____

_____

_____

_____

_____

⭐6 Un(e) babysitter catastrophique!

Un soir vous faites du babysitting chez des amis qui sont allés au cinéma. Malheureusement vous vous êtes endormi(e) devant la télé, et les enfants, André, 5 ans, et Paul, 7, se sont réveillés et ils ont complètement désorganisé la maison. Utilisez les mots interrogatifs pour leur poser des questions.

One evening you are babysitting for some friends who have gone to the movies. Unfortunately you fell asleep in front of the TV, and the kids, André, 5, and Paul, 7, woke up and caused havoc in the house. Use interrogatives to ask them questions.

Exemples:
—Qu'est-ce que vous avez fait de mes chaussures?
—Pourquoi avez-vous ouvert toutes les fenêtres?
—Pourquoi avez-vous allumé la cuisinière à gaz?
—Que va dire votre mère?

_____

_____

_____

_____

_____

17 What a Language! What a Lot of Rules!
exclamations

Ā vos marques!

Some of the words used to ask questions in the previous chapter are also used to make exclamations.

Quel, quelle, quels, quelles . . . !

Quel is used with a noun to mean "what a . . . !", "what _____s!"

Quelle langue!	**What a** language!
Quel professeur!	**What a** teacher!
Quels problèmes!	**What** problems!
Quelles difficultés!	**What** difficulties!
Quels bon élèves!	**What** good students!

Que de . . . ! "what a lot of . . . !"

Que de règles!	**What a lot of** rules!
Que de mots à apprendre!	**What a lot of** words to learn!

Qu'est-ce que + verb . . . "how . . . !" "look how . . . !"

Qu'est-ce que je suis bête!	**How** silly I am!
Qu'est-ce que tu es intelligent!	**How** intelligent you are!
Qu'est-ce qu'il neige!	**Look how** it's snowing!

Prêts?

▶ **1** La parade de Disneyland

Vous êtes mêlé(e) à la foule qui admire la parade de Disneyland et vous entendez les réflexions des spectateurs admiratifs. Retrouvez ces exclamations à partir des suggestions données ci-dessous.

You are in a crowd watching the Disneyland parade, and you hear the comments of the admiring spectators. Make up exclamations from the suggestions given below.

a.
Exemple:

Il y a beaucoup de monde!
Que de monde il y a!

1. Il y a de beaux chars (*floats*)!

_____

2. Les musiciens ont de beaux uniformes!

_____

3. Il y a beaucoup de personnages sur le char de Blanche Neige!

_____

b.
Exemple:

La fanfare (*brass band*) est vraiment bonne!
Quelle bonne fanfare!

4. La musique est vraiment entraînante (*lively*)!

_____

5. Le char du Livre de la Jungle est amusant!

_____

6. Le Grand Méchant Loup (*the Big Bad Wolf*) a l'air féroce (*fierce, ferocious*)!

_____

7. Les Trois Petits Cochons sont fabuleux!

_____

8. Minnie et Mickey sont des personnages extraordinaires!

_____

➡

c.

Exemple:

La fanfare joue bien!
Qu'est-ce que la fanfare joue bien!

   9. Mowgli court vite!

   _____

   10. Robin des Bois (*Robin Hood*) se bat bien!

   _____

   11. Mary Poppins danse gracieusement (*gracefully*)!

   _____

   12. Dingo amuse les enfants!

   _____

Partez!

▶ 2 Que d'exclamations vous faites!

Vous imaginez des situations et les exclamations que vous pourriez faire dans ces situations.

You imagine some situations and the exclamations you might make in these situations.

Exemples:

   1. Vous êtes au match de football:
   Qu'est-ce que cette équipe joue mal aujourd'hui!
   Quel but (*goal*)!
   Que de spectateurs!

   _____

   _____

   _____

   2. Vous êtes au bord de la mer en été:
   Qu'est-ce qu'il fait chaud aujourd'hui!
   Que de monde sur la plage!
   Quelle pollution!

   _____

   _____

   _____

Watch That Pronunciation and Spelling!

À vos marques!

You must have noticed by now that French sounds are very different from English ones, and that words that may be spelled the same in both languages in fact sound very different. We will simply concentrate here on the points that are sometimes challenging for English-speaking students.

Conseil!

You can't learn sounds from a printed book: you have to hear them. So use these notes on pronunciation together with your teacher, your French *assistant(e),* or other native French speaker.

Vowels, consonants, and syllables

You need to know what these are:

- **Vowel** sounds in French are *a, e, i, o, u,* and also combinations of these, such as *ai, au, eau, eu, oi, ou;* also *y* when pronounced the same as *-i-,* and the "nasal" sounds ending in *-n* (see the section on "nasal" vowels below).

- **Consonant** sounds mean all other sounds: *b, c/k/qu, ch, d, f/ph, g, j, l, ll, m, n, gn, p, r, s/ç, t/th, v, x, y, z/s.*

- **Syllables** are the consonant + vowel-sound components that make up a word: *fran-çais, li-vre, man-gez, in-tel-li-gent, Pa-ris, Bor-deaux.*

Accents

Accents **do matter**! They are part and parcel of French spelling and usually indicate that the vowel they are over is pronounced differently from how it would be pronounced if there were no accent.

There are three main accents which you put on top of a vowel:

■ (´) *accent aigu,* or "acute accent," found only on *é: été, mangé, événement*

■ (`) *accent grave,* or "grave accent," mainly on *è* (*boulangère, frère*) but also used to distinguish words otherwise spelled the same—such as *à* "to" / *(il) a* "(he) has," *où* "where" / *ou* "or," *là* "there" / *la* "the"—and on *voilà*

■ (^) *accent circonflexe,* or "circumflex accent," found on any vowel: *théâtre, (vous) êtes, gîte, hôte, flûte*

■ There are also the *cédille,* or "cedilla," which you put under *ç* in the combinations *ça, ço, çu* to show that the *c* is pronounced "soft," like an *s*—*ça, lançait, garçon, reçu*— and the *tréma,* or dieresis (¨), which you will find just occasionally to separate two vowels, as in *Noël.*

Vowels

E sounds

There are three different *e* sounds:

■ "Closed" *e:* this is a "tight" sound, usually spelled *-é, -er, -ez,* and also *-ai:*

préparer, préparé, préparez, préparerai.

■ "Open" *e:* pronounced with your mouth further open, usually spelled *-è, -e* + double consonant (*-elle, -ette*), *-et,* and the imperfect/conditional endings: *-ais, -ait, -aient: elle, jette, jouet, allais, allait, allaient.*

■ "Mute" *e:* this is *e* without an accent and appears in all other places:

1. When it comes at the end of a word of more than one syllable and in the *-ent* verb ending, it is hardly sounded, except in certain regional accents: *mange, manges, mangent, travaille, gomme, Marseille.*

2. Otherwise, it is pronounced as in *le: me, se, ce, je, je te regarde, appeler, jeter.*

Ou and *u*

These are two different sounds, so practice both listening/identifying them and pronouncing them!

tout/tu   vous/vu   dessous/dessus   nous/nu   d'où/du   oui/huit

O sounds

There are two *o* sounds. Practice and contrast:

■ *homme, gomme, pomme, bonne, trottoir, tricoter, vol, voleur, folle*

with

■ *hôte, rose, oser, gros,* **au,** *gâteau, chevaux*

Unless there is a circumflex on the *ô,* you just have to learn which sound the *o* has!

"Nasal" vowels

The ones you pronounce through your nose! There are four different nasal sounds, all ending in *-n-,* which English speakers often fail to distinguish.

Practice and contrast these groups with each other:

■ *an/en:* **en,** *dans, grand, vent, sent, sans, tante, tente, France*

■ *on: bon, son, ont, font, vont, allons, montons,* **on** *monte*

■ *in/ain/ein: vin, pain, peint, inquiet, insecte*
 also: *ien: italien, mécanicien*

■ *un:* **un,** *lundi*

Oi/oy sounds

Be careful with the pronunciation of the very common combination *oi/oy:*

Practice: *moi, toi, joie, oie, soit, voix, boîte, noir, croire, crois, croissant, envoie, envoyé.*

Consonants

Consonants at the end of a word

The following consonants are not usually pronounced when they come alone or in combination with each other at the end of a word: *d, g, s, t, x, z: bord, bords, lourd, lourds, sans, les, mes, et, est, jouet, choux, mangez, rez-de-chaussée.*

Conseil!

> An *-s* or *-x* added to make a noun or adjective plural is not heard, and you have to listen for the "agreement" marker to indicate that the noun is plural: **mon** *frère*   **mes** *frères.* This is fully explained in Chapter 1.

However, the last consonant in a word is carried on to the next word of a phrase if that word begins with a vowel. This is called "liaison":

un bon enfant, sans elle, mes amis, dix hommes, est il? prend il? allez-y!

A final *r* is usually sounded (*fleur, amour, car*), except at the end of a word ending *-er*, which has the *-é* sound, as in many infinitives. Exceptions: *mer, cher, fier, amer.*

Consonants to pay particular attention to

■ *h* at the beginning of a word: most are completely ignored; they are not pronounced and the word is regarded as beginning with a vowel: *l'homme, s'habiller, je m'habille, un hôtel.* However, *h* is sometimes "aspirate." This means that although it is still not sounded, it forms a barrier between the preceding word and the first vowel; articles don't contract and there is no liaison: *le: haricot, les: haricots, en: haut.*

■ *ll* is usually pronounced *y: réveiller, mouillé, grillade, fille* (but not in *ville, village,* or after *e: intelligent*). So is *l* in the endings *-ail, -eil, -euil: ail, réveil, deuil.*

■ *n* at the end of a syllable usually forms a nasal vowel (see the section on "nasal" vowels above).

■ *gn* is always pronounced like the *ni* in "onion": *oignon, espagnol, signe.*

■ *th* is sounded the same as *t: thé*

■ *qu* is always sounded *k*, never *kw: quel, qui, que, question.*

Prêts?

▶1 Entraînez-vous!

Entraînez-vous aux sons décrits ci-dessus avec votre professeur, assistant(e) de français ou une autre personne dont la langue maternelle est le français.

Practice the sounds described above with your teacher, French *assistant(e),* or other French native speaker.

▶2 Vous n'avez pas d'accent!

Voici la lettre que Vanessa, une fille américaine, a écrit à sa nouvelle correspondante française. Malheureusement elle ne sait pas comment imprimer les accents à son ordinateur. Alors, mettez les trente-deux accents (´ ` ^ ç)!

This is the letter that Vanessa, an American girl, has written to her new French pen pal. Unfortunately she doesn't know how to print the accents on her computer. Put the 32 accents on for her (´ ` ^ ç)!

Je m'appelle Vanessa. J'ai quinze ans. Je suis nee a San Francisco. J'habite maintenant a San Diego, mais autrefois, j'ai habite pres de Los Angeles. Mon pere est ingenieur et ma mere est infirmiere a l'hopital de la region. Tous les deux parlent bien le francais, parce qu'ils ont passe beaucoup de temps en France. Mon frere s'appelle Tom et il va a l'ecole primaire a cote de chez nous. C'est un garcon sympa. Au college, j'etudie huit matieres au total, mais je prefere la geographie et les mathematiques. Dans mon temps libre, j'aime aller au cinema et au theatre. Et toi, que fais-tu et ou vas-tu dans tes heures libres?

Partez!

▶3 Où sont les accents?

a. Écrivez le passage ci-dessus à l'ordinateur, en mettant tous les accents.

Write the above passage on a computer, putting in all the accents.

b. Choisissez un autre passage de votre manuel principal de français et écrivez-le à l'ordinateur avec tous ses accents.

Choose another passage from your main textbook and write it on the computer with all its accents.

19 Doing Things . . .
verbs, tenses, persons, and infinitives

Conseil!

Chapters 20 to 40 will give you detailed information and practice on verbs and their tenses, but study this chapter before going any further!

What is a verb?

A verb tells you what someone or something **does.** In other words, it describes an **action,** such as "make," "sing," "walk," "write," "be."

What is a tense?

A tense tells you **when** an action happens, happened, or will happen: in other words, it sets the action within a time framework. Chapters 20 to 29 explain in full the main tenses in French.

What is a "person"?

Person refers to **who** is doing the action (I/we, you, he/she/they). The numbering of the persons is rather selfish: you always think of yourself/-selves first! Then the person(s) you are talking **to** second, and the rest (he/she/it/they) third! Nouns always take the third person, for example, my dad **is** great, the children **are** very small, the bus **arrives.** "I" is "first-person **singular**" because there's only one of you, and "we" is "first-person **plural**" because there are two or more. Here are the first, second, and third persons, in both French and English:

	Singular		**Plural**	
1st person	*je*	I	*nous*	we
2nd person	*tu*	you	*vous*	you
3rd person	*il/elle*	he/she/it	*ils/elles*	they

ojo Attention!

French tenses have six endings—one for each person, singular and plural, for example: *je regarde, tu regardes, il/elle regarde, nous regardons, vous regardez, ils/elles regardent.* You need to pay particular attention to learning these endings. English verbs, unlike French verbs, have few changes in their endings. In English we have I/you/we/they **run,** he/she **runs**; I/you/he/she/we/they **ran** (no ending change at all!).

What is an ending?

You've guessed: it's the part that comes at the end and tells you which tense you are in and which person of the verb you are using.

What is a stem?

It's what's left when you've removed the ending: the part you add the endings to.

What is the infinitive?

The infinitive is the form of the verb, the "title," if you like, that you find in a dictionary or vocabulary list. You may come across the term "finite verb": this means a verb in a tense. The infinitive is not a tense—it is "in-finite." You could also describe it as the verb "in neutral," before you put it in a tense.

French infinitives usually end in *-er* (the biggest group), *-ir,* or *-re.* These are the three conjugations, or "families" of verbs, and the tense endings you use will in most cases be indicated by the infinitive ending. These verbs are called **regular.**

Verbs which don't fall into these three categories are called **irregular,** and you have to learn the forms that don't obey the rules. Both regular and irregular verbs are listed in full in the verb charts in Chapter 40.

Conseil!

Here's a useful tip for practicing verb endings (which your teacher may already use with you, but you can do it at home or by yourself). Take an ordinary die, and let each number represent one of the six persons of the verb: 1 = *je,* 2 = *tu,* 3 = *il/elle,* 4 = *nous,* 5 = *vous,* 6 = *ils/elles.* Select a verb and tense, throw the die, and say or write down the form shown by the die: for example, present of *manger,* throw 4 for *nous* and write *nous mangeons.* You could make a game of it with a partner, scoring a point for each correct ending.

20 Doing Things Now
the present tense of regular verbs

À vos marques!

What is the present tense?

The present tells you what happens as a general rule or what is happening at this moment.

How to form the present tense

Totally regular verbs

Remove the *-er, -ir,* or *-re* from the infinitive and add the endings as shown below:

regarder	to look	*finir*	to finish	*vendre*	to sell
je regarde	I look	*je finis*	I finish	*je vends*	I sell
tu regardes	you look	*tu finis*	you finish	*tu vends*	you sell
il/elle regarde	he/she looks	*il/elle finit*	he/she finishes	*il/elle vend*	he/she sells
nous regardons	we look	*nous finissons*	we finish	*nous vendons*	we sell
vous regardez	you look	*vous finissez*	you finish	*vous vendez*	you sell
ils regardent	they look	*ils finissent*	they finish	*ils vendent*	they sell

Conseil!

- The *nous* form always ends in *-ons*.
- The *vous* form always ends in *-ez*.
- The *ils/elles* form always ends in *-ent*, which you don't pronounce!
- The plural forms of *-ir* verbs have the additional *-iss-* in the middle.
- The *il* form of an *-re* verb ends with the *-d* of the stem.

"Boot" verbs

Small but important spelling adjustments occur in 1-2-3-6 verbs, or "boot verbs"!

The following groups of *-er* verbs are not really irregular, but they do change their sound and their spelling in the singular and third-person plural, that is, in forms 1, 2, 3, and 6:

■ Verbs like *acheter* "to buy": *e* becomes *è*

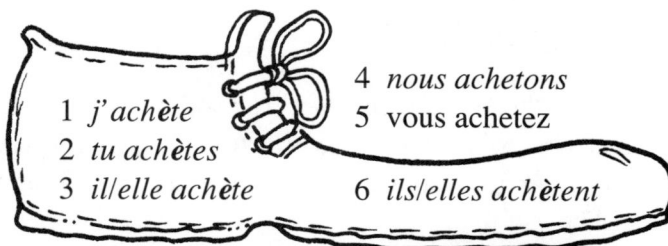

1 j'ach**è**te   4 *nous achetons*
2 tu ach**è**tes   5 vous achetez
3 il/elle ach**è**te 6 ils/elles ach**è**tent

Also in this category are *amener* "to bring," *emmener* "to take away," *mener* "to lead," *se lever* "to get/stand up," *se promener* "to go for a walk/ride," *peser* "to weigh."

■ Verbs like *appeler* "to call," *jeter* "to throw": double the final consonant (*l* becomes *ll*, *t* becomes *tt*)

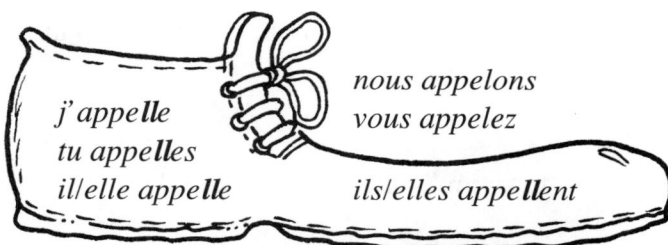

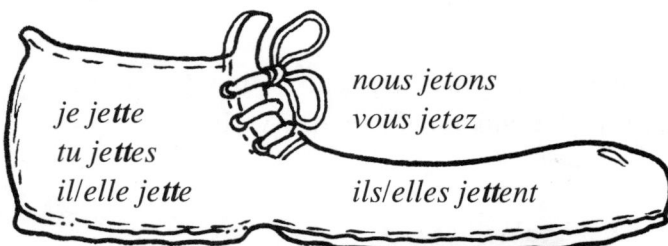

j'appe**ll**e   nous appelons
tu appe**ll**es   vous appelez
il/elle appe**ll**e ils/elles appe**ll**ent

je je**tt**e   nous jetons
tu je**tt**es   vous jetez
il/elle je**tt**e   ils/elles je**tt**ent

Also *rappeler* "to remember," "to phone back."

■ Verbs like *espérer* "to hope": change acute accent *é* to grave accent *è*

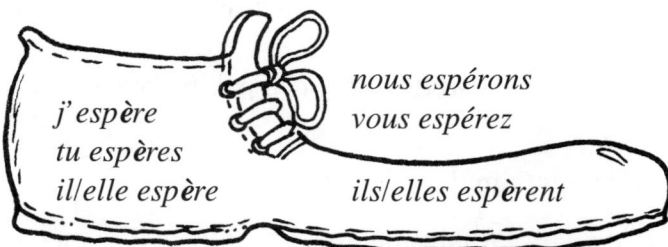

j'esp**è**re   nous espérons
tu esp**è**res   vous espérez
il/elle esp**è**re   ils/elles esp**è**rent

Also *s'inquiéter* "to worry," *préférer* "to prefer," *protéger* "to protect," *répéter* "to repeat," *sécher* "to dry."

■ Verbs like *employer* "to use": *y* becomes *i*

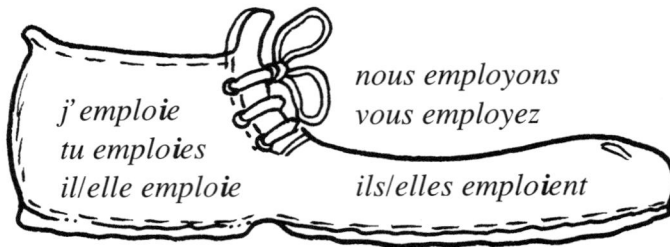

j'emplo*ie*   nous employons
tu emplo*ies*   vous employez
il/elle emplo*ie*   ils/elles emplo*ient*

Also *appuyer* "to lean, press," *envoyer* "to send," *renvoyer* "to send back," *essuyer* "to wipe," *nettoyer* "to clean," *se noyer* "to drown." *Essayer* "to try" (*j'essaie*), *payer* "to pay," and other verbs ending in *-ayer* are also usually spelled that way, though the change is not required.

As you can see, a good way to remember where these changes happen is to draw a line around them, *et voilà*—you have a boot! Call them "boot verbs" or *verbes bottés,* if you like, though those aren't "official" grammar terms!

■ Note also:

manger "to eat," *lancer* "to throw," and other *-er* verbs which have a *g* or a *c* before the ending are spelled *ge* or *ç* respectively in the *nous* form in order to keep the "soft" sound of the *g* and *c*.

nous mangeons   *nous lançons*

Also *s'allonger* "to lie down," *nager* "to swim," *partager* "to share," *protéger* "to protect"; *annoncer* "to announce."

Uses of the present tense

Note: some examples contain irregular verbs, which are dealt with in full in the next chapter. The uses are the same, of course, for both regular and irregular verbs.

The present is used:

■ To say what happens repeatedly, at certain intervals:

*Chaque année **nous allons** au bord de la mer.*	Every year **we go** to the seashore.
***Chantal se douche** tous les matins.*	**Chantal showers** every morning.
*D'habitude **Alain passe l'aspirateur** dans la salle de séjour.*	**Alain** usually **vacuums** the living room.
***J'écris** à mon correspondant au Canada tous les mois.*	**I write** to my pen pal in Canada every month.

■ To say what **is happening** at the present time:

*Dans cette photo **nous faisons une pique-nique** sur la plage.*	In this photo **we're picnicking** on the beach.

Chantal ne peut pas venir au téléphone: elle se douche.

Chantal can't come to the phone: **she's taking a shower.**

Alain passe l'aspirateur dans la salle de séjour.

Alain is vacuuming the living room.

J'écris à mon correspondant au Canada.

I'm writing to my pen pal in Canada.

■ To say what is happening in the immediate future, as in English:

*Qu'est-ce que **tu fais** ce soir?*

What **are you doing** this evening?

Je joue au tennis avec mes copines.

I'm playing tennis with my friends.

ojo Attention!

There is only one form of the present tense in French: there is no literal equivalent of **I'm playing**—you always say *je joue.*

See also Chapter 21 for the use of the present with *depuis*.

Prêts?

▶1 Travailler à Disneyland

Isabelle travaille à Disneyland à Paris. Elle décrit ce qu'elle et ses camarades de travail font. Trouvez la forme correcte du présent.

Isabelle works at Disneyland in Paris. She describes what she and her coworkers do. Find the correct form of the present.

1. Je (travaille/travaillons/travaillent) _____ à Disneyland.

2. Les visiteurs (arrives/arrive/arrivent) _____ en voiture ou par le RER (*Paris suburban railway*) du centre de Paris.

3. Nous (commencons/commençons/commencez) _____ le matin à 8h

   et nous (finis/finissez/finissons) _____ à 16h.

4. En été, le parc (restes/reste/restent) _____ ouvert jusqu'à 24h.

5. L'hiver, ils (fermez/fermes/ferment) _____ le parc à 21h et quelquefois à 19h quand il fait froid.

6. Au bureau de renseignements, je (répond/répondent/réponds) _____ aux questions des visiteurs.

7. Ma copine, Audrey, (vend/vends/vendent) _____ les glaces.

→

8. Mes amis et moi nous (mangeons/mangent/mangons) _____ à l'Auberge de Cendrillon ou au Chalet de la Marionnette.

9. Les touristes (achetez/achète/achètent) _____ beaucoup de souvenirs à Frontierland.

10. Je me (proméne/promène/promenne) _____ dans le parc après mon travail.

11. Voici une conversation que j'ai entendue entre deux touristes:

—Tu (envoies/envoyez/envoie) _____ des cartes postales à ta famille?

—Oh non! Je (préfères/préfèrent/préfère) _____ garder mon argent pour aller à la Rustler Round-up Shootin' Gallery! C'est fantastique! On se croirait au Wild West!

▶ **2 Les personnages de Walt Disney**

Isabelle va maintenant vous parler des personnages de Walt Disney qu'elle adore. Complétez les phrases en employant les verbes dans la case ci-dessous.

Isabelle is now going to tell you about the Walt Disney characters she loves. Complete the sentences using the verbs in the box below.

Tu te **(1)** _____ Baloo? Il se **(2)** _____ dans le parc et

(3) _____ la main des visiteurs. Il est formidable! Il **(4)** _____

superbement le swing. Les Sept Nains **(5)** _____ beaucoup les enfants dans

l'attraction "Blanche Neige et les Sept Nains," mais les enfants **(6)** _____ surtout

Blanche Neige et son Prince Charmant! Moi, je **(7)** _____ Geppetto et

Pinocchio. Mon amie et moi, nous **(8)** _____ quelquefois l'attraction des

Voyages de Pinocchio. C'est super! On **(9)** _____ de l'Italie! Et toi, quels

personnages **(10)** _____-tu? Avec ta famille, vous **(11)** _____ pour

la parade? C'est sensass! On **(12)** _____ tous les personnages de Disney!

aimes	adorent	danse	rêve	admire	restez	visitons
promène	préfère	rappelles	serre	amusent		

▶**3 Une invitation**

Vous êtes au Camp Davy Crockett à Disneyland et vous écrivez à votre correspondant(e)
et sa famille pour leur raconter ce que vous faites et les inviter à passer quelques jours avec
vous et votre famille. Mettez les verbes entre parenthèses à la forme qui convient.

You are at Camp Davy Crockett at Disneyland and you are writing to your pen pal and his
or her family to tell them what you are doing and to invite them to spend a few days with you
and your family. Put the verb in parentheses into the correct form.

Chers amis,

   Nous voici à Disneyland. Avec mes parents, nous (loger) **(1)** _____

dans un bungalow au Camp Davy Crockett, à cinq kilomètres environ du parc

Disneyland. Le bungalow est bien équipé mais nous (cuisiner) **(2)** _____

sur le barbecue et nous (manger) **(3)** _____ dehors. Mes parents

(acheter) **(4)** _____ la nourriture en ville au "Alamo Trading Post."

Tous les matins mon père se (baigner) **(5)** _____ dans la piscine et

ensuite nous (jouer) **(6)** _____ au tennis. L'après-midi, nous

(choisir) **(7)** _____ une autre activité. Quand viendrez-vous nous voir?

Pourquoi ne nous (téléphoner) **(8)** _____-vous pas pour dire quand vous

(arriver) **(9)** _____? Nous nous (amuser) **(10)** _____

beaucoup et nous serons contents de vous faire partager tout ceci.

   À bientôt

Partez!

4 Pendant les vacances

a. Dites 10 choses que vous faites pendant les vacances, en utilisant les verbes suivants.

Say 10 things you do during vacation, using the following verbs.

se lever	manger	regarder	se promener	se reposer	acheter
se coucher	se détendre (*to relax*)		jouer	s'amuser	se baigner

Exemple:

Je me lève tard / de bonne heure / à neuf heures

_____

_____

_____

_____

_____

_____

b. Maintenant dites 10 choses que vous *ne faites pas* pendant les vacances. Utilisez quelques verbes de "la section a" ou peut-être ces autres ci-dessous.

Now say 10 things you *don't* do on vacation. Use some verbs from "part a" and perhaps those below.

travailler	s'habiller en uniforme	attendre le bus chaque matin

_____

_____

_____

_____

_____

_____

c. Maintenant dites ce que vos parents ou vos frères ou sœurs font et ne font pas pendant les vacances.

Now say what your parents or brothers or sisters do and do not do on vacation.

_____

_____

_____

_____

_____

_____

▶5 Interview

Travail par deux. Vous interviewez un personnage sur sa vie quotidienne. Votre camarade de classe est le personnage qui répond à vos questions. Utilisez quelques verbes de l'exercice 4, et aussi *arriver au travail, terminer le travail, déjeuner, dîner, choisir.*

Pair work. You are interviewing a personality about his or her daily life. Your partner is the personality who answers your questions. Use some verbs from exercise 4 and also *arriver au travail, terminer le travail, déjeuner, dîner, choisir.*

Exemples:

—À quelle heure est-ce que vous vous levez le matin?
—Je me lève vers huit heures.

—Pour travailler, quels vêtements choisissez-vous?
—Pour le travail, je choisis un costume bleu.

21 Doing Things Now
the present tense of irregular verbs

Ā vos marques!

There are quite a lot of French verbs that don't follow the "regular" patterns set out in Chapter 20. However, we have broken down irregular verbs into types in order to help you learn them.

Groups of irregular verbs

There are several small groups of irregular verbs which follow the same pattern of irregularity in the present tense.

-ir verbs with *-er* endings

ouvrir "to open"

j'ouvre	*nous ouvrons*
tu ouvres	*vous ouvrez*
il/elle ouvre	*ils/elles ouvrent*

Also in this group are *accueillir* "to welcome," *cueillir* "to gather," *couvrir* "to cover," *découvrir* "to discover," *offrir* "to offer," *souffrir* "to suffer."

-ir verbs without *-i-*

sortir "to go out"

je sors	*nous sortons*
tu sors	*vous sortez*
il/elle sort	*ils/elles sortent*

Also *courir* "to run," *dormir* "to sleep," *s'endormir* "to go to sleep," *mentir* "to lie / tell lies," *partir* "to leave," *sentir* "to feel/smell," *servir* "to serve."

The following groups of *-re* verbs

éteindre "to put out, extinguish"

j'éteins	*nous éteignons*
tu éteins	*vous éteignez*
il/elle éteint	*ils/elles éteignent*

Also *craindre* "to fear," *joindre* "to join," *peindre* "to paint," *se plaindre* "to complain."

conduire "to drive"

je conduis	*nous conduisons*
tu conduis	*vous conduisez*
il/elle conduit	*ils/elles conduisent*

Also *détruire* "to destroy," *produire* "to produce," *réduire* "to reduce," *traduire* "to translate."

Completely irregular verbs

These are the most important irregular verbs. We advise you to learn them because they are frequently used! However, here are a few helpful hints:

- ■ Most have the singular endings *-s, -s, -t: je bois, tu bois, il boit.*

- ■ When the stem ends in *-d* there is no *-t* in the third-person singular: *il prend.*

- ■ The vowel often changes in the plural: *je bois → nous buvons.*

- ■ The vowel may change back in the third-person plural: *ils boivent*

- ■ Or it may stay the same: *nous savons → ils savent.* Watch out also for a possible consonant change: *nous prenons → ils prennent.*

- ■ The key forms are therefore 1–4–6: *bois–buvons–boivent:* the other endings usually follow as normal.

s'asseoir	to sit	*je m'assieds, tu t'assieds, il s'assied, nous nous asseyons, vous vous asseyez, ils s'asseyent*
boire	to drink	*je bois, tu bois, il boit, nous buvons, vous buvez, ils boivent*
connaître	to know	*je connais, tu connais, il connaît, nous connaissons, vous connaissez, ils connaissent*

Also *paraître* "to seem," *reconnaître* "to recognize."

coudre	to sew	*je couds, tu couds, il coud, nous cousons, vous cousez, ils cousent*
croire	to believe/think	*je crois, tu crois, il croit, nous croyons, vous croyez, ils croient*
devoir	must/to have to	*je dois, tu dois, il doit, nous devons, vous devez, ils doivent*
écrire	to write	*j'écris, tu écris, il écrit, nous écrivons, vous écrivez, ils écrivent*

Also *décrire* "to describe."

falloir	to be necessary	*il faut* only: it is necessary
mettre	to put	*je **mets**, tu **mets**, il **met**, nous **mettons**, vous **mettez**, ils **mettent***

Also *promettre* "to promise," *remettre* "to put back."

mourir	to die	*je **meurs**, tu **meurs**, il **meurt**, nous **mourons**, vous **mourez**, ils **meurent***
pleuvoir	to rain	*il **pleut*** only
pouvoir	to be able / can	*je **peux**, tu **peux**, il **peut**, nous **pouvons**, vous **pouvez**, ils **peuvent***
prendre	to take	*je **prends**, tu **prends**, il **prend**, nous **prenons**, vous **prenez**, ils **prennent***
recevoir	to receive	*je **reçois**, tu **reçois**, il **reçoit**, nous **recevons**, vous **recevez**, ils **reçoivent***
rire	to laugh	*je **ris**, tu **ris**, il **rit**, nous **rions**, vous **riez**, ils **rient***

Also *sourire* "to smile."

rompre	to break	*je **romps**, tu **romps**, il **rompt**, nous **rompons**, vous **rompez**, ils **rompent***

Also *interrompre* "to interrupt."

savoir	to know	*je **sais**, tu **sais**, il **sait**, nous **savons**, vous **savez**, ils **savent***
suivre	to follow	*je **suis**, tu **suis**, il **suit**, nous **suivons**, vous **suivez**, ils **suivent***
venir	to come	*je **viens**, tu **viens**, il **vient**, nous **venons**, vous **venez**, ils **viennent***

Also *devenir* "to become," *revenir* "to come back," *se souvenir* "to remember"; *tenir* "to hold," *appartenir* "to belong," *obtenir* "to obtain," *retenir* "to retain, hold back."

vivre	to live	*je **vis**, tu **vis**, il **vit**, nous **vivons**, vous **vivez**, ils **vivent***
voir	to see	*je **vois**, tu **vois**, il **voit**, nous **voyons**, vous **voyez**, ils **voient***
vouloir	to want	*je **veux**, tu **veux**, il **veut**, nous **voulons**, vous **voulez**, ils **veulent***

The following verbs are very irregular—and very common, so you will want to memorize them.

aller	to go	*je **vais**, tu **vas**, il **va**, nous **allons**, vous **allez**, ils **vont***
avoir	to have	*j'**ai**, tu **as**, il **a**, nous **avons**, vous **avez**, ils **ont***
dire	to say/tell	*je **dis**, tu **dis**, il **dit**, nous **disons**, vous **dites**, ils **disent***
être	to be	*je **suis**, tu **es**, il **est**, nous **sommes**, vous **êtes**, ils **sont***
faire	to do/make	*je **fais**, tu **fais**, il **fait**, nous **faisons**, vous **faites**, ils **font***

Uses of the present tense

The same uses apply as for regular verbs in Chapter 20, pages 136–37. Another use which also applies to all verbs is to say what has been happening for a period of time or since a particular time **and is still happening**—that is, how long you have been doing something for.

ojo Attention!

Pay particular attention to this way of saying things because in English a past tense is used. In French you use the present tense + *depuis* + the amount of time the action has been going on or the time when it started.

Depuis quand attendez-vous le bus?
How long have you been waiting for the bus?

Nous attendons ici depuis vingt minutes.
We've been waiting here **for** twenty minutes.

Joël joue au tennis depuis 1998.
Joël has been playing tennis **since** 1998.

Martine travaille pour Air France depuis l'année dernière.
Martine has been working for Air France **since** last year.

Prêts?

1 Que font-ils?

a. Utilisez les verbes donnés pour dire ce que font ces personnes et ces animaux.

Use the verbs given to say what these people and animals are doing.

1. Il _____ à l'école. (aller)

2. Elle _____ du supermarché. (venir)

3. Il _____ une lettre. (recevoir)

4. Elle _____ du vélo. (faire)

5. Ils _____ des cartes postales. (écrire)

6. Ils _____ devant le feu. (dormir)

7. Elles _____. (courir)

8. Je _____ très bien! (conduire)

→

b. Choisissez la légende qui convient. Encerclez la bonne réponse.

Choose the right caption. Circle the correct response.

1. il peut
   il pleut
   il prend

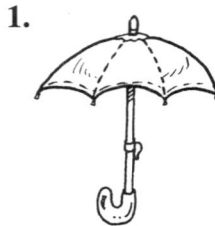

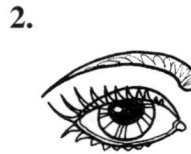

2. il va
   il veut
   il voit

3. elle sort
   elle sait
   elle sent

4. il suit
   il sait
   il sert

5. ils croient
   ils doivent
   ils boivent

▶2 Le camping sous la pluie

Vous êtes en vacances avec vos parents en France, mais il pleut tout le temps. Ce n'est pas drôle! Pour passer le temps sous la tente, vous écrivez à votre correspondant(e) dans le Midi et vous lui expliquez ce que vous faites. Mettez les verbes entre parenthèses à la forme du présent qui convient.

You are on vacation with your parents in France, but it's raining all the time. It isn't funny! You write to your pen pal in the south of France and explain what you are doing. Complete the following paragraph with the correct forms of the verbs in parentheses.

Il (faire) **(1)** _____ mauvais ici à Abbeville. Il (pleuvoir) **(2)** _____

tout le temps! Je (sortir) **(3)** _____ avec mes parents et quelquefois

je (aller) **(4)** _____ au cinéma, mais je ne (comprendre) **(5)** _____

pas bien les films en français! Je (dormir) **(6)** _____ beaucoup, mais sous

la tente, ce n'est pas amusant. J'(entendre) **(7)** _____ la pluie qui tombe

toute la nuit et le matin, quand j'(ouvrir) **(8)** _____ la tente,

je (voir) **(9)** _____ que tout (être) **(10)** _____ mouillé et je me (dire) **(11)** _____, "Qu'est-ce que nous (aller) **(12)** _____

faire aujourd'hui?" Est-ce que nous (pouvoir) **(13)** _____ descendre

chez toi dans le Sud? Moi, je (vouloir) **(14)** _____ bien, et si tu es d'accord,

je (pouvoir) **(15)** _____ demander à mes parents.

▶ 3 Une journée à Paris

Avec vos parents vous décidez de passer une journée à Paris. Vous allez au syndicat d'initiative à Abbeville où l'on vous donne quelques renseignements. Choisissez la forme convenable du verbe pour chaque phrase.

With your parents you decide to spend a day in Paris. You go to the tourist office in Abbeville where you are given some information. Choose the right form of the verb for each sentence.

—Comment (peut/peux/peuvent) **(1)** _____-on aller à Paris en partant

d'Abbeville?

—Oh! Il (falloir/faut) **(2)** _____ prendre le train. C'est ce qu'il y a de mieux.

En voiture, vous ne (sait/savent/savez) **(3)** _____ jamais où vous garer à Paris.

(Connaissons/connaît/connaissez) **(4)** _____-vous Paris?

—Non, mais mon père y (va/vais/allons) **(5)** _____ quelquefois pour ses affaires.

—Alors, vous (avez/avons/ont) **(6)** _____ un plan du métro?

—Non. (Pouvons/peuvent/pouvez) **(7)** _____-vous nous en donner un?

—Voici. Que (voulons/veulent/voulez) **(8)** _____-vous voir à Paris?

—Mes parents (voulons/veulent/veut) **(9)** _____ voir quelque chose d'amusant.

—Alors, vous (prenez/prenons/prennent) **(10)** _____ le métro jusqu'à Anvers,

et vous (va/allez/vont) **(11)** _____ jusqu'à la place du Tertre pour voir

les peintres. Ils (peignez/peint/peignent) **(12)** _____ très bien.

Ils (fait/faites/font) **(13)** _____ même d'excellentes caricatures!

—Quelle bonne idée! On y (vont/allons/va) **(14)** _____!

Partez!

▶5 Le matin

a. Travail en classe entière comme un jeu, ou par deux. Vous vous posez des questions sur vos activités le matin, en utilisant les verbes suivants avec *tu*.

Whole class game or pair work. You ask each other questions about your morning activities, using the following verbs with *tu*.

aller (à l'école, au supermarché, etc.)	devoir (aider tes parents)
faire (la vaisselle, les devoirs, etc.)	mettre (le couvert, l'uniforme)
venir (en bus, à vélo, à pied, etc.)	partir
prendre (une douche, le petit déjeuner, etc.)	voir (tes amis, tes profs, etc.)

Exemples:

Comment viens-tu à l'école? Je viens en bus.
Est-ce que tu prends du thé ou du café? Je prends du thé.

b. Maintenant posez des questions semblables à votre professeur, en utilisant *vous*.

Now ask your teacher similar questions using *vous*.

▶6 Travail à trois

Divisez-vous en groupes de trois. L'un d'entre vous choisit un des verbes de la liste de la section *À vos marques!* et en fait une phrase avec *je*. Les deux autres doivent dire que "nous aussi, nous faisons la même chose," c'est-à-dire qu'ils répètent la même phrase, mais au pluriel. Écrivez vos phrases ci-dessous.

Work in groups of three. One of you chooses a verb from the list in *À vos marques!* and makes a sentence beginning with *je*. The two others have to say that they do the same thing, but in the plural, of course. Write your sentences below.

Exemples:

—Je lis le journal tous les jours.
—Nous aussi, nous lisons le journal tous les jours!

—Je bois un verre d'eau en déjeunant.
—Nous aussi, nous buvons un verre d'eau en déjeunant!

Pour compliquer un peu les choses, vous pouvez utiliser la troisième personne.

Exemple:

—Mon frère écrit à une fille en France.
—Nos frères aussi écrivent à des filles en France!

_____

_____

_____

_____

_____

_____

_____

_____

▶**7** **Depuis quand?**

Mettez les mots dans le bon ordre.

Put the words in the right order.

1. habitez-vous quand depuis ici?

_____

2. et mois moi ma vivons six depuis sœur ici

_____

3. trois frère mois seconde est depuis en mon

_____

4. du je depuis cinq français fais ans

_____

5. ans ici le vingt-cinq est collège depuis

_____

6. hier chimie Colin depuis la comprend

_____

7. et ans jouent deux Karim depuis rugby Mustapha au

_____

8. est une français malade semaine professeur depuis notre de

_____

22 Do's and Don'ts
imperatives or commands

À vos marques!

What is an imperative?

An imperative is a command—"do" or "don't," for example—"Eat your breakfast!" "Don't feed the animals!" It also includes suggestions such as "let's": "Let's go to the movies."

How to form the imperative

Forming the imperative is easy, except that you should remember that there are two words for "you," *tu* and *vous,* and so there are two forms of the "you" imperative.

Tu

For -*er* verbs, you simply remove the -*s* from the *tu* form of the present tense and omit *tu:*

tu pousses	you push	*pousse!*	push!
tu tires	you pull	*tire!*	pull!

For other verbs, you simply use the *tu* form without *tu:*

tu choisis	you choose	*choisis!*	choose!
tu réponds	you answer	*réponds!*	answer!
tu bois	you drink	*bois!*	drink!

Exception: *tu vas* "you go" becomes *va!* "go!" except in *vas-y!* "go ahead, get on with it!"

Vous

You simply use the *vous* form of the present without *vous:*

vous poussez	you push	*poussez!*	push!
vous choisissez	you choose	*choisissez!*	choose!
vous répondez	you answer	*répondez!*	answer!

vous buvez	you drink	*buvez!*	drink!
vous allez	you go	*allez!*	go!
vous faites quelque chose	you do something	*faites quelque chose!*	do something!

"Let's"

To say "let's do something," use the *nous* form of the present, without *nous:*

| *nous voyons* | we see | *voyons!* | let's see! |
| *nous allons* | we go | *allons!* | let's go! |

Exceptions

Just three verbs don't follow the usual pattern:

		tu	*vous*	*nous*
être	to be	*sois*	*soyez*	*soyons*
avoir	to have	*aie*	*ayez*	*ayons*
savoir	to know	*sache*	*sachez*	*sachons*

Don't! Let's not!—making the command negative

Just place *ne . . . pas* around the verb, as usual:

ne pousse pas!	don't push!
ne répondez pas!	don't answer!
n'allons pas!	let's not go!

Do it, don't do it

The imperative may be used with object pronouns. (To review object pronouns, look at Chapters 8, 9, and 10.)

■ Positive commands: pronouns come at the end, joined with hyphens:

*Envoyez-**les-lui**!*	Send **them to her**!
*Faites-**le** bien!*	Do **it** well!
*Donne-**le-leur**!*	Give **it to them**!
*Arrêtez-**vous**!*	Stop!

ojo Attention!

For "me" and "you" (familiar), use *moi* and *toi,* which come last:

*Écrivez-**moi**!*	Write **to me**!
*Montre-le-**moi**!*	Show it **to me**!
*Lève-**toi**!*	Stand up!

■ Negative commands: pronouns come before the verb, as in any other tense:

*Ne **les lui** envoyez pas!*	Don't send **them to her**!
*Ne **vous** arrêtez pas!*	Don't stop!
*Ne **t'**inquiète pas!*	Don't worry!

Other ways of expressing commands

■ The infinitive is often used in instructions:

Ne pas toucher!	Don't touch!
Ouvrir ici!	Open here!

■ To soften a command and sound more polite, you can ask someone to do something, rather than telling them to, using *pourriez-vous?* "could you?":

***Pourriez-vous parler** un peu plus lentement, s'il vous plaît?*	**Could you speak** a little more slowly, please?

Prêts?

▶1 Le dressage du chien

Vous avez un jeune chien à la maison et vous lui enseignez des ordres simples. Que lui dites-vous?

You have a young dog at home and you are teaching him some simple commands. What do you say to him?

1. manger

2. boire

_____

_____

3. venir

4. s'asseoir

_____

_____

5. aller chercher

_____

6. prendre

_____

7. ne pas bouger

_____

8. ne pas tirer

_____

▶**2** Sophie entre au collège

Sophie a 11 ans. Elle entre au collège. Le professeur principal donne les règles à respecter en classe. Faites correspondre les impératifs avec la fin de phrase qui convient.

Sophie is 11. She's starting junior high. The homeroom teacher is stating the class rules. Match up the commands with the rest of the sentence.

_____ **1.** Demandez

_____ **2.** Ne buvez pas

_____ **3.** Ne mangez pas

_____ **4.** Attendez

_____ **5.** Levez-vous

_____ **6.** Participez

_____ **7.** Ne parlez pas

_____ **8.** Levez

a. quand un professeur entre dans la classe.

b. à vos camarades lorsque le professeur parle.

c. le doigt pour demander la parole (_to ask to speak_).

d. de coca pendant les cours.

e. la fin du cours pour boire et manger.

f. de chewing-gum en class.

g. la permission si vous voulez sortir.

h. activement à la classe.

▶3 Le départ en vacances

La famille Dupuis part en vacances. Ils préparent les bagages et se donnent des ordres les uns aux autres à la première personne du pluriel.

The Dupuis family is going on vacation. As they pack they give each other commands in the first-person plural.

Exemple:

(Prendre) la crème solaire
Prenons la crème solaire!

1. (Aller) faire le plein d'essence!

   _____

2. (Ne pas oublier) les passeports!

   _____

3. (Prendre) de l'argent liquide!

   _____

4. (Passer) chez l'épicier pour acheter des fruits et des boissons pour la route!

   _____

5. (Ne pas boire) trop avant le départ!

   _____

6. (Mettre) le répondeur automatique (*answering machine*) en marche!

   _____

7. (Vérifier) que la garage est bien fermé!

   _____

8. (Fermer) la porte de la maison à clef!

   _____

Partez!

▶4 À notre collège . . .

Préparez une liste des règles de votre collège pour un groupe de jeunes Français qui vont y passer quelques jours comme élèves. Utilisez la forme *vous*.

Prepare a list of your school's rules for a group of French students who are going to spend a few days at your school. Use the *vous* form because you are addressing the group.

Exemples:

Portez l'uniforme!
Ne courez pas dans les couloirs!

_____

_____

_____

_____

_____

_____

▶5 À l'auberge de jeunesse

Faites une liste de 5 règles d'une auberge de jeunesse. Utilisez la forme *tu*.

Make a list of 5 rules for a youth hostel. Use the *tu* form because you are addressing each individual.

Exemples:

Laisse l'évier propre après l'avoir utilisé!
Fais ton lit!

_____

_____

_____

_____

_____

▶6 Faisons quelque chose d'intéressant

Vous discutez avec vos copains et copines de la façon dont vous allez passer un jour des vacances scolaires. Faites des propositions, en utilisant la forme *-ons.*

You are discussing with your friends how you are going to spend one of your school vacation days. Make some proposals using the *-ons* form.

Exemples:

Faisons une randonnée à vélo!
Allons au Parc Astérix!

_____

_____

_____

_____

What Will Happen?
the future tense

23

À vos marques!

What is the future tense?

The future tense tells you what **will happen,** what you **will do**—in the future!

How to form the future

Verb endings

The endings *-ai, -as, -a, -ons, -ez, -ont* are always the same. For the majority of verbs you add them to the end of the **infinitive.** You drop the *-e* from the end of *-re* infinitives:

regarder	finir	vendre	
je regarderai	*je finirai*	*je vendrai*	I will look/finish/sell
tu regarderas	*tu finiras*	*je vendras*	you will . . .
il/elle regardera	*il/elle finira*	*il/elle vendra*	he/she will . . .
nous regarderons	*nous finirons*	*nous vendrons*	we will . . .
vous regarderez	*vous finirez*	*vous vendrez*	you will . . .
ils/elles regarderont	*ils/elles finiront*	*ils/elles vendront*	they will . . .

Conseil!

Note that the future endings resemble the present tense of *avoir*—except for *avons* and *avez,* which lose the *av-*!

157

Spelling changes in some *-er* verbs

Verbs ending in *-er* that have a spelling change in the present tense (see Chapter 20) also have the same change in the stem of the future:

Infinitive		Present	Future
appeler	to call	*j'appelle*	*j'appellerai*
jeter	to throw	*je jette*	*je jetterai*
acheter	to buy	*j'achète*	*j'achèterai*
employer	to use	*j'emploie*	*j'emploierai* (not *envoyer*—see below)

ojo Attention!

Verbs like *espérer* do not have a spelling change in the future:

espérer   to hope   *j'espère*   *j'espérerai*

Irregular verbs

ojo Attention!

Irregularities are always in the **stem,** never in the endings.

Irregular *-er* verbs: only

aller	to go	*j'irai*
envoyer	to send	*j'enverrai* (and *renvoyer* "to send back")

Irregular *-ir* verbs:

courir	to run	*je courrai*
mourir	to die	*je mourrai*
tenir	to hold	*je tiendrai* (also *obtenir* "to obtain," *retenir* "to retain")
venir	to come	*je viendrai* (also *devenir* "to become," *revenir* "to come back," *se souvenir* "to remember")

Irregular *-re* verbs: only

être	to be	*je serai*
faire	to do/make	*je ferai*

Conseil!

Even though many otherwise irregular verbs have an infinitive that ends in *-re,* they behave normally in the future.

Irregular *-oir* verbs:

This is a small group which you should just commit to memory.

s'asseoir	to sit down	*je m'**assié**rai*
avoir	to have	*j'**aur**ai*
devoir	to have to	*je **dev**rai*
falloir	to be necessary	*il **faud**ra*
pleuvoir	to rain	*il **pleuv**ra*
pouvoir	to be able, can	*je **pour**rai*
recevoir	to receive	*je **recev**rai*
savoir	to know	*je **sau**rai*
voir	to see	*je **ver**rai*

Conseil!

Have you noticed how the future stem **always ends in -r,** whether the verb is regular or irregular?

How do you use the future?

Saying what will happen

Tu finiras **tes devoirs tout de suite!**
You'll finish your homework right now!

Nous ne verrons pas **le château aujourd'hui.**
We won't see the castle today.

Pendante ta visite, ***nous irons*** *à Paris,* ***nous ferons*** *des promenades à vélo,* ***tu pourras*** *pratiquer ton français et* ***nous nous amuserons*** *bien.*
During your visit, **we'll go** to Paris, **we'll do** some biking, **you'll be able to** practice your French, and **we'll have a good time.**

Attention!

Don't be tempted to use the future for expressions like "Will you help me set the table?" where "will" means "are you willing to," not "will you do it at some time in the future?"

Tu veux m'aider **à mettre le couvert?**
Will you help me set the table?

After time expressions

You have to use the future after time expressions such as *quand* or *lorsque* "when" and *aussitôt que* "as soon as" when the action has not yet taken place:

Quand vous arriverez *à Paris, vous retrouverez notre représentant.*
When you arrive in Paris, you will meet our representative. (You haven't arrived yet!)

Aussitôt qu'il* *vous verra, *il vous mènera à votre hôtel.*
As soon as he sees you, he will take you to your hotel. (He hasn't seen you yet!)

ojo Attention!

> Be careful here because the present tense is used in English, but the future is used in French!

Other ways of expressing the future

■ In French, as in English, you can say what **you are going to do** in the immediate future by using *aller* + the infinitive:

*Qu'est-ce que **tu vas faire** ce soir? **Je vais me laver** les cheveux!*
What **are you going to do** this evening? **I'm going to wash** my hair!

■ You can also use the present tense to talk about the immediate future (see also Chapter 20):

*Qu'est-ce que **tu fais** ce soir? **Je me lave** les cheveux!*
What **are you doing** this evening? **I'm washing** my hair!

Prêts?

▶1 Quand j'aurai de l'argent

Avec votre correspondant(e) vous discutez de ce que vous ferez de votre argent quand vous aurez vos premiers salaires. Choisissez la forme du verbe qui convient dans la conversation.

With your pen pal you are discussing what you will do with your money when you get your first paycheck. Choose the correct form of the verb.

—Quand j'(aura/aurons/aurai) **(1)** _____ mon premier salaire, je

(passerai/passerez/passeras) *(to take an exam)* **(2)** _____ mon permis

de conduire et je m'(achètera/achèterai/achèterez) **(3)** _____ une voiture.

Avec mes copains et mes copines, nous (irons/iront/iras) **(4)** _____ sur

la Côte d'Azur et nous nous (baigneront/baignerez/baignerons) **(5)** _____

sur les plages de Nice, Cannes et St-Tropez. Et toi, qu'est-ce que tu (ferai/fera/feras)

(6) _____ de ton premier salaire?

—Oh! Moi, je dois beaucoup d'argent à mes parents. Je leur (rendra/rendrai/rendras)

(7) _____ ce que je leur dois. Ils (pourront/pourrez/pourrons)

(8) _____ en faire ce qu'ils (voudrons/voudras/voudront)

(9) _____: partir en vacances ou changer l'ordinateur!

▶ 2 Les "cabotans (*puppets*) d'Amiens"

Vous vous proposez de passer une semaine de vacances à Amiens, en Picardie, et vous en avez écrit les détails avec précision à l'ordinateur. Malheureusement votre ordinateur est devenu fou et il s'est trompé dans les terminaisons du futur. Corrigez ses fautes.

You are planning on a weeklong vacation in Amiens, in Picardie, and you have carefully typed the details into your computer. Unfortunately, the computer has gone crazy and has gotten the future endings all wrong! Correct them.

Nous *logerez* **(1)** _____ à l'hôtel Carlton en face de la gare. Mes parents

visitera **(2)** _____ le musée de la Picardie et la cathédrale. Moi, je *partirez*

(3) _____ à vélo avec mon copain au bord de la Somme. C'est très beau.

Mes parents et moi, nous *iras* **(4)** _____ voir les spectacles à la maison de

la culture et nous *monteront* **(5)** _____ en haut de la tour Perret pour voir le

paysage autour de la ville d'Amiens. Mais je *voudrons* **(6)** _____ surtout voir

le théâtre de marionnettes "Les cabotans d'Amiens." Je *parleront* **(7)** _____ aux

marionnettistes. Je leur *direz* **(8)** _____: "Vous *voudra* **(9)** _____

bien que je vienne voir vos répétitions (*rehearsal*)? J'aime beaucoup vos marionnettes Lafleur

et Tchot Blaise. Et puis, vous m'*apprendrai* **(10)** _____ un peu de picard

(*the Picardy dialect*): ça m'amuse!"

▶3 Une lettre d'invitation

Vous vous êtes lié(e) d'amitié avec un des marionnettistes de la troupe des "Cabotans d'Amiens" et vous lui écrivez pour l'inviter aux États-Unis. Mettez les verbes entre parenthèses au futur.

You have made friends with one of the puppeteers of the "Cabotans d'Amiens" troupe and you are writing to invite him to America. Put the verbs in parentheses into the future.

Cher Jean-Louis,

Quand tu (venir) **(1)** _____ aux États-Unis, tu (pouvoir)

(2) _____ visiter ma ville. Nous (aller) **(3)** _____

voir d'autres spectacles de marionnettes, puisque tu aimes ça. Tu

(amener) **(4)** _____ deux de tes marionnettes si tu peux, et nous

les (montrer) **(5)** _____ ici. Tu (voir) **(6)** _____ ,

tout le monde (dire) **(7)** _____ qu'elles sont très belles.

Il (falloir) **(8)** _____ amener un imperméable parce qu'il pleut souvent

ici. Mes parents (être) **(9)** _____ très contents de te recevoir.

Ma mère (cuisiner) **(10)** _____ des spécialités américaines pour toi

et tu (devoir) **(11)** _____ goûter à tout. Mais quelquefois,

nous (acheter) **(12)** _____ des hot-dogs et nous

(partir) **(13)** _____ nous promener.

▶4 Que va-t-on faire?

Quand vous aurez complété les exercices 2 et 3, regardez-les encore une fois et répondez à ces questions, en utilisant *aller* avec l'infinitif.

When you have completed exercises 2 and 3, look at them again and answer these questions using *aller* and the infinitive.

Exemple:

Où allez-vous loger?
Nous allons loger à l'hôtel Carlton.

1. Qu'est-ce que vous allez faire pendant que vos parents visitent la cathédrale?

_____

2. Où allez-vous monter, vous et vos parents?

_____

3. À qui allez-vous parler?

_____

4. Qu'est-ce que vous allez apprendre?

_____

5. Qui va venir aux États-Unis?

_____

6. Qu'est-ce qu'il va amener?

_____

7. Que va faire ta mère?

_____

8. Qu'est-ce que vous allez acheter de très typique?

_____

Partez!

▶**5** Au futur

a. Commencez au mois où nous sommes et faites une prédiction pour chacun des 6 mois prochains.

Beginning with the month we are in now, make a prediction for each of the next 6 months.

Exemples:

Ce mois je me préparerai pour mes examens.
En juin je passerai mes examens.
En juillet . . .

_____

_____

_____

_____

_____

_____

→

b. Maintenant essayez de prévoir votre vie et celle de vos amis pour les dix prochains ans.

Now try to predict your life and those of your friends for the next ten years.

Exemples:

En 2002 nous entrerons au terminale (*12th grade*).
En 2003 Martin(e) commencera sa formation professionnelle (*professional training*).

_____

_____

_____

_____

▶6 Vos premiers salaires

Utilisez l'exercice 1 comme base pour dire ce que vous ferez de vos premiers salaires.

Use exercise 1 as a model to describe what you will do with your first paycheck.

_____

_____

_____

_____

▶7 Une situation

Un élève décrit une situation et les autres disent ce qu'ils/elles vont faire dans cette situation.

One student describes a situation and the others say what they are going to do about it.

Exemples:

—Je vois un incendie.
—Je vais téléphoner aux sapeurs-pompiers.

—Nous avons froid.
—Nous allons chercher/mettre nos pulls.

_____

_____

_____

_____

What Would Happen?
the conditional tense

![running figure] **À vos marques!**

What is the conditional?

The conditional tells you mainly what **would happen**—what you **would do** under certain conditions—therefore its name!

How do you form the conditional?

The endings are *-ais, -ais, -ait, -ions, -iez, -aient*. You add them to the end of the infinitive.

regarder	finir	vendre	
je regarderais	*je finirais*	*je vendrais*	I would look/finish/sell
tu regarderais	*tu finirais*	*tu vendrais*	you would . . .
il/elle regarderait	*il/elle finirait*	*il/elle vendrait*	he/she would . . .
nous regarderions	*nous finirions*	*nous vendrions*	we would . . .
vous regarderiez	*vous finiriez*	*vous vendriez*	you would . . .
ils/elles regarderaient	*ils/elles finiraient*	*ils/elles vendraient*	they would . . .

Or you add them to the future stem as explained in Chapter 23. Here are just a few examples; for the full list turn back to pages 158–59.

aller	to go	*j'irais*	I would go
venir	to come	*je viendrais*	I would come
pouvoir	to be able	*je pourrais*	I would be able, I could
être	to be	*je serais*	I would be
avoir	to have	*j'aurais*	I would have

ᎾᏂᏩ Attention!

The conditional endings are the same as the imperfect endings. However, for the mperfect you remove the infinitive ending; for the conditional you leave he infinitive complete (less *-e* for *-re* verbs) or use the future stem ending in *-r*. So, just like the future, **the stem always ends in *r*.**

How do you use the conditional?

■ The conditional is used mainly to say what **would happen,** what you **would do:**

Je gagnerais beaucoup d'argent.	**I would make** a lot of money.
Nous irions au bord de la mer.	**We would go** to the seashore.

It is often used in combination with *si* + the imperfect to express a condition "if . . .":

*Si j'avais assez d'argent, **je partirais** en vacances en Italie.*
imperfect   conditional

If I had enough money, **I would go** on vacation to Italy.

*Si nous écoutions notre prof, **nous apprendrions** beaucoup de français!*
imperfect   conditional

If we listened to our teacher, **we'd learn** a lot of French!

ᎾᏂᏩ Attention!

1. Beware of trying to use the conditional for the French equivalent of "In the evening **we would go** for a walk," when this simply indicates what you **used to do.** You should use the imperfect here: *Le soir nous faisions des promenades.*

2. When somebody/something "would or wouldn't do something," this indicates willingness, and you should use the imperfect of *vouloir: Luc ne voulait pas se lever.* Luc **wouldn't** get up.

■ The conditional forms of *pouvoir* and *vouloir* are particularly useful to soften a command or request:

Pourriez-vous *fermer la porte, s'il vous plaît?*
Could you shut the door, please?

Je voudrais *encore du potage, s'il vous plaît.*
I'd like some more soup, please.

See also *devoir,* Chapter 32, which is used in the conditional for "ought to."

■ The conditional is used in reported speech after verbs such as *dire, répondre,* and so forth.

Jacques a répondu **qu'il ne serait pas** *chez lui ce soir-là.*
Jacques replied **that he wouldn't be** at home that evening.

Prêts?

▶1 Jamais content!

Clément est un jeune garçon qui n'est jamais content. Il rêve d'une vie différente.
Dans ce qu'il dit à sa mère, vous trouverez la forme convenable du verbe au conditionnel.

Clément is a young boy who is never happy. He dreams of a different life. Find out what he says to his mom by using the right form of the conditional.

1. Maman! Si nous habitions dans les Alpes, je (pourrait/pourraient/pourrais)

   _____ skier plus souvent!

2. Si nous avions un chien, je ne (serais/serait/seraient) _____ pas si seul

   (*lonely*)!

3. Maman! Si tu travaillais, tu (aurais/aurions/auriez) _____ plus d'argent et

   nous (achèterions/achèteriez/achèterait) _____ un plus grand appartement!

4. Si papa et toi, vous aviez vos vacances en même temps, vous m'(emmènerions/

   emmèneraient/emmèneriez) _____ à Biarritz pendant un mois!

5. Si papy (*Grandpa*) et mamy (*Grandma*) étaient plus jeunes, ils (viendront/viendraient/

   viendrait) _____ en vacances avec nous!

6. Si la voiture n'était pas si vieille, elle (roulerait/roulera/rouleraient) _____

   plus vite!

▶2 Ah! Si j'étais à Biarritz

C'est l'hiver. Il fait très froid. Vous faites un échange scolaire à Doullens, une petite ville de Picardie, et vous entendez à la météo qu'il fait vingt degrés à Biarritz dans le sud-ouest. Dites ce que vous feriez si vous étiez là, en mettant les verbes entre parenthèses au conditionnel.

It's winter and it's very cold. You are on a school exchange in Doullens, a small town in Picardy, and you hear on the weather forecast that it's 70° F in Biarritz, in the southwest. Say what you would do there, putting the verbs in parentheses into the conditional.

Ah! Si j'étais à Biarritz, je (prendre) **(1)** _____ le soleil. Je (voir)

(2) _____ la Côte Sauvage. Je (manger) **(3)** _____

des fruits de mer. Avec mon correspondant / ma correspondante, nous nous (baigner)

(4) _____ peut-être et nous nous (promener) **(5)** _____ sur

la plage. Nous (pouvoir) **(6)** _____ aussi surfer sur les vagues (*waves*).

Je (faire) **(7)** _____ un tas de (*heaps of, a lot of*) photos. Le bus de l'école

nous (amener) **(8)** _____ peut-être jusqu'aux Pyrénées ou à la frontière

espagnole. Il (faire) **(9)** _____ chaud! Je (être) **(10)** _____

ravi(e). Mais me voici à Doullens et j'ai très froid. Brrrrrrr!

⭐3 Respectez les consignes (*instructions*)!

a. Vous voyez des personnes qui ne respectent pas ces panneaux. Que leur diriez-vous? Utilisez la forme polie, *pourriez-vous/pourrais-tu* ou *voudriez-vous/voudrais-tu,* selon les circonstances.

You see people ignoring the signs. What would you say to them? Use the polite conditional form, *pourriez-vous/pourrais-tu* or *voudriez-vous/voudrais-t,* depending on the circumstances.

Exemple:

Voudriez-vous ne pas pique-niquer ici, s'il vous plaît?

1.

2.

3.

4.

5.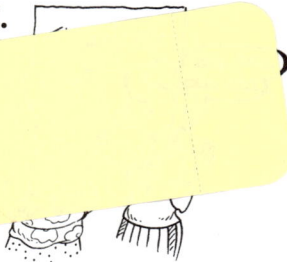

6.

7.

Present

8.

1. _____

2. _____

3. _____

4. _____

5. _____

6. _____

7. _____

8. _____

b. Et vous, que feriez-vous dans chacune des situations illustrées dans "la section a"?

And what would you do in each of the situations depicted in "section a?"

Exemple:

Naturellement, je ne pique-niquerais pas!

Partez!

▶4 Travail par deux

L'un imagine une situation, et l'autre dit ce qu'il/elle ferait ou ce que vous feriez tous les deux. Écrivez vos phrases.

Pair work. One of you imagines a situation, and the other says what he or she or both of you would do. Write your sentences.

Exemples:

—Tu t'es déchiré le jean.
—J'irais changer de pantalon.

—Le professeur est tombé dans la salle de classe.
—Nous l'aiderions à se lever.

_____

_____

_____

_____

_____

_____

▶5 Il ne le ferait pas! Elle ne le ferait pas!

Imaginez l'élève modèle, et dites ce qu'il/elle ne ferait pas!

Imagine the model student and say what he or she would not do!

Exemples:

Il/elle ne bavarderait pas en classe.
Il/elle ne taquinerait pas le prof!

(Vous pourriez employer aussi *manger, boire, jouer, hurler* "to shout, yell," *se battre* "to fight," *tricher* "to cheat" et d'autres verbes.)

_____

_____

_____

_____

▶**6** Voudriez-vous le faire, s'il vous plaît!

Dites (poliment!) à vos parents, vos frères et sœurs ou vos professeurs ce que vous voudriez qu'ils fassent ou ne fassent pas.

Tell your parents, brothers and sisters, or teachers (politely!) what you would like them to do or not to do.

Exemples:

—Sacha, pourrais-tu frapper avant d'entrer dans ma chambre?
—Maman, voudrais-tu m'apporter le petit déjeuner au lit?

_____

_____

_____

_____

_____

25 What You Were Doing or What You Used to Do

the imperfect tense

À vos marques!

What is the imperfect?

The imperfect is a past tense that is used to describe what used to happen or what was going on at some point in the past. It is called "imperfect" because we are not concerned about whether the activity it describes was completed or not. If you say "When I lived in Marseille I used to go to school in the suburbs," we are not interested in when you stopped doing it. With the statement "When you phoned, I was taking a shower," we're concerned only with what you were doing (showering) at that moment: we're not interested in when you finished!

How do you form the imperfect?

The imperfect endings are *-ais, -ais, -ait, -ions, -iez, -aient*. They are added to the first-person plural (*nous*) form of the present, after you remove the *-ons*. This applies equally to regular and irregular verbs:

		regarder to look	finir to finish	vendre to sell	
Present	*nous*	**regard**ons	**finiss**ons	**vend**ons	
Imperfect	*je*	regard**ais**	finiss**ais**	vend**ais**	I was looking/finishing/selling I used to look/finish/sell
	tu	regard**ais**	finiss**ais**	vend**ais**	you were . . . you used to . . .
	il/elle	regard**ait**	finiss**ait**	vend**ait**	he/she was looking, etc. he/she used to look, etc.
	nous	regard**ions**	finiss**ions**	vend**ions**	we were . . . we used to . . .
	vous	regard**iez**	finiss**iez**	vend**iez**	we were . . . we used to . . .
	ils/elles	regard**aient**	finiss**aient**	vend**aient**	they were . . . they used to . . .

Conseil!

You need to know the *nous* form of the present tense of irregular verbs!
Here are some examples of some common ones:

		boire to drink	dire to say/tell	écrire to write	ouvrir to open
Present	*nous*	**buv**ons	**dis**ons	**écriv**ons	**ouvr**ons
Imperfect was/were used to		*je* **buv**ais *tu* **buv**ais drinking drink	*je* **dis**ais *tu* **dis**ais saying/telling say/tell	*j'***écriv**ais *tu* **écriv**ais writing write	*j'***ouvr**ais *tu* **ouvr**ais opening open

Other irregular verbs in the imperfect are:

aller	to go	*j'***allais**
avoir	to have	*j'***avais**
conduire	to drive	*je* **conduis**ais
croire	to believe	*je* **croy**ais
connaître	to know	*je* **connaiss**ais
coudre	to sew	*je* **cous**ais
devoir	to have to	*je* **dev**ais
être	to be	*j'***étais***

*Only *être* is totally irregular: *j'***étais**, *tu* **étais**,etc.

faire	to do, make	*je **fais**ais*
falloir (il faut)	to be necessary	*il **fall**ait*
lire	to read	*je **lis**ais*
mettre	to put	*je **mett**ais*
ouvrir	to open	*j'**ouvr**ais (couvrir, offrir, souffrir)*
pleuvoir	to rain	*il **pleuv**ait*
prendre	to take	*je **pren**ais*
recevoir	to receive	*je **recev**ais*
rire	to laugh	*je **ri**ais*
savoir	to know	*je **sav**ais*
sortir	to go out	*je **sort**ais (dormir, partir, sentir, servir)*
suivre	to follow	*je **suiv**ais*
voir	to see	*je **voy**ais*
vouloir	to want	*je **voul**ais*

OJO Attention!

Verbs ending in *-ger, -cer,* like *manger, lancer,* take *ge* or *ç* before the endings *-ais, -ait, -aient: je/tu man**ge**ais, il man**ge**ait, ils man**ge**aient; je/tu lan**ç**ais, il lan**ç**ait, ils lan**ç**aient.*

How do you use the imperfect?

The imperfect has three main uses:

■ To say what **was happening,** what you **were doing** at some time in the past:

*Qu'est-ce que **tu faisais**?*	What **were you doing**?
*Je **prenais** une douche!*	I **was taking** a shower!
*Je **regardais** le tennis à la télé.*	I **was watching** tennis on TV.

The imperfect is often used to describe **what was going on** when something else happened (in the *passé composé*):

*Qu'est-ce que **tu faisais** quand **je t'ai téléphoné** hier soir?*

        imperfect   *passé composé*

What **were you doing** when **I phoned** you last night?

*Quand **tu m'as téléphoné** hier soir **je regardais** le tennis à la télé.*

     passé composé   imperfect

When **you phoned** me last night I **was watching** tennis on TV.

■ To say what **used to happen,** such as habitual or repeated actions:

*Quand **nous allions** à l'école primaire, **nous sortions** à seize heures trente.*
When **we went** (= **used to go**) to grade school, **we got out** (= **used to get out**) at 4:30 P.M.

It is often used with such time expressions/adverbs as *de temps en temps* "from time to time," *souvent* "often," *tous les jours* "every day," which help to emphasize that the activity was repeated:

***Nous entrions souvent** dans le magasin en face de l'école où **nous achetions** des bonbons.*
We often went into the shop opposite the school and **bought** some candy.

***De temps en temps** l'institutrice me **punissait** parce que **je mangeais** ces bonbons en classe.*
From time to time the teacher punished me because **I ate** candy in class.

■ To describe how a situation or state of affairs was in the past:

Annette ne voulait pas** sortir avec Martin parce qu'**elle ne l'aimait pas.
Annette didn't want to go out with Martin because **she didn't like** him.

*Selon ma grand-mère **la vie était** beaucoup plus simple quand **elle était** jeune il y a cinquante ans.*
According to my grandmother **life was** much simpler when **she was** young fifty years ago.

Prêts?

▶ **1 Un petit déjeuner mouvementé**

Chantal Leroy raconte à ses copines ce qui s'est passé chez elle pendant que sa famille et elle prenaient le petit déjeuner. Choisissez la forme correcte de l'imparfait.

Chantal Leroy is telling her friends what happened at her house while she and her family were having breakfast. Choose the correct form of the imperfect.

1. Pendant que maman (faisiez/faisais/faisait) _____ le café, le téléphone

    a sonné.

2. Pendant que mes frères (mettait/mettaient/mettions) _____ la table,

    ils ont cassé une tasse.

3. Quand ma grand-mère (descendais/descendaient/descendait) _____

    l'escalier, elle est tombée.

4. Pendant que j'(aidais/aidait/aidiez) _____ ma grand-mère à se lever,

    le facteur est arrivé.

→

5. Pendant que nous (buviez/buvions/buvais) _____ notre café, le chien a

   volé le poulet que mon père (prépariez/préparaient/préparait) _____ pour

   le déjeuner.

6. Et chez vous, Florence et Édouard, qu'est-ce qui s'est passé pendant que vous

   (prenais/prenions/preniez) _____ votre petit déjeuner?

▶2 Au salon de coiffure

Jojo Détecto, détective privé, est entré au salon de coiffure de Mireille, car elle est accusée d'un vol. Voici ce qu'il raconte à son patron quand il rentre au bureau. Mettez les verbes à l'imparfait.

Jojo Détecto, a private detective, goes into Mireille's hair salon because she is suspected of a theft. This is what he tells his boss when he returns to the office. Put the verbs into the imperfect.

1. Quand je suis entré, Mireille (couper) _____ les cheveux d'un client.

2. Son employée (laver) _____ les cheveux d'un autre client.

3. Une deuxième employée (faire) _____ un brushing à une dame.

4. Deux dames (parler) _____ en attendant leur tour.

5. Un enfant (manger) _____ des caramels et (lancer) _____

   des papiers dans le salon.

6. Et un monsieur (lire) _____ un magazine pendant qu'il (attendre)

   _____ son tour.

▶3 Un voyage en Eurostar

Benjamin et Clément sont allés en Angleterre pour la première fois et ils ont pris le train Eurostar. Benjamin a écrit ses impressions à un camarade en France. Complétez ce qu'il a écrit à l'aide des verbes contenus dans la case.

Benjamin and Clément went to England for the first time by Eurostar train. Benjamin has written his impressions to a friend in France. Complete his letter with the help of the verbs in the box.

dormait	entrions	brillait	lisaient	approchions	essayions	regardais
faisait	roulaient	était	attendaient	jouaient	allait	

Quand le train est sorti du tunnel sous la Manche, il **(1)** _____ beau

temps et le soleil **(2)** _____. On a annoncé dans le train qu'il

(3) _____ seize heures cinq—une heure de moins qu'en France.

Pendant que je **(4)** _____ par la fenêtre du train, j'ai vu les voitures

et les camions sur l'autoroute M20, et vraiment ils **(5)** _____ à gauche!

Quelques personnes dans le train **(6)** _____ le journal, des enfants

(7) _____ avec leur mère, un monsieur **(8)** _____.

Clément et moi, nous **(9)** _____ de lire les noms des gares, mais le train

(10) _____ trop vite. Après une heure les maisons ont commencé à

devenir plus nombreuses: nous nous **(11)** _____ de Londres. Encore une

demi-heure et nous **(12)** _____ dans la gare de Waterloo, où nos

correspondants anglais, Kevin et Daniel, nous **(13)** _____.

▶4 Il y a cent ans

Vous racontez comment vivaient les gens il y a cent ans. Mettez les verbes à l'imparfait.

You are discussing how people lived 100 years ago. Put the verbs into the imperfect,
making sure you use the right endings!

1. Les gens (être) _____ plus pauvres que maintenant.

2. Beaucoup de personnes (vivre) _____ à la campagne.

3. Elles (cultiver) _____ la terre . . .

4. . . . et (manger) _____ leurs fruits et légumes.

5. On (envoyer) _____ les enfants à l'usine pour travailler.

6. On (utiliser) _____ les chevaux pour travailler et pour voyager.

7. Il n'y (avoir) _____ pas d'avions.

8. Les gens n'(aller) _____ pas beaucoup à l'étranger.

9. Il (falloir) _____ prendre le bateau pour aller en France.

10. Naturellement, je n'(être) _____ pas là: j'ai vu tout ça à la télévision!

Partez!

▶5 Samedi dernier, à midi

Chaque élève doit raconter ce qu'il/elle faisait samedi dernier à midi.

Each member of the class or group says what he or she was doing at noon last Saturday.

Exemples:

Moi, je faisais mes devoirs.
Moi, j'étais chez ma grand-mère.
Moi, je faisais des courses en ville.

▶6 Dans mon école primaire

Avec un copain / une copine de classe, posez-vous des questions l'un à l'autre sur la vie dans votre école primaire.

With a partner, take turns asking each other questions about how things were in school.

Exemples:

Quelles matières étudiais-tu?
Quelles matières aimais-tu le plus?
Qui étaient tes profs, et comment étaient-ils?
À quelle heure est-ce que tu entrais et sortais?
Prenais-tu le déjeuner au collège ou est-ce que tu rentrais à la maison?
Comment allais-tu au collège?
Est-ce que tu travaillais mieux ou pas si bien que maintenant?

Continuez tous les deux à poser d'autres questions.

★7 Il y a cinquante ans

Imaginez que votre ville est jumelée avec une ville en France. De temps en temps, vous échangez un bulletin de renseignements sur vos villes. Comme vous savez écrire le français, on vous a demandé d'écrire une courte description de votre ville il y a 50 ans.

Imagine that your town has a sister city in France. From time to time you exchange information sheets about your towns. Because you know French, they have asked you to write a brief description of your town 50 years ago.

Comment étaient les gens?
Que faisaient-ils?
Où travaillaient-ils?
Comment étaient les rues, les maisons, les bâtiments, etc.?
Est-ce qu'il y avait beaucoup de circulation? de supermarchés?
Qu'est-ce qu'il n'y avait pas?

Il y a 50 ans

Maintenant

26 What You Have Done, What You Did
the *passé composé: avoir* verbs

À vos marques!

What is the *passé composé*?

The *passé composé* is a **past** tense that tells you what **has happened,** what you **have done** in the recent past, or what **happened**—what you **did** at a point in the past.

How do you form the *passé composé*?

The *passé composé* is a "compound" tense, that is, it consists of **two** words, the **auxiliary verb** and the **past participle.**

The "auxiliary verb" is usually *avoir* "to have."

Regular verbs

The past participles and *passé composé* of regular verbs are formed as follows:

-er verbs: *regarder* "to look" → *regardé* → *j'ai regardé:*

j'ai regardé	I have looked	I looked
tu as regardé	you have looked	you looked
il/elle a regardé	he/she has looked	he/she looked
nous avons regardé	we have looked	we looked
vous avez regardé	you have looked	you looked
ils/elles ont regardé	they have looked	they looked

-ir verbs: *finir* "to finish" → *fini* → *j'ai fini:*

j'ai fini	I have finished	I finished
tu as fini	you have finished	you finished
il/elle a fini	he/she has finished	he/she finished

nous avons fini	we have finished	we finished
vous avez fini	you have finished	you finished
ils/elles ont fini	they have finished	they finished

-re verbs: *vendre* "to sell" → *vendu* → *j'ai vendu:*

j'ai vendu	I have sold	I sold
tu as vendu	you have sold	you sold
il/elle a vendu	he/she has sold	he/she sold
nous avons vendu	we have sold	we sold
vous avez vendu	you have sold	you sold
ils/elles ont vendu	they have sold	they sold

Examples of some other regular verbs in the *passé composé:*

Nous avons commandé *trois cafés.*	**We've ordered** three coffees.
*Hier **notre équipe a gagné**.*	**Our team won** yesterday.
*Qu'est-ce que **tu as choisi**?*	{ What **have you chosen**? What **did you choose**?
***Ta mère**, qu'est-ce qu'elle **a répondu**?*	What **did your mother answer**?

Irregular verbs

There are a number of irregular past participles. To make it easier for you to learn them, we have broken the list down according to their endings:

Ending in -*é*:

| *être* | to be | *j'ai été* | I have been | I was |

Ending in -*u*:

courir	to run	*j'ai couru*	I have run	I ran
avoir	to have	*j'ai eu*	I have had	I had
boire	to drink	*j'ai bu*	I have drunk	I drank
connaître	to know	*j'ai connu*	I have known	I knew
reconnaître	to recognize	*j'ai reconnu*	I have recognized	I recognized
coudre	to sew	*j'ai cousu*	I have sewn	I sewed
croire	to believe	*j'ai cru*	I have believed	I believed
devoir	to have to	*j'ai dû*	I have had to	I had to
falloir	to be necessary	*il a fallu*	it has been necessary	it was necessary
lire	to read	*j'ai lu*	I have read	I read
pleuvoir	to rain	*il a plu*	it has rained	it rained
pouvoir	to be able / can	*j'ai pu*	I have been able	I was able / could
recevoir	to receive	*j'ai reçu*	I have received	I received
savoir	to know	*j'ai su*	I have known	I knew
voir	to see	*j'ai vu*	I have seen	I saw
vouloir	to want	*j'ai voulu*	I have wanted	I wanted

Ending in *-i:*

rire	to laugh	*j'ai ri*	I have laughed	I laughed
sourire	to smile	*j'ai souri*	I have smiled	I smiled

Ending in *-is:*

mettre	to put	*j'ai mis*	I have put	I put
promettre	to promise	*j'ai promis*	I have promised	I promised
prendre	to take	*j'ai pris*	I have taken	I took
apprendre	to learn	*j'ai appris*	I have learned	I learned

Ending in *-t:*

dire	to say/tell	*j'ai dit*	I have said/told	I said/told
écrire	to write	*j'ai écrit*	I have written	I wrote
faire	to do/make	*j'ai fait*	I have done/made	I did/made
conduire	to drive	*j'ai conduit*	I have driven	I drove
traduire	to translate	*j'ai traduit*	I have translated	I translated
couvrir	to cover	*j'ai couvert*	I have covered	I covered
ouvrir	to open	*j'ai ouvert*	I have opened	I opened
découvrir	to discover	*j'ai découvert*	I have discovered	I discovered
éteindre	to put out	*j'ai éteint*	I have put out	I put out
peindre	to paint	*j'ai peint*	I have painted	I painted

Asking questions: have you . . . ? did you . . . ?

You invert the auxiliary verb and the subject, and follow with the past participle:

As-tu écrit à ta tante?	**Have you** written to your aunt?
Avez-vous acheté des cartes postales?	**Did you** buy some postcards?

When you use *est-ce que?* the verb follows the subject (see Chapter 16 on interrogatives):

Est-ce que vous avez acheté des cartes postales?	**Did you** buy postcards?

Making the *passé composé* negative: I haven't, I didn't

You place *ne . . . pas* around the auxiliary verb, so the past participle comes last:

Je n'ai pas écrit à ma tante.	I **haven't** written to my aunt.
Nous n'avons pas acheté de cartes postales.	We **didn't** buy any postcards.

For other negative words with the *passé composé*, see Chapter 38.

Object pronouns with the *passé composé*

These come before the auxiliary verb and are used in the usual way:

Où est-ce que vous m'avez vu?	Where did you see **me**?
Nous le lui avons envoyé.	We have sent **it to him**.

(ojo) *Attention!*

The auxiliary can sometimes be separated from the past participle by an adverb:

Nous avons déjà vu ce film.	**We've already seen** that film.
Paulette n'a pas encore reçu le paquet.	**Paulette hasn't yet received** the package.

How is the *passé composé* used?

■ As the literal equivalent of the English you use the *passé composé* to say what **has happened,** what you **have done**:

*Maman **a fait** un gâteau pour demain.*	Mom **has made** a cake for tomorrow.
*Nous **n'avons pas encore pris** notre café.*	We **haven't yet had** our coffee.

■ As the usual equivalent of the English simple past to say what **happened,** what you **did**:

*Maman **a fait** un gâteau hier.*	Mom **made** a cake yesterday.
*Nous **avons reçu** le paquet la semaine dernière.*	We **received** the package last week.

■ See the next chapter (27) for a note on past participle agreements.

Prêts?

▶1 Qu'est-ce qu'ils ont vu aux États-Unis?

On interviewe des jeunes français qui visitent les États-Unis et qui décrivent ce qu'ils y ont vu. Complétez les phrases, en choisissant dans la case la forme correcte d'*avoir*!

Some French teenagers, visiting the U.S., are being interviewed and are describing what they have seen. Complete the sentences, choosing the correct form of *avoir* from the box.

ai	as	a	avons	avez	ont

1. À New York, tous les jeunes _____ vu la statue de Liberté.

2. À Boston, Jérémie _____ vu les collèges de l'université.

3. —À Phoenix, moi, j'_____ vu le Grand Canyon, dit Frédéric.

4. —Et nous, à Chicago, nous _____ vu la Sears Tower, répondent Sylvie et Véronique.

→

5. À San Francisco, Myriam _____ vu le pont Golden Gate.

6. Et toi, Édouard, qu'est-ce que tu _____ vu à la Nouvelle-Orléans?

7. Et vous, Céline et Pamela, _____-vous vu les plages quand vous êtes arrivées en Floride?

▶2 Participes mélangés

Combien de participes passés trouvez-vous? Il y en a des horizontaux, des verticaux et des diagonaux. Pouvez-vous en trouver 20? Après les avoir trouvés, faites une liste des verbes correspondants à l'infinitif.

How many past participles can you find across, down, and diagonally? Can you find 20? After you have found them, make a list of their infinitives.

V	F	F	P	R	I	S	V	E
E	A	É	I	Q	T	D	P	U
N	I	T	S	N	B	I	O	J
D	T	É	C	R	I	T	U	K
U	C	Z	L	R	L	D	V	P
A	H	H	M	B	U	W	E	C
M	O	K	A	F	R	Y	R	O
O	I	V	N	B	I	E	T	N
S	S	S	G	T	P	V	Ç	N
Q	I	R	É	P	O	N	D	U

▶3 Une visite dans le Marquenterre

Le Marquenterre est une réserve naturelle d'oiseaux située près de l'estuaire de la Somme. Mark le visite avec la famille de son correspondant Nicolas, et de retour aux États-Unis, il raconte à son professeur de français ce qu'il a vu. Mettez les verbes au passé composé.

Le Marquenterre is a bird reserve situated near the estuary of the River Somme. Mark visits it with his pen pal Nicolas's family and back in the U.S. he tells his French teacher about it. Put the verbs into the *passé composé*.

C'était formidable! J' (voir) **(1)** _____ des milliers (*thousands of*)

d'oiseaux. J' (reconnaître) **(2)** _____ les oies, les canards, les hérons, les

mouettes (*seagulls*). Nous (marcher) **(3)** _____ pendant trois heures dans les dunes et nous (observer) **(4)** _____ tous ces oiseaux. Le père de Nicolas

(indiquer) (*to point out*) **(5)** _____ dix sortes d'oiseaux différents,

et il (prendre) **(6)** _____ des photos. Il (faire) **(7)** _____

beau temps! Avec Nicolas nous (courir) **(8)** _____ dans les dunes,

mais sa mère nous (dire) **(9)** _____ de ne pas courir, alors nous

(promettre) **(10)** _____ de ne plus le faire. Le soir, j' (ouvrir)

(11) _____ mon dictionnaire et j' (traduire) **(12)** _____

les noms des oiseaux que je ne connaissais pas.

▶4 Un pique-nique raté

Votre correspondant(e) vous décrit un pique-nique un peu désastreux qu'il/elle a fait avec ses camarades. Malheureusement les participes passés ont été effacés par la pluie! Remettez les participes passés effacés, que vous retrouverez dans la case.

Your pen pal is describing a somewhat disastrous picnic he or she had with his or her friends. Unfortunately the past participles got washed out by the rain. Rewrite the missing past participles, which you will find in the box.

Hier, j'ai **(1)** _____ un pique-nique avec mes camarades de classe.

J'ai **(2)** _____ des chips et du poulet à cuire au barbecue. Marion

a **(3)** _____ une salade composée. Arrivés sur le lieu du pique-nique,

nous avons **(4)** _____ du papier et du bois et nous avons

(5) _____ le barbecue. Puis nous avons **(6)** _____

le poulet à cuire et nous avons **(7)** _____ du coca. Alors, j'ai

(8) _____ un grand bruit. Mes camarades et moi, nous avons

(9) _____ que c'était un avion mais non! C'était l'orage! Il a beaucoup

(10) _____ et le poulet n'a pas **(11)** _____. Alors nous

avons **(12)** _____ le feu, et il a **(13)** _____ tout ranger

et rentrer à la maison.

grillé	fait	entendu	plu	acheté	éteint	préparé
cherché	allumé	bu	fallu	mis	cru	

Partez!

▶ 5 Hier

En prenant huit verbes choisis parmi ceux de la case ci-dessous, écrivez dans votre journal intime huit choses que vous avez faites hier.

Choosing eight verbs from the box below, write in your journal eight things you did yesterday.

manger	travailler	acheter	choisir	finir	perdre
vendre	cuisiner	jouer	préparer	gagner	nettoyer

_____

_____

_____

_____

_____

_____

_____

_____

▶ 6 Qu'est-ce que tu as fait?

En utilisant seulement les participes passés irréguliers aux pages 181–82, faites des phrases pour décrire ce que vous et votre famille avez fait le week-end dernier.

Using only irregular past participles from pages 181–82, make up some sentences to describe what you did last weekend.

Exemples:

Moi, j'ai reçu une carte postale de mon amie suisse.
Mon père a peint le salon.

_____

_____

_____

_____

⭐**7** Il a beaucoup voyagé

Travail par deux, ou pour la classe entière. Un ami français de votre famille, artiste, a beaucoup voyagé. Vous lui posez des questions sur l'endroit où il a été, ce qu'il a vu, fait, mangé, bu, dessiné, peint, etc. Votre camarade de classe ou les autres élèves y répondent.

Pair or whole-class work. A French friend of your family, an artist, has traveled a great deal. You ask him questions about where he has been, what he has seen, done, eaten, drunk, drawn, painted, etc. Your partner or the other members of the class reply.

Exemples:

—Quels pays avez-vous visités?
—J'ai visité beaucoup de pays, au moins vingt.

—Qu'est-ce que vous avez vu à Sydney?
—J'ai vu le pont sur le port et l'Opéra.

—Qu'est-ce que vous avez dessiné en Italie?
—J'ai dessiné la tour penchée de Pise.

_____

_____

_____

_____

_____

_____

_____

27 What You Have Done, What You Did

the *passé composé: être* verbs

À vos marques!

The *passé composé* of *être* verbs is used in the same way as the *avoir* verbs in the last chapter, but it is formed somewhat differently. There are two groups of *être* verbs.

Verbs of motion

■ There is a small group of verbs which use *être* as their auxiliary instead of *avoir*. These are mainly verbs of motion. It may help you to remember them to learn them as pairs of opposites, reading ADVENT down the first letters of the first column:

Arriver	to arrive	*partir*	to leave
Descendre	to go down	*monter*	to go up
Venir*	to come	*aller*	to go
Entrer	to enter, go in	*sortir*	to go out
Naître*	to be born	*mourir**	to die
Tomber	to fall	*rester*	to stay, remain

Also *passer* "to pass (by), go by," *retourner* "to return," and compounds of (that is, verbs based on) the above verbs: *devenir* "to become," *revenir* "to come back, return," *rentrer* "to come back, to go/come home."

---

*Irregular past participles:

venir	*venu*
naître	*né*
mourir	*mort*

■ Formation of the *passé composé* and agreement of the past participle:

With *être* verbs you have to make the past participle agree with the person or thing that is doing the action, that is, the subject:

arriver to arrive		
Masculine subject	**Feminine subject**	
je suis arrivé	*je suis arrivée*	I (have) arrived
tu es arrivé	*tu es arrivée*	you (have) arrived
il est arrivé	*elle est arrivée*	he/she/it (has) arrived
nous sommes arrivés	*nous sommes arrivées*	we (have) arrived
vous êtes arrivés*	*vous êtes arrivées**	you (have) arrived
ils sont arrivés	*elles sont arrivées*	they (*m./f.*) (have) arrived

*If *vous* is used when talking to one person only, singular agreements are used:

vous êtes arrivé   *vous êtes arrivée*   you (have) arrived

If "we," "you," or "they" is a mixture of masculine and feminine, the agreement is always masculine.

Les filles et les garçons anglais sont *arrivés ce matin.*	**The English girls and boys** arrived this morning.
Suzanne est tombée de son vélo.	**Suzanne** fell off her bike.
Mes parents sont restés en Angleterre.	**My parents** stayed in England.
Yvette, à quelle heure es-tu partie?	**Yvette,** at what time did **you** leave?
"Je suis née en 1985," a écrit **Jeanne.**	"**I** was born in 1985," wrote **Jeanne.**

ojo Attention!

When *descendre, monter, passer,* and *sortir* mean "to take down," "to take up," "to pass/spend," and "to take out" respectively, and have a direct object, that is, they are used "transitively," they have *avoir* as their auxiliary. In this case these verbs obey *avoir* agreement rules (see page 191). Compare:

Monique est passée devant la fenêtre.	**Monique passed/went by** the window.
Monique **a passé quelques jours** *chez nous.*	Monique **spent a few days** at our house.
Nous sommes montés au troisième étage.	**We went up** to the third floor.
Nous **avons monté les bagages** *au troisième étage.*	We **took the suitcases up** to the third floor.

Notice that you also say *j'ai monté/descendu l'escalier* "I went up/down the stairs":

Nous **avons monté l'escalier** *au troisième étage.*	We **went upstairs** to the third floor.

Reflexive verbs

Reflexive verbs (such as *se lever* "to get up," *s'habiller* "to get dressed") are explained fully in Chapter 30, but their *passé composé* requires further special treatment here, since they also use *être* as their auxiliary.

OJO Attention!

When the subject and direct object are the same person (the majority of times), the past participle agrees with them. Mixed gender agreement is masculine, as explained.

se lever to get up		
Masculine subject	**Feminine subject**	
je me suis levé	*je me suis levée*	I got up
tu t'es levé	*tu t'es levée*	you got up
il s'est levé	*elle s'est levée*	he/she/it got up
nous nous sommes levés	*nous nous sommes levées*	we got up
*vous vous êtes levés**	*vous vous êtes levées**	you got up
ils se sont levés	*elles se sont levées*	they (*m./f.*) got up

*If *vous* is used talking to one person:

vous vous êtes levé   *vous vous êtes levée*   you got up

***Élodie s'est levée** à sept heures. **Elle est allée** dans la salle de bains, où **elle s'est douchée.**
Puis **elle s'est habillée.***
Élodie got up at 7 o'clock. **She went** into the bathroom, where **she took a shower.**
Then **she got dressed.**

***Deux cars se sont arrêtés** devant le collège.*
Two buses stopped outside the school.

■ Negatives and questions are formed as explained in the last chapter:

*Martin **n'est pas encore parti.***	Martin **hasn't** yet **left.**
*Où **sont-ils** allés?*	Where **did they** go?
*Le car **ne s'est pas** arrêté.*	The bus **didn't** stop.

More about past participle agreements

■ If you use a reflexive verb to say that you did something to a part of yourself (such as wash your hair), you don't need to make the past participle agree:

Élodie s'est lavé les cheveux et puis elle s'est brossé les dents.
Élodie **washed her hair** and then she **brushed her teeth.**

■ *Attention les filles!* If you are a girl, remember that if you are describing (in a letter or essay) what you yourself have done or did, you must add an *-e* to the past participle when you use the twelve "motion" verbs or a reflexive verb:

Je suis tombée mais je ne me suis pas blessée.
I fell but I didn't hurt myself.

■ We didn't quite tell you the whole story about the *passé composé* formed with *avoir* in the last chapter, because we thought there was enough to absorb without this slight complication! Past participles *do* have to agree, *but only sometimes:* they agree with the **direct object** when it comes before the verb. This occurs most often after an object pronoun:

Ma chemise? Je l'ai mise dans le tiroir.
My shirt? I've put **it** in the drawer.

Où avez-vous acheté ces chaussures? Je les ai achetées au grand magasin.
Where did you buy **those shoes**? I bought **them** at the department store.

It may also occur after *que* referring to a noun:

Les chaussures que vous avez achetées au grand magasin sont très belles.
The shoes which you bought at the department store are very nice.

Conseil!

It is when you are **writing** French that you need to pay attention to various past participle agreement rules. When you are **speaking**, you actually hear the feminine agreement only on the small number of past participles that end in *-s* or *-t: mise(s), écrite(s)*.

Prêts?

▶1 Joyeux anniversaire!

Elsa décrit ce que sa famille a fait pour fêter son anniversaire. Choisissez la bonne forme du participe passé.

Elsa describes what her family did to celebrate her birthday. Choose the correct form of the past participle.

Un matin des vacances, je me suis (réveillé/réveillées/réveillée) **(1)** _____

à neuf heures. Ma mère est (venus/venue/venu) **(2)** _____ me voir dans ma

chambre et mon père est (allée/allés/allé) **(3)** _____ me préparer mon petit

déjeuner. Puis je suis (montée/montés/monté) **(4)** _____ dans la salle de bains,

et j'ai entendu une musique étrange en bas, alors je suis (descendus/descendue/descendues)

(5) _____ dans la cuisine, et mes parents et mon frère se sont (levé/levées/levés)

(6) _____, sont (venue/venues/venus) **(7)** _____ vers moi et ont

chanté «Joyeux Anniversaire», en m'offrant des cadeaux. C'était mon anniversaire: je suis

(née/né/nés) **(8)** _____ le 23 juillet. Après, ma mère et moi, nous sommes

(parti/partis/parties) **(9)** _____ en ville pour faire des courses.

▶2 La bataille d'Azincourt

Benoît est allé visiter le centre médiéval d'Azincourt dans le nord de la France. Voici ce qu'il a retenu. Préoccupé par l'histoire, il a oublié de conjuguer les verbes. Conjuguez-les à sa place!

Benoît went to visit the medieval section of Azincourt (site of a famous battle in 1415, better known in English as Agincourt) in the north of France. Concerned with the story of the battle, he forgot to put the verbs into the *passé composé*. Do it for him!

Le 25 octobre 1415, de nombreux soldats anglais (arriver) **(1)** _____

à Azincourt. Ils (se préparer) **(2)** _____ à la bataille. Ils (aller)

(3) _____ à la rencontre des Français. Dix mille Français (mourir)

(4) _____ et 1.500 (rester) **(5)** _____

prisonniers des Anglais. Même les chevaux des français (tomber)

(6) _____. Le roi des Anglais, Henri V, (rentrer)

(7) _____ très heureux en Angleterre, et en 1420 il (devenir)

(8) _____ roi d'une grande partie de la France.

⭐3 Le jeu de piste

Johann a suivi ces instructions qui font partie du règlement d'un jeu de piste. Qu'a-t-il fait? Attention! Quelquefois vous devez utiliser *être,* d'autres fois, *avoir.*

Johann has followed these instructions on a trail. Say what he has done. Careful! Sometimes you need to use *être* and sometimes *avoir.*

Exemple:

Arrêtez-vous!
Il s'est arrêté.

1. Tournez à droite!

   _____

2. Avancez jusqu'au premier panneau!

   _____

3. Asseyez-vous sur le banc!

   _____

4. Finissez le questionnaire!

   _____

5. Levez-vous!

   _____

6. Prenez le premier chemin à gauche!

   _____

7. Passez devant l'église!

   _____

8. Allez jusqu'au bout!

   _____

9. Entrez dans la dernière maison sur la droite!

   _____

10. Montez l'escalier!

    _____

⭐4 Quelle mère!

Madame Albaret pense que sa fille Muriel est étourdie. Elle vérifie toujours si Muriel fait bien les choses. Vous répondrez à la place de Muriel. N'oubliez pas l'accord des participes passés, que vous pourrez entendre!

Madame Albaret thinks her daughter Muriel is forgetful. She always checks whether Muriel does things properly. You reply for Muriel. Don't forget the past participle agreements: these are all ones you can hear!

Exemple:

—Muriel, qu'as-tu fait des lettres? (mettre sur la table)
—Je les ai mises sur la table, maman.

1. Et des cartes postales? (écrire)

   _____

2. Et des lettres? (mettre à la poste)

   _____

3. Et les courses? (faire ce matin)

   _____

4. Et la boîte de sardines? (ouvrir)

   _____

5. Et les crudités (*raw vegetables*)? (couvrir de scellofrais [*plastic wrap*])

   _____

6. Et la lettre de ton amie américaine? (traduire)

   _____

7. Et la lumière de ta chambre? (éteindre)

   _____

8. Et ta limonade? (prendre)

   _____

Partez!

▶**5** Soir et matin

Décrivez au passé composé trois choses que vous avez faites avant de vous endormir hier soir et trois choses que vous avez faites ce matin. Attention aux verbes auxiliaires!

Describe in the *passé composé* three things you did last night before going to sleep and three you did this morning. Pay attention to the auxiliary verbs!

_____

_____

_____

_____

_____

_____

_____

_____

_____

_____

▶**6** Une montre perdue

Travail par deux. Vous êtes sorti(e) un jour avec votre correspondant(e), et soudain vous vous rendez compte que vous avez perdu votre montre. Les deux ensemble, vous remémorez ce que vous avez fait depuis que vous êtes sorti(e)s.

Pair work. You have gone out one day with your pen pal, and suddenly, you realize that you have lost your watch. Together, you reconstruct what you have done since you left the house.

Exemple:

—Alors, nous sommes parti(e)s de la maison à dix heures.
—Oui, et nous sommes allé(e)s à l'arrêt de bus.
—Et puis . . .

_____

_____

_____

_____

→

_____

_____

_____

_____

⭐7 Quelle histoire!

Racontez le plus important de ce qui s'est passé dans un épisode récent de votre feuilleton favori. Utilisez au moins cinq verbes au passé composé.

Recount the gist of what happened in a recent episode of your favorite daytime drama. Use at least five verbs in the perfect.

_____

_____

_____

_____

_____

_____

What Had Already Happened?

the pluperfect and other compound tenses

Ã vos marques!

What is a compound tense?

As already explained in Chapter 26 (the *passé composé*), a compound tense consists of two words: in this case the auxiliary verb *avoir* or *être* and the past participle. All the rules about auxiliary verbs, formation of questions and negatives, and formation and agreement of the past participle as explained in Chapters 26 and 27 apply to these tenses. Only the tense of the auxiliary verb is different.

The pluperfect tense

This tense goes further back than the perfect and tells you what **had** (already) happened.

Formation

You form it with the **imperfect** of *avoir* or *être* + the past participle:

avoir **verbs**

j'avais regardé/fini/vendu	**I had** looked/finished/sold
tu avais regardé/fini/vendu	**you had** . . .
il/elle avait regardé/fini/vendu	**he/she had** . . .
nous avions regardé/fini/vendu	**we had** . . .
vous aviez regardé/fini/vendu	**you had** . . .
ils/elles avaient regardé/fini/vendu	**they had** . . .

être **verbs**

j'étais allé(e)	**I had** gone
tu étais allé(e)	**you had** gone
il était allé	**he had** gone
elle était allée	**she had** gone
nous étions allé(e)s	**we had** gone
vous étiez allé(e)(s)	**you had** gone
ils étaient allés	**they** (*m.*) **had** gone
elles étaient allées	**they** (*f.*) **had** gone

Reflexive verbs use *être*

je m'étais habillé(e)	**I had** gotten dressed
tu t'étais habillé(e)	**you had** gotten dressed
il s'était habillé	**he had** gotten dressed
elle s'était habillée	**she had** gotten dressed
nous nous étions habillé(e)s	**we had** gotten dressed
vous vous étiez habillé(e)(s)	**you had** gotten dressed
ils s'étaient habillés	**they** (*m.*) **had** gotten dressed
elles s'étaient habillées	**they** (*f.*) **had** gotten dressed

Uses

■ The most common use of the pluperfect is to say **what had (already) happened** before another event:

*Quand nous sommes arrivés à la fête, **les enfants avaient mangé** tous les gâteaux!*
When we arrived at the party, **the children had eaten** all the cakes!
    (The eating happened before we arrived.)

*Qu'est-ce que **tu avais fait** pour fâcher ta mère?*
What **had you done** to make your mother angry?
    (The action happened before mother got angry.)

*Nous **étions déjà partis** quand la pluie a commencé.*
We had already left when the rain started.

*Annette **s'était déjà couchée** quand sa sœur est rentrée.*
Annette had already gone to bed when her sister came home.

■ The pluperfect is also often used in "reported" speech:

*Étienne a dit qu'il **avait fini** de réparer son vélo.*
Étienne said that he **had finished** repairing his bike.

Future perfect

Another compound tense that you will come across is the "future perfect." It tells you what you **will have done** (usually at or by a certain time). It is formed with the **future** of the auxiliary *avoir* or *être* and the past participle:

À cette heure demain j'aurai terminé mes examens!
By this time tomorrow **I will have finished** my exams!

Et aujourd'hui en huit nous serons partis en vacances!
And a week from today **we will have gone** on vacation.

Je me serai déjà baigné(e) dans la mer.
I will already have gone swimming in the sea.

Conditional perfect

You will also need to recognize and perhaps use the "conditional perfect," which tells what you **would have done.** It is formed with the conditional of *avoir* or *être* and the past participle:

Nous aurions préféré un hôtel à un camping.
We would have preferred a hotel to a campsite.

This tense is often used in conjunction with *si* ("if") + the pluperfect:

Qu'auriez-vous fait du chien si vous étiez allés en France? Nous l'aurions mis dans un chenil.
What **would you have done** with the dog **if you had gone** to France? **We would have put him** in a kennel.

Si j'avais su l'heure, je me serais levé(e)!
If I had known the time, **I would have gotten up**!

Prêts?

⭐1 Au restaurant

Les élèves du troisième ont décidé de fêter la fin de l'année scolaire au restaurant. Mais, comme toujours, Tiphaine est très en retard. Qu'est-ce que ses copains **avaient déjà fait** quand elle est arrivée? Choisissez la forme correcte d'*avoir* ou *être* pour former le plus-que-parfait.

The students in ninth grade decided to celebrate the end of the school year at a restaurant. But, as usual, Tiphaine is very late. What **had her friends already done** when she arrived? Choose the right form of *avoir* or *être* to create the pluperfect.

1. Quand elle est arrivée, ses copains (auraient/ont/avaient) _____ déjà commandé.

2. Ils (avait/avaient/auront) _____ déjà bu un coca.

3. Le serveur (aura/a/avait) _____ apporté les hors-d'œuvre et le pain sur la table.

4. Muriel (a/avait/aurait) _____ mangé son hors-d'œuvre.

5. Pierre et Cédric (étaient/avaient/était) _____ partis téléphoner pour savoir si elle venait.

6. Rachida (avait/est/était) _____ rentrée chez elle pour se changer.

7. La discussion sur le prof de maths (a/avait/aura) _____ bien commencé.

⭐2 Dans trois jours . . .

Sandrine vient de passer le brevet. Elle aura les résultats dans trois jours. Elle rêve . . . Mettez les verbes entre parenthèses au futur antérieur. Attention aux accords des participes passés!

Sandrine has just taken her *brevet* (exam taken at the end of middle school). She will have the results in three days. Put the verbs into the future perfect, paying attention to past participle agreement!

Dans trois jours j' (apprendre) **(1)** _____ que je suis reçue.

Mes parents m' (féliciter) **(2)** _____ et ma grand-mère m' (faire)

(3) _____ un cadeau. Avec mes copains, nous (aller)

(4) _____ faire la fête et nous (aller) (5) _____

dîner chez la mère de Fabrice. J' (déjà mettre) (6) _____

tous mes vêtements dans ma valise pour partir en vacances, et ma sœur (partir)

(7) _____ en Italie. Mes frères (préparer)

(8) _____ la voiture pour le départ en vacances.

⭐3 Mamy, ne t'en fais pas!

Mélanie, une Belge très sûre d'elle, passe quelques jours à Montréal pour son travail. De là, elle appelle sa grand-mère, qui se préoccupe beaucoup pour elle. Combinez les expressions des deux colonnes.

Mélanie, a very self-confident Belgian, is in Montreal for a few days for her work. From there, she phones her grandmother, who worries a great deal about her. Match the phrases in the two columns.

_____ **1.** Mamy, ne t'en fais pas! si la voiture était tombée en panne,

_____ **2.** Si je n'avais pas trouvé de restaurant ouvert,

_____ **3.** Si le vol de onze heures avait été complet,

_____ **4.** Si tous les hôtels avaient été complets,

_____ **5.** Si je m'étais perdue dans les rues de Montréal,

_____ **6.** Si le bureau de change avait été fermé,

a. j'aurais dormi à une auberge de jeunesse.

b. j'aurais pris le prochain vol.

c. j'aurais changé de l'argent à l'hôtel.

d. j'aurais acheté de la nourriture au supermarché.

e. je serais allée au garage.

f. j'aurais demandé le chemin à un beau garçon montréalais!

Partez!

⭐4 Vous arrivez en retard

Hier vous êtes arrivé(e) au collège à midi parce que vous aviez été malade le matin. Qu'est-ce que vos camarades avaient déjà fait? Il doivent vous le dire.

Yesterday you arrived at school at noon because you had been ill in the morning. What had your classmates already done? They have to tell you.

Exemple:

Nous étions déjà arrivé(e)s vers huit heures et demie.

_____

_____

_____

_____

_____

⭐5 Quel chien!

La semaine dernière vous avez laissé votre nouveau chiot (*puppy*) seul dans la maison pendant que vous passiez la journée en ville à faire des courses. Qu'est-ce qu'il avait fait quand vous êtes rentré(e)? Chaque élève doit penser à un méfait.

Last week you left your new puppy alone in the house while you spent the day shopping. What had he done when you got back? Each student has to think of a misdemeanor.

Exemple:

Il avait mangé les pantoufles de papa!

Voici quelques verbes utiles: *renverser* "to knock over," *abîmer* "to ruin," *déchirer, salir, ronger* "to gnaw."

_____

_____

_____

_____

_____

⭐6 Aujourd'hui en huit

Qu'aurez-vous fait d'ici huit jours? Pensez à une chose pour chaque jour.

What will you have done by this time next week? Think of one thing for each day.

Exemple:

Je serai allé(e) chez ma grand-mère.

_____

_____

_____

_____

_____

_____

_____

⭐7 Qu'auriez-vous fait?

Qu'auriez-vous fait dans cette situation? Le professeur ou votre camarade de classe vous donne une situation, et vous devez dire ce que vous auriez fait.

What would you have done in this situation? Your teacher or classmate gives you a situation and you have to say what you would have done. (The situation is best described by using *si* and the pluperfect.)

Exemples:

—Si tu avais perdu ton porte-monnaie . . .
—Je serais allé(e) au commissariat de police / au bureau des objets trouvés.

—Si une guêpe (*wasp*) t'avait piqué(e) . . .
—Je serais allé(e) à la pharmacie.

29 Stating Formally What Happened

the *passé simple*

À vos marques!

What is the *passé simple*?

The *passé simple* is another past tense which tells you what happened at some point in the past. You will need to be able to recognize it. To help you be able to recognize it, there are a couple of practice activities below.

The *passé simple* is never used in conversation. Instead, the *passé composé* is always used. In fact, the *passé simple* is a tense that is mainly seen and not heard, since it is used only in writing, and formal writing at that. (You would never use it in a letter, for example.) You will find it mainly in books (novels, biographies, etc.) and in some newspaper or magazine reports or articles. We will give you the stems and endings here, so that you can recognize it when you come across it.

Formation

Regular verbs

regarder	finir	vendre
je regardai	*je finis*	*je vendis*
tu regardas	*tu finis*	*tu vendis*
il/elle regarda	*il/elle finit*	*il/elle vendit*
nous regardâmes	*nous finîmes*	*nous vendîmes*
vous regardâtes	*vous finîtes*	*vous vendîtes*
ils/elles regardèrent	*ils/elles finirent*	*ils/elles vendirent*

We have boxed the third-person singular and plural forms because they are the forms you are most likely to come across. If you think about it, you are not going to use the "I, we, you" forms very often in a tense not used in conversation!

Irregular verbs

Nearly all irregular verbs have the endings *-is, -is, -it, -îmes, -îtes, -irent,* with an *-i-* throughout, or *-us, -us, -ut, -ûmes, -ûtes, -urent,* with a *-u-* throughout.

> **Conseil!**
>
> We have listed the third-person forms of the *passé simple.* They are the forms which you are most likely to encounter.

-i- verbs

il/elle apprit	*ils/elles apprirent*	he/she/they learned	*apprendre*
il/elle s'assit	*ils/elles s'assirent*	he/she/they sat down	*s'asseoir*
il/elle conduisit	*ils/elles conduisirent*	he/she/they drove	*conduire*
il/elle dit	*ils/elles dirent*	he/she/they said	*dire*
il/elle écrivit	*ils/elles écrivirent*	he/she/they wrote	*écrire*
il/elle fit	*ils/elles firent*	he/she/they did/made	*faire*
il/elle mit	*ils/elles mirent*	he/she/they put	*mettre*
il/elle naquit	*lis/elles naquirent*	he/she was; they were born	*naître*
il/elle peignit	*ils/elles peignirent*	he/she/they painted	*peindre*
il/elle prit	*ils/elles prirent*	he/she/they took	*prendre*
il/elle promit	*ils/elles promirent*	he/she/they promised	*promettre*
il/elle rit	*ils/elles rirent*	he/she/they laughed	*rire*
il/elle sourit	*ils/elles sourirent*	he/she/they smiled	*sourire*
il/elle suivit	*ils/elles suivirent*	he/she/they followed	*suivre*
il/elle vit	*ils/elles virent*	he/she/they saw	*voir*

-u- verbs

il/elle but	*ils/elles burent*	he/she/they drank	*boire*
il/elle connut	*ils/elles connurent*	he/she/they knew	*connaître*
il/elle courut	*ils/elles coururent*	he/she/they ran	*courir*
il/elle crut	*ils/elles crurent*	he/she/they believed	*croire*
il/elle dut	*ils/elles durent*	he/she/they had to	*devoir*
il/elle eut	*ils/elles eurent*	he/she/they had	*avoir*
il fallut		it was necessary to	*falloir*
il/elle fut	*ils/elles furent*	he/she was; they were	*être*
il/elle lut	*ils/elles lurent*	he/she/they read	*lire*
il/elle mourut	*ils/elles moururent*	he/she/they died	*mourir*
il plut		it rained	*pleuvoir*
il/elle put	*ils/elles purent*	he/she was; they were able	*pouvoir*
il/elle reçut	*ils/elles reçurent*	he/she/they received	*recevoir*

il/elle sut	*ils/elles surent*	he/she/they knew	*savoir*
il/elle vécut	*ils/elles vécurent*	he/she/they lived	*vivre*
il/elle voulut	*ils/elles voulurent*	he/she/they wanted	*vouloir*

Note also:

| *il/elle tint* | *ils/elles tinrent* | he/she/they held | *tenir* |
| *il/elle vint* | *ils/elles vinrent* | he/she/they came | *venir* |

Also *devenir, revenir, obtenir,* and other verbs based on them.

Some examples of the *passé simple* in use

Napoléon Bonaparte naquit *en 1769 et* **mourut** *en 1821.*
Napoleon Bonaparte was born in 1769 and **died** in 1821.

Il vécut *aux dix-huitième et dix-neuvième siècles.*
He lived in the 18th and 19th centuries.

La tour Eiffel fut *construite en 1889.*
The Eiffel Tower was built in 1889.

La Seconde Guerre mondiale commença *en 1939 et* **se termina** *en 1945.*
World War II began in 1939 and **ended** in 1945.

Conseil!

Remember: you never say the *passé simple*. In spoken French you would use the *passé composé;* therefore the last example above would be:

La Seconde Guerre mondiale ***a commencé*** *en 1939 et* ***s'est terminée*** *en 1945.*

Prêts?

⭐ 1 L'anniversaire du jumelage

Voici un article de journal, racontant l'anniversaire du jumelage entre la ville d'Amiens et la ville de Darlington. Cet article raconte l'événement au passé simple. Mais vous étiez là en personne, et vous le racontez à la famille de votre ami(e) français(e), en mettant les verbes au passé composé, naturellement!

Here is a newspaper article describing the anniversary celebration for the sister cities of Amiens and Darlington. This article gives the account in the *passé simple*. But you were there in person and tell your French friends' family all about it using the *passé composé,* of course. Change the verbs in italics from the *passé simple* to the *passé composé*.

Hier à onze heures, la cérémonie du 40ᵉ anniversaire du jumelage *se déroula* (*to take place*)

(1) _____ à la mairie d'Amiens. Tout d'abord on *entendit*

(2) _____ le "God Save the Queen" et la "Marseillaise." Puis, les maires

de Darlington et Amiens accompagnés par des personnalités locales *entrèrent*

(3) _____ dans la grande salle de réception et *rappelèrent*

(4) _____ en de longs discours (*speech*) l'histoire du jumelage.

Ils *félicitèrent* **(5)** _____ les comités de jumelage très dynamiques de part

et d'autre (*on both sides*) de la Manche. Puis le président du Comité de Jumelage (*Sister Cities*

International) amiénois *prit* **(6)** _____ la parole (*to make a speech*)

et *évoqua* (*to describe*) **(7)** _____ les nombreux échanges entre les deux

villes. La Musique Municipale *joua* **(8)** _____ l'Hymne à la Joie, puis les

participants *burent* **(9)** _____ le verre d'Amitié (*to drink to friendship*)

avant de se réunir (*to gather, meet*) autour d'un bon repas.

⭐2 Victor Hugo

Voici quelques extraits d'une biographie de Victor Hugo, écrivain célèbre français du dix-neuvième siècle. Transformez le passé composé des verbes en passé simple, ce qui est plus formel.

Here are some extracts from the biography of Victor Hugo, the famous nineteenth-century French writer. Change the verbs from the *passé composé* to the more formal *passé simple*.

Victor Hugo *est né* **(1)** _____ à Besançon en 1802. Il *a fait*

(2) _____ ses études à Paris. Il *a eu* **(3)** _____ cinq enfants.

Il *a écrit* **(4)** _____ des romans et des poésies (*poems*). Il *est devenu*

(5) _____ homme politique à partir de 1848. Il *a connu* **(6)** _____

la gloire. La France *a célébré* **(7)** _____ son 80ᵉ anniversaire en 1882.

Il *est mort* **(8)** _____ en 1885. Beaucoup de Français *sont venus*

(9) _____ à ses funérailles.

Partez!

⭐3 L'histoire du collège

Vous préparez une courte histoire de votre collège en français pour un groupe de jeunes Français qui vont bientôt vous rendre visite. Choisissez environ cinq événements importants et écrivez votre histoire au passé simple.

You are preparing a brief history of your school in French for a group of French students who will visit you soon. Choose about 5 significant events and write your account in the *passé simple.*

_____

_____

_____

_____

_____

⭐4 Petite biographie

Choisissez un personnage bien connu du monde de la musique moderne, du cinéma, du sport, etc., et racontez au passé simple les événements principaux de sa vie.

Choose a well-known personality of the world of music, film, sports, etc., and give an account in the *passé simple* of the main events of his or her life.

_____

_____

_____

_____

_____

Actions with "Myself," "Each Other"

30

reflexive verbs

Ā vos marques!

What is a reflexive verb?

A reflexive verb describes an action that the subject of the verb performs to or for himself or herself. There are some reflexive verbs in English, such as "behave yourself!" but there are many more in French, for the reasons explained below.

How do you make a verb reflexive?

To make a verb reflexive, use the reflexive pronoun, which comes before the verb in most cases. When you learn the infinitive of a reflexive verb, you learn it with *se* "oneself": *se laver* "to wash (oneself)," *se raser* "to shave (oneself)." As in English, the reflexive pronoun changes according to the person:

*je **me** lave*	I wash **myself**
*tu **te** laves*	you wash **yourself**
*il **se** lave*	he washes **himself**
*elle **se** lave*	she washes **herself**
*on **se** lave*	one washes **oneself**
*nous **nous** lavons*	we wash **ourselves**
*vous **vous** lavez*	you wash **yourself/yourselves**
*ils **se** lavent*	they (*m.*) wash **themselves**
*elles **se** lavent*	they (*f.*) wash **themselves**

This applies in all tenses:

*je **me** lavais*	I was washing (myself)
*nous **nous** laverons*	we will wash (ourselves)

ojo Attention!

1. Remember that the *passé composé*, pluperfect, and other compound tenses of reflexive verbs use *être* as the auxiliary: this is fully explained in Chapters 27 and 28.

Nous nous sommes baignés *dans la rivière.*	**We bathed** in the river.
Robert s'était *déjà* ***levé.***	**Robert had** already **gotten up.**

2. When you use the infinitive, you have to use the reflexive pronoun to correspond to the subject:

Thibaut, ***tu*** *vas* ***t'habiller?***	Thibaut, are **you** going to get dressed?

3. In affirmative commands (Chapter 22), the reflexive pronoun comes at the end:

*Asseyez-**vous**!*	Sit down!
*Asseyons-**nous**!*	Let's sit down!

    and *te* becomes *toi:*

*Assieds-**toi**!*	Sit down!

When do you use reflexive verbs?

Daily routine

A lot of routine actions are reflexive:

se réveiller	to wake up
se lever	to get up
se doucher	to shower
se baigner	to bathe, take a bath
se laver	to wash
se peigner	to comb one's hair
se coiffer	to do one's hair
se raser	to shave
se coucher	to go to bed

Je me suis réveillé(e) à sept heures.	**I woke up** at seven o'clock.
Ma sœur s'est couchée à dix heures.	**My sister went to bed** at ten o'clock.

Classroom requirements

s'asseoir	to sit down
se taire	to be quiet, shut up
se lever	to stand up

*Assieds-**toi** et tais-**toi**!*	Sit down and be quiet!
*Levez-**vous**!*	Stand up!

Performing an action to oneself

The verb is reflexive when you perform an action or cause an injury to a part of yourself:

se couper	to cut oneself
se brûler	to burn oneself
se casser	to break
se tordre	to twist
se faire mal (au genou)	to hurt one's (knee)

In addition to these verbs, some of those listed as "routine" above can be used in this way:

*Je **me suis coupé le doigt**.*	I've **cut my finger.**
*Martine **s'est cassé la jambe**.*	Martine **has broken her leg.**
*Josette **s'est lavé les mains**.*	Josette **washed her hands.**

¿Conseil!

Reminder: there is no past participle agreement when you have done something to a part of yourself!

S'en aller

s'en aller   to go away

*Nos invités **s'en vont** demain.*	**Our guests are going away** tomorrow.

Verbs used intransitively

Some verbs are made reflexive when used intransitively, that is, when the subject does the action himself or herself. Here are three common ones:

*J'ai arrêté **le bus** en faisant un signe de la main.*	I stopped **the bus** by giving a hand signal.
*Le bus **s'est arrêté**.*	**The bus** stopped.
*J'ai ouvert **la porte**.*	I opened **the door.**
*La porte **s'est ouverte**.*	**The door** opened.
*Henri essayait de fermer **le tiroir** mais il ne **se fermait** pas.*	**Henri** was trying to close **the drawer,** but it didn't close.

(S')allumer "to light up" and *(s')éteindre* "to put out / go out" are used in the same way when referring to lights or fires.

oʃǿ Attention!

Have you noticed that when these verbs are not reflexive they use *avoir* in the *passé composé*?

Each other, one another

You use a reflexive verb when people perform an action on or to each other:

*Maxime et Francine **se** téléphonent tous les jours. Ils **s'**aiment beaucoup.*
Maxime and Francine phone **each other** every day. They love **each other** very much.

*Nous **nous** écrivons chaque mois, ma cousine et moi.*
My cousin and I write **to each other** every month.

Prêts?

▶1 La veille de l'examen

Yannick et ses camarades de classe échangent leurs idées sur ce qu'ils aiment faire pour se détendre la veille de l'examen. Mettez les verbes entre parenthèses au présent à la personne qui convient.

Yannick and his classmates are exchanging their ideas about what they like to do to relax the day before an exam. Put the verbs into the appropriate form of the present tense. Don't forget to change the reflexive pronoun!

Yannick: Moi, je (se lever) **(1)** _____ très tôt et je (se baigner)

(2) _____ à la piscine pendant trois ou quatre heures. Et toi,

Nathalie, qu'est-ce que tu fais?

Nathalie: Oh, moi, je (se réveiller) **(3)** _____ très tard et je reste au lit

jusqu'à midi. L'après-midi, je (se promener) **(4)** _____ avec

mes copines, et le soir, je (se coucher) **(5)** _____ très tôt.

Mon frère, lui, il (s'amuser) **(6)** _____ toute la journée avec ses

copains, et le soir il (s'endormir) **(7)** _____ très tard.

Yannick: Et Sandrine et Aurélie, qu'est-ce qu'elles font?

Nathalie: Elles sont folles! Elles (se dépêcher) **(8)** _____ de travailler

jusqu'au dernier moment. Elles ne (s'arrêter) **(9)** _____

que tard le soir.

Yannick: Et toi, Romain?

Romain: Ma mère et moi, nous (se payer) **(10)** _____ un bon petit repas

au restaurant, et l'après-midi nous (s'offrir) **(11)** _____ une

bonne séance de cinéma.

▶2 C'est dur de se lever!

Tiphaine a beaucoup de mal à se lever le matin. Elle a envie de dormir. Voici ce qu'elle a fait. Imaginez les ordres de sa mère!

Tiphaine has trouble getting up in the morning. She wants to sleep in. This is what she did: imagine her mom's orders!

Exemple:

Les ordres de sa mère   **Ce que Tiphaine a fait**

Tiphaine, **réveille-toi**!   Elle s'est réveillée.

1. Tiphaine, _____!   Elle s'est levée.

2. Tiphaine, _____!   Elle s'est douchée.

3. Tiphaine, _____!   Elle s'est habillée.

4. Tiphaine, _____!   Elle s'est coiffée.

5. Tiphaine, _____

   _____!   Elle s'est assise à table pour le petit déjeuner.

6. Tiphaine, _____!   Elle s'est brossé les dents.

7. Tiphaine, _____!   Elle s'est lavé les mains.

8. Tiphaine, _____

   _____!   Elle s'est préparée pour partir à l'école.

▶ **3 Une journée à la pêche**

a. Thomas (12 ans) et Rudy (9 ans) sont allés passer la journée au bord de la rivière, mais tout ne s'est pas passé comme ils avaient prévu, et ils ont dû s'excuser à leur mère à leur retour à la maison. Dites au passé composé ce qu'ils ont fait selon les dessins. Utilisez les verbes dans la case.

Thomas and Rudy went to spend the day by the river, but everything didn't quite go as planned, and they had to apologize to their mother on their return. Describe in the *passé composé* what they did according to the drawings, using the verbs from the box.

Exemple:

Ils se sont baignés dans la rivière.

1. _____

2. _____

3. _____

4. _____

5. _____

6. _____

7. _____

s'habiller   se réveiller   se tordre la cheville   s'excuser   se baigner se couper le doigt   se sécher   s'endormir

b. Maintenant, imaginez les mots exacts qu'ils ont dits à leur mère.

Now imagine the exact words they said to their mother.

Exemple:

Nous nous sommes baignés dans la rivière.

1. _____

2. _____

3. _____

4. _____

5. _____

6. _____

7. _____

Partez!

►4 La première heure de la journée

Décrivez la première heure de la journée de votre famille, en utilisant autant de verbes pronominaux que possible au présent.

Describe the first hour of your family's day, using as many reflexive verbs as possible in the present.

Exemple:

Mon père se réveille à . . . Je me lève à . . . Etc.

_____

_____

_____

_____

_____

_____

►5 Simon dit . . .

On joue à "Simon dit." Un des élèves donne des ordres aux autres, en employant les verbes pronominaux à l'impératif.

Playing "Simon Says," one student gives the others orders using the imperatives of reflexive verbs. Use the verbs listed on page 210 and in exercise 2.

Exemple:

—Simon dit, "Levez-vous!" (tout le monde se lève / *everybody stands up*)
—Asseyez-vous! (personne ne se lève / *nobody stands up*)

►6 Au poste de secours

Vous êtes au poste de secours. En employant des verbes pronominaux au passé composé, chacun doit expliquer ce qui lui est arrivé.

You are at a first aid station. Using reflexive verbs in the *passé composé,* each student explains what has happened to him or her.

Exemple:

Je me suis brûlé la main.

The Name of the Verb
the infinitive

31

À vos marques!

What is the infinitive?

An infinitive is the basic form of a verb which you find when you look in a dictionary or vocabulary list. It is, if you like, the verb "in neutral," before you choose a tense and start adding endings. English infinitives begin with "to"; French ones, as you will have already seen many times, end in *-er, -ir, -re,* which usually tells you how the tenses are formed. There are also a few ending in *-oir,* whose forms are irregular.

How do you use the infinitive?

Basic form

The infinitive is used as the basic form of the verb to be found in a dictionary. With regular verbs, it's an indicator of which sets of endings you should use to form tenses. The relationship between endings and infinitives also enables you to work back the other way, that is, from a person and tense to the infinitive:

*nous choisissons → chois**ir***
*ils vendraient → vend**re***
*j'ai travaillé → travaill**er***

Command

The infinitive is sometimes used instead of a command, especially in instructions, notices, recipes, and so forth:

Ne pas toucher!	**Don't touch!**
Ouvrir ici.	**Open** here.
Battre les œufs.	**Beat** the eggs.

ojo Attention!

Ne and *pas* both come **before** the infinitive!

Following a preposition

All prepositions are followed by the infinitive (**except** *en,* which takes the present participle: see Chapter 35). Those most commonly used with a verb are:

Avant de: before (doing something)

*Il faut composter votre billet **avant d'aller** sur le quai.*
You must validate your ticket **before going** onto the platform.

Pour: to, in order to

*Qu'est-ce qu'il faut faire **pour composter** mon billet?*
What do I have to do **(in order) to validate** my ticket?

Sans: without (doing something)

*Je ne peux pas manger **sans boire.***
I can't eat **without drinking something.**

Au lieu de: instead of

***Au lieu de jouer** au tennis, nous avons décidé d'aller au cinéma.*
Instead of playing tennis, we decided to go to the movies.

Après: after

ojo Attention!

Après "after (doing something)" is followed by *avoir* or *être* (depending on the auxiliary) + the past participle (in other words, it needs a "perfect" infinitive—"after **having** (done something)":

*Après **avoir acheté** ce T-shirt, je l'ai porté toute la journée.*
After having bought (after buying) this T-shirt, I wore it all day.

*Après **être descendus** à la rivière, nous y avons fait notre pique-nique.*
After having gone down (after going down) to the river, we had our picnic there.

*Après **s'être habillée,** Muriel est sortie voir son petit ami.*
After having gotten (getting) dressed, Muriel went out to see her boyfriend.

Following other verbs

The infinitive is used following other verbs, such as "must do," "try to do," "continue to do." This is a very common use that is explained in the next two chapters.

Prêts?

▶1 Respectez les consignes!

Vous allez en France en autobus. Vous trouvez ce panneau à l'intérieur et vous expliquez les réglementations au petit frère de votre ami(e) français(e). Utilisez les phrases de la case.

You are traveling by bus in France. You find this sign inside and you explain the rules to your French friend's little brother. Use the phrases from the box.

Exemple   **1.**   **2.**   **3.**

 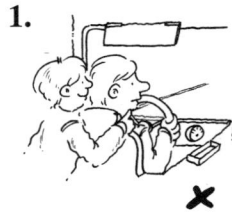  

4.   **5.**   **6.**   **7.**

Exemple:

Ne pas manger.

1. _____

2. _____

3. _____

4. _____

5. _____

6. _____

7. _____

écouter la radio   parler au chauffeur   mettre les bagages dans la soute (*luggage hold*)
jeter les papiers par terre   fumer   montrer votre billet   boire

▶2 La mayonnaise

Voici la recette de la mayonnaise. Mettez les verbes à l'infinitif.

Here is the recipe for mayonnaise. Put the verbs into the infinitive.

1. On prend un œuf et de la moutarde.

_____

2. On met l'œuf et la moutarde dans un bol.

_____

3. On bat l'œuf et la moutarde.

_____

4. On ajoute de l'huile, très lentement.

_____

5. On ne s'arrête pas de battre le mélange (*mixture*).

_____

6. On ajoute du sel.

_____

★3 Un voyage bien organisé

Paul est un jeune Américain qui part rejoindre son correspondant français à Besançon. Ensemble, ils iront faire du camping en Alsace. Voici ce qu'il raconte à de nouveaux amis qu'il rencontre au camping. Malheureusement, il s'embrouille dans ses phrases. Faites coïncider les éléments des deux colonnes.

Paul is an American teenager who goes to join his French pen pal in Besançon. They are going camping together in Alsace. Here is what he tells the new friends he meets at the campsite, but, unfortunately he gets his sentences mixed up. Match the parts from the two columns.

_____ **1.** J'ai préparé mon sac à dos

_____ **2.** J'ai pris mon sac de couchage

_____ **3.** J'ai pris l'avion

_____ **4.** L'avion est arrivé à Amiens

_____ **5.** À Amiens j'ai bu une Orangina

_____ **6.** Je me suis reposé quelques jours chez mon correspondant

_____ **7.** J'ai passé ma première journée en France

a. sans boire une goutte (*drop*) de Coca-Cola.

b. après avoir traversé l'Atlantique.

c. sans oublier les cadeaux pour la famille de mon correspondant.

d. pour payer moins cher.

e. avant de repartir en Alsace.

f. pour partir en camping avec mon correspondant.

g. avant de prendre le car pour Péronne.

Partez!

▶**4** Changer les consignes

Choisissez n'importe quel(s) chapitre(s) de ce livre et mettez à l'infinitif les consignes des exercices qui sont à l'impératif.

Choose any chapter(s) of this book and put the imperatives in the exercise instruction lines into the infinitive.

Exemple:

L'exercice 2 ci-dessus: Mettre les verbes à l'infinitif.

_____

_____

_____

_____

⭐**5** On ne peut pas aller à Paris sans . . .

Complétez les phrases suivantes avec des expressions qui contiennent un infinitif. Combien de phrases pouvez-vous inventer?

Complete the following sentences with phrases containing an infinitive. How many sentences can you invent?

1. On ne peut pas aller à Paris sans . . .
2. Nous restons à la maison au lieu de/d' . . .
3. Je travaille pour . . .
4. Il faut bien regarder avant de/d' . . .
5. Il faut se doucher après . . . (*Attention! Voir la section "Following a preposition" à la page 218!*)

Exemples:

1. On ne peut pas aller à Paris **sans monter** à la tour Eiffel.
4. Il faut bien regarder **avant d'**acheter.
5. Il faut se doucher **après avoir joué** au football.

_____

_____

_____

→

Can I? Must I?
I Don't Want to . . .

32

À vos marques!

Pouvoir: can, may, to be able

Pouvoir is used in most cases for "can" or "to be able." You will find its conjugation in the verb charts in Chapter 40.

Est-ce que tu peux sortir aujourd'hui?	**Can you go out** today? Yes, **I can,** I'm not
Oui, je peux, je ne travaille pas.	working.
Nous n'avons pas pu acheter de croissants.	**We haven't been able to buy** any croissants.

Attention!

Je peux "I can," but *puis-je* "can I?" "may I?"

Puis-je entrer?	**May I** come in?

The conditional of *pouvoir* means "could," and is often used to ask a favor:

Pourriez-vous me dire l'heure,	**Could you** tell me the time, please?
s'il vous plaît?	

ojo Attention!

"Could" in the preceding example means "would you be able to?" but "could" in English can also be a past tense, in which case the imperfect or *passé composé* is necessary in French:

Je ne pouvais pas voir l'écran.	**I couldn't** (= **wasn't able to**) see the screen.
Je n'ai pas pu l'aider.	**I couldn't** (= **wasn't able to**) help him.

Conseil!

If in doubt, convert "could" to "was" or "would be able" to determine which tense to use in French.

Savoir: can = to know how to

If "can"/"can't" refers to a skill you have or haven't learned, you use *savoir,* not *pouvoir:*

Est-ce que tu sais nager?	**Can you** swim?
Oui, mais je ne sais pas faire de planche à voile.	Yes, but **I can't** windsurf.

Devoir and *il faut:* two ways of saying "must"

■ *Devoir* mostly works like any other verb:

Nous devons terminer avant sept heures.	**We must / have to** finish before 7 o'clock.
Philippe a dû attendre le car.	**Philippe had to** wait for the bus.
Vous devrez écrire à la mairie.	**You will have to** write to city hall.

ojo Attention!

The conditional of *devoir* means "ought (not) to" or "should (not)":

Tu devrais mettre un pull.	**You should** put on a sweater.
Je ne devrais pas vous dire ça!	**I should not** tell you that!

and the conditional perfect + infinitive means "should (not) have":

Tu aurais dû mettre un pull.	**You should have put on** a sweater.

■ *Il faut* means "it is necessary to" and is used only in the third-person singular. It is often used to convey the idea of "must," especially when **who** has to do the action is understood from the context:

Il faut terminer avant sept heures.	I/you/we/he/she/they (according to context) **must** finish before 7 o'clock.
Il ne faut pas réveiller le bébé!	**We/you mustn't** wake the baby!
Il a fallu changer de train à Amiens.	**We had to** change trains at Amiens.

See also *il faut que* in Chapter 39 (page 272).

Vouloir

The uses of *vouloir* are fairly straightforward:

Je ne veux pas me coucher!	**I don't want to** go to bed!

ojo Attention!

Remember that

1. *Veux-tu/voulez-vous?* is used for "will you do something" in the sense of "are you willing?":

Veux-tu ranger tes jouets?	**Will you** put your toys away?
Non, je ne veux pas!	No, **I won't!**

2. The conditional *je voudrais,* etc., is used for "would like to":

Nous voudrions voir le tennis à la télé cet après-midi.	**We'd like to** see tennis on TV this afternoon.

and also in polite requests:

Voudriez-vous ouvrir la fenêtre, s'il vous plaît?	**Would you** open the window, please?

Aller

Aller + the infinitive gives you the "immediate future," saying what you are going to do (see also Chapter 23):

Nous allons regarder une vidéo ce soir.	**We're going to watch** a video this evening.

Venir de

The present tense of *venir de* + the infinitive tells you what **has just happened,** what you **have just done:**

Je viens de préparer un repas.	**I've just prepared** a meal.

The imperfect of *venir de* tells you what **had just** happened, what you **had just** done:

Nous venions de sortir *quand le courrier*   **We had just gone out** when the mail arrived.
   est arrivé.

 *Prêts?*

▶ **1 Le départ en vacances**

Que faut-il faire avant de partir en vacances? Choisissez dans la case la phrase qui correspond au dessin.

What do you have to do before you go on vacation? From the box, choose the phrase which fits the drawing.

Exemple:

Il faut faire les valises.

1.

2.

3.

4.

5.

6.

7.

1. _____

2. _____

3. _____

4. _____

5. _____

6. _____

7. _____

> mettre la table et les chaises de jardin dans la maison
> prendre les billets et les passeports
> fermer la porte à clef
> faire les valises
> mettre l'alarme
> ranger la maison
> fermer les fenêtres
> vider (*to empty*) le frigo

▶2 Arrivée chez un(e) correspondant(e)

Vous arrivez chez votre correspondant(e) français(e), et sa mère vous pose une série de questions pour mieux vous connaître. Vous devez répondre à ses questions.

You arrive at your French pen pal's house and his or her mother asks you a series of questions in order to get to know you better. You reply to the questions. (No need to repeat the whole question!)

Exemple:

—Est-ce que tu veux voir la maison? —Oui, je . . .
—Oui, je veux bien.

1. Est-ce que tu veux partager la chambre de ton/ta correspondant(e) ou avoir une chambre pour toi tout(e) seul(e)? —Je . . .

   _____

2. Est-ce que tu veux téléphoner à tes parents aux États-Unis? —Oui, je . . .

   _____

3. Est-ce que tu veux prendre des croissants au petit déjeuner? —Non, merci, je . . .

   _____

→

4. Est-ce que tu sais jouer au basket? —Non, je . . .

_____

5. Est-ce que tu peux sortir tard le soir aux États-Unis? —Oui, je . . .

_____

6. Est-ce que tu dois faire des devoirs pendant que tu es en France? —Non, je . . .

_____

7. Est-ce que tu veux dîner maintenant, ou tu viens de dîner dans l'avion? —Je . . .

_____

8. Est-ce que tu veux aller au village m'acheter la baguette demain matin? —Oui, je . . .

_____

9. Est-ce que tu sais faire du vélo? —Oui, je . . .

_____

▶3 L'installation au gîte

Vous arrivez dans un gîte rural en France, et vous discutez avec le propriétaire. Dans les extraits de conversation qui suivent, choisissez le verbe entre parenthèses qui convient.

You arrive at a country cottage in France, and you discuss matters with the owner.
Choose the right verb in the snippets of conversation below.

1. —Il manque un lit pour la petite.

   —Alors (il faut / nous venons d' / nous voulons) _____ en ajouter un.

2. —Il y a un barbecue dans le jardin.

   —Alors on (devra/pourra/saura) _____ faire des grillades.

3. —Il y a des bicyclettes dans le garage.

   —Alors on (doit/veut/peut) _____ aller faire un tour demain.

4. —Il y a un film à la télé après les informations de 20h.

   —Alors nous (allons / venons de / savons) _____ le regarder.

5. —Nous avons un lac au village. Vous ne savez pas faire de planche à voile? Alors vous

   (voudriez/sauriez/devriez) _____ apprendre. Il y a des cours.

6. —Les enfants ont très chaud ici l'été. Alors nous (allons/pourrons/saurons)

   _____ construire une piscine. Elle sera faite l'année prochaine.

7. —J'ai beaucoup d'animaux à la maison. (Sauriez-vous/voudriez-vous/devriez-vous)

   _____ emmener la petite pour lui montrer?

▶4 Le jour du départ du gîte

Quand on loue un gîte rural il faut faire le ménage. Le jour du départ, M. Dupuis,
qui a distribué les tâches, vérifie que tout est fait avant de prendre la route. Répondez
à ses questions selon le modèle.

When you rent a country cottage you have to do the housework. The day they are leaving,
Mr. Dupuis, who has given out the tasks, checks that everything has been done before heading
out. Answer according to the model.

Exemple:

—Richard, tu as nettoyé la douche?
—Oui, je viens de la nettoyer.

1. —Mélanie, tu as passé l'aspirateur?

   _____

2. —Sébastien, tu as vérifié les pneus de la voiture?

   _____

3. —Francine et Élodie, vous avez rangé la vaisselle?

   _____

4. —Est-ce que Sylvie a vidé les ordures?

   _____

5. —Est-ce que les enfants ont fait leurs lits?

   _____

6. —Chérie, est-ce que la petite est allée aux toilettes?

   _____

Partez!

▶5 Où faut-il aller pour . . . ?

a. La classe se divise en deux équipes. L'équipe A demande à l'équipe B "Où faut-il aller pour acheter . . . ?" Si l'équipe répond correctement, elle gagne un point, et ainsi de suite.

The class divides into two teams. Team A asks team B *"Où faut-il aller pour acheter . . . ?"* If team B replies correctly, they win a point, and so on.

Exemple:

—Où faut-il aller pour acheter de l'aspirine?
—Il faut aller à la pharmacie.

b. Presque le même jeu, mais cette fois on donne une situation et l'autre équipe dit ce qu'il faut faire pour s'en sortir.

Almost the same game, but this time one side gives a situation and the other has to offer a way of getting out of it.

Exemple:

—Votre camarade a des problèmes avec les maths.
—Il faut l'aider.

c. Continuez à inventer des situations, mais cette fois on répond avec *vous devriez* ou *vous pourriez.*

Continue inventing situations, but this time you reply using *vous devriez* or *vous pourriez.*

Exemple:

—J'ai très chaud!
—Vous pourriez/devriez enlever un de vos pulls!

⭐6 On a tout fait!

Travail par deux ou en deux équipes. L'un(e) est employé(e) du syndicat d'initiative d'une ville en Suisse francophone, l'autre est touriste. L'employé(e) fait des suggestions pour des activités, mais il semblerait que le/la touriste vient justement de tout faire. Écrivez vos questions et vos réponses.

Pair or team work. One is an assistant in the tourist office in a town in French-speaking Switzerland. He or she makes suggestions for various activities, but the tourist seems to have just done everything. Write your questions and your answers.

Exemple:

—Pourquoi ne pas monter dans les montagnes?
—Non, nous venons d'y monter ce matin.

Continuez à faire d'autres suggestions (faire une promenade sur le lac, visiter le musée, aller voir le château, etc.).

_____

_____

_____

_____

_____

_____

_____

33 Saying What You Love Doing, What You'll Try to Do

verbs + the infinitive

À vos marques!

There are many verbs in French which are linked to a following infinitive. Sometimes these verbs are followed directly by the infinitive and sometimes they are joined by *à* or *de*.

*Mon frère **adore aller** à la pêche.* My brother **loves going** fishing.
*Ce livre **vous aidera à réussir** à l'examen.* This book **will help you pass** your test.

Attention!

If an English "-ing" word follows a verb ("I love shopping"), don't try to use the present participle ending in *-ant* (Chapter 35) in French: stick with the **infinitive**!

Here are the verbs you are most likely to need.

Verbs that tend to be followed by the infinitive

devoir	to have to, must, ought
il faut	it is necessary to
pouvoir	to be able to, can
savoir	to know how to
aller	to be going to, to go and . . .
vouloir	to want to

(These are explained fully in Chapter 32.)

adorer	to adore _____ing
aimer	to love _____ing
descendre	to go down and . . .
désirer	to want to
détester	to detest _____ing
entrer	to go in and . . .
espérer	to hope to
laisser	to let
monter	to go up and . . .
oser	to dare to
paraître	to appear to, seem to
penser	to think of _____ing
préférer	to prefer to, to prefer _____ing
rentrer	to come back and . . .
sembler	to seem to
il vaut mieux	it's best to
venir	to come and . . .

*Mais il **déteste faire** les courses.*	But he **hates** shopping.
*Nous **espérons vous voir** bientôt.*	We **hope to see you** soon.
***Laisse ta sœur prendre** son déjeuner!*	**Let your sister eat** her lunch!
*Les enfants **préféreraient aller** au Futuroscope.*	The children **would prefer to go** to the Futuroscope.

Verbs joined with *à*, followed by the infinitive

aider (quelqu'un) à	to help (someone) to
apprendre à	to learn to
s'attendre à	to expect to
commencer à	to begin/start to
continuer à	to continue, carry on _____ing
encourager quelqu'un à	to encourage someone to
enseigner à quelqu'un à	to teach someone to
hésiter à	to hesitate to
inviter quelqu'un à	to invite someone to
se mettre à	to start, begin _____ing
se préparer à	to get ready to
réussir à	to succeed in _____ing
servir à	to be used for _____ing
tarder à	to take a long time to

*Quand **as**-tu **commencé à apprendre** le français?*	When **did** you **begin learning** French?
*Nous **vous invitons à passer la journée** chez nous samedi prochain.*	We **invite you to spend the day** with us next Saturday.
*Ce truc-là **sert à attraper** les mouches.*	That gadget **is used to catch** flies.

Verbs joined with *de*, followed by the infinitive

avoir besoin de	to need to
avoir envie de	to want to, feel like _____ing
avoir honte de	to be ashamed to
avoir l'intention de	to intend to
avoir peur de	to be afraid to
cesser de	to stop, cease _____ing
décider de	to decide to
essayer de	to try to
menacer de	to threaten to
offrir de	to offer to
oublier de	to forget to
refuser de	to refuse to
suggérer de	to suggest _____ing
terminer de	to finish _____ing

J'ai envie de danser!	I **want to dance / feel like dancing!**
*Nous **avons décidé de rentrer** à la maison.*	We **decided to go** home.
*Mon père **a oublié de faire le plein** d'essence.*	My dad **forgot to fill up** with gas.

Commander à quelqu'un de . . . , followed by the infinitive

Verbs which get other people to do something or stop them from doing something are also joined with *de:*

commander à quelqu'un de	to order someone to
conseiller à quelqu'un de	to advise someone to
demander à quelqu'un de	to ask someone to
empêcher quelqu'un de	to stop/prevent someone from _____ing
dire à quelqu'un de	to tell someone to
permettre à quelqu'un de	to allow someone to
recommander à quelqu'un de	to recommend to someone to

***Dis à ton frère de changer** ses chaussures.*	**Tell your brother to change** his shoes.
*Nos amis **nous ont demandé de garder** leurs enfants.*	Our friends **asked us to watch** their children.
*Le gros camion **nous empêchait de sortir**.*	The big truck **was stopping us from getting out.**

Prêts?

▶1 Une surprise pour grand-mère

Voici l'histoire de Dorian, qui veut faire une surprise à sa grand-mère pour son anniversaire. Faites coïncider les phrases des deux colonnes. Les prépositions peuvent vous guider!

This is the story of Dorian, who wants to give his grandmother a birthday surprise. Match phrases from each column. The prepositions may guide you!

_____ **1.** Dorian veut	**a.** de préparer la mousse quand sa grand-mère arrive.
_____ **2.** Il hésite	**b.** de casser les œufs.
_____ **3.** Il décide	**c.** faire une surprise à sa grand-mère.
_____ **4.** Il descend	**d.** de faire une mousse au chocolat.
_____ **5.** Il essaie	**e.** à faire un gâteau parce que c'est trop cher!
_____ **6.** Il se met	**f.** acheter des œufs au supermarché.
_____ **7.** Il termine	**g.** à les battre.

▶2 Le bagage oublié

Toby arrive à l'aéroport de Roissy–Charles de Gaulle. Mais en descendant de l'avion, il se rend compte qu'il a laissé un bagage dans la salle d'embarquement à Chicago. Il faut qu'il aille au bureau des réclamations bagages. Complétez les phrases avec *à* ou *de* si c'est nécessaire.

Toby arrives at Roissy–Charles de Gaulle Airport, but as he gets off the plane he realizes he has left a bag at the gate in Chicago. He has to go to the baggage claim office. Complete the sentences with *à* or *de* where necessary.

1. Toby va _____ demander où se trouve le bureau des réclamations.

2. Il hésite _____ entrer dans le bureau.

3. Il n'ose pas _____ parler français, car il pense qu'il parle mal.

4. Il commence _____ expliquer son histoire, et l'hôtesse l'encourage _____ parler français.

5. Elle lui demande _____ lui donner son adresse à Chicago.

6. Elle dit qu'elle va _____ envoyer un fax à Chicago.

7. Elle suggère _____ téléphoner plus tard dans la journée.

8. Rassuré, Toby décide _____ prendre un autobus pour aller à Paris et il se met _____ parler sans hésitation.

✪**3 Un job pour l'été**

Olivier est étudiant. Il veut partir en Écosse mais il a besoin d'argent. Répondez aux questions ci-dessous en choisissant une phrase de la case et en ajoutant la préposition *à* ou *de* si c'est nécessaire.

Olivier is a student. He wants to go to Scotland but he needs money. Answer the questions, choosing a phrase from the box and adding the preposition *à* or *de* if necessary.

1. De quoi Olivier a-t-il besoin?

_____

2. Que réussit-il?

_____

3. Qu'espère-t-il?

_____

4. Que pense-t-il faire avec cet argent?

_____

5. Que refuse-t-il?

_____

6. Que lui enseigne-t-on le premier jour?

_____

7. Que lui permet-on?

_____

8. Que décide-t-il?

_____

---

commencer à cinq heures du matin
travailler pendant deux mois
trouver un job pour l'été dans un supermarché
mettre les étiquettes (*labels*) sur les produits (*products*)
gagner de l'argent
s'arrêter un quart d'heure pour prendre un café
gagner 3000 francs
partir en Écosse et rester chez sa cousine

✪ 4 Quelle sœur autoritaire!

Votre grande sœur est très autoritaire et vous commande toujours de faire quelque chose. Dites ce qu'elle vous a demandé, commandé, etc., de faire cette semaine!

Your big sister is very bossy and is always ordering you to do something. Say what she has asked, ordered, etc., you to do this week.

Exemple:

Qu'est-ce qu'elle vous a demandé de faire dimanche?
Elle m'a demandé d'acheter des croissants.

1. Qu'est-ce qu'elle vous a commandé de faire lundi?

   _____

   _____

2. Qu'est-ce qu'elle vous a dit de faire mardi?

   _____

   _____

3. Qu'est-ce qu'elle vous a recommandé de faire mercredi?

   _____

   _____

4. Qu'est-ce qu'elle vous a empêché de faire jeudi?

   _____

   _____

→

5. Qu'est-ce qu'elle ne vous a pas permis de faire vendredi?

_____

_____

6. Qu'est-ce qu'elle vous a demandé de faire samedi?

_____

_____

7. Qu'est-ce qu'elle vous a conseillé de faire dimanche?

_____

_____

Partez!

▶5 Pour mieux vous connaître

Travail par deux. Imaginez que vous et votre camarade de classe, vous ne vous connaissez pas et que vous vous posez des questions pour mieux vous connaître. Utilisez dans vos questions les verbes _aimer, adorer, détester, espérer, penser, préférer_. Écrivez vos questions et réponses.

Pair work. Imagine that you and your partner do not know each other and that you are asking each other questions in order to get to know each other better. In your questions use the verbs _aimer, adorer, détester, espérer, penser, préférer_. Write your questions and answers.

Exemples:

—Qu'est-ce que tu aimes faire le week-end?
—Le samedi j'aime aller en ville, et le dimanche j'adore aller à la piscine.

—Que penses-tu faire après les examens?
—Je pense aller en vacances avec mes copains/copines.

_____

_____

_____

_____

_____

_____

_____

_____

✪6 Qu'est-ce qui se passe?

Un élève choisit un verbe des listes des sections "Verbs joined with _à/de_ . . ." (pages 233–34) plus un autre verbe à l'infinitif et le mime. Les autres doivent deviner ce qui se passe.

One student chooses a verb from the lists in the sections "Verbs joined with _à/de_ . . ." (pages 233–34) plus another verb in the infinitive and mimes it. The others have to guess what is happening.

Exemples:

—Tu essaies d'ouvrir une bouteille!
—Tu aides quelqu'un à traverser la rue!

34 Look at This!
verbs and their objects

À vos marques!

What are direct and indirect objects?

You learned all about direct and indirect objects in Chapter 8. Look back if you have forgotten! You may have noticed that some verbs take different kinds of objects in English and French: for example, *regarder* takes a direct object in French, but the English is to "look **at**" something. The following lists will help you to sort out the most common verbs whose objects differ in French and English.

Direct object verbs

Verbs taking a direct object in French but a preposition in English:

attendre	to wait **for**
chercher	to look **for**
écouter	to listen **to**
regarder	to look **at**

Attendez les enfants!	Wait **for** the children!
Regarde cette robe!	Look **at** that dress!

Indirect object verbs

Verbs taking an indirect object (with *à*) in French but a direct object in English:

jouer à	to play (a game)
obéir à	to obey
téléphoner à	to phone

*Allons jouer **au** football!*	Let's go and play soccer!
*Il faut obéir **à** ton prof!*	You must obey your teacher!
*Je vais téléphoner **à** ma mère.*	I'm going to phone my mother.

Verbs with *à* for "from"

Verbs which use *à* where "from" is used in English:

A small number of French verbs that express actions involving removal of something **from** a person use *à*:

*acheter quelque chose **à** quelqu'un*	to buy something **from** somebody
*enlever quelque chose **à** quelqu'un*	to take something away **from** someone
*emprunter quelque chose **à** quelqu'un*	to borrow something **from** somebody
*voler quelque chose **à** quelqu'un*	to steal something **from** somebody
*Nous avons acheté notre voiture **à** un mécanicien.*	We bought our car **from** a mechanic.

Note also:

*demander quelque chose **à** quelqu'un*	to ask someone **for** something
Ils nous ont demandé l'argent.	They demanded (asked us **for**) our money (*nous* is an indirect object pronoun).

Verbs + *de* + object

Verbs + *de* + object in French, but verb + direct object in English:

*s'apercevoir **de***	to notice
*s'approcher **de***	to approach
*avoir besoin **de***	to need
*changer **de***	to change
*discuter **de***	to discuss
*jouer **de***	to play (an instrument)
*se souvenir **de***	to remember
*se tromper **de***	to make a mistake about (see example below)

*Mesdames, messieurs, nous nous approchons **de** l'aéroport de Paris–Charles de Gaulle.*	Ladies and gentlemen, we are approaching Paris–Charles de Gaulle Airport.
*Marc, va changer **de** chemise.*	Marc, go and change your shirt.
*Tu te souviens **de** cet homme?*	Do you remember that man?
*Nous nous sommes trompés **de** train!*	We're on the wrong train!

 *Prêts?*

▶ 1 C'est la rentrée!

C'est le jour de la rentrée scolaire à la cité scolaire d'Amiens. Tout le monde est un peu perdu dans ce grand lycée. Faites coïncider les éléments des deux colonnes.

It's "back to school" at the cité scolaire (junior and senior high school campus) in Amiens. Everyone is a bit lost in this large school. Match the parts in the two columns.

_____ **1.** Tous les élèves attendent

_____ **2.** Les élèves discutent

_____ **3.** Claire cherche

_____ **4.** Un nouvel élève demande

_____ **5.** Un professeur s'approche

_____ **6.** Ludovic va téléphoner

_____ **7.** Le professeur de musique a changé

_____ **8.** Un nouveau professeur se trompe

a. à sa mère pour lui dire qui sont ses professeurs.

b. des élèves pour leur demander s'ils ont passé de bonnes vacances.

c. de leurs vacances.

d. à Claire où se trouve la salle 104.

e. de salle: il ne connaît pas l'école.

f. de look: il s'est coupé la barbe.

g. leurs professeurs principaux dans la cour.

h. ses amies mais ne les trouve pas.

 *Partez!*

▶ 2 Encore des mimes!

Choisissez un des verbes des listes de la section *À vos marques!* et mimez-le. Les autres devinent ce que vous faites.

Choose a verb from the lists in the *À vos marques!* section and mime it. The others guess what you are doing.

Exemples:

Tu écoutes la radio!
Tu joues de la guitare!

Going, Gone
participles

À vos marques!

What are participles?

There are two participles, present and past, and their functions are best explained with the examples which follow.

The present participle

-ant, "-ing"

The French present participle ends in -ant, and corresponds with **some but not all** of the uses of words ending in "-ing" in English. The stem is the first-person plural (*nous* form) of the present tense, for both regular and irregular verbs:

	Regular			Irregular	
	regarder to look	*finir* to finish	*vendre* to sell	*boire* to drink	*recevoir* to receive
nous	**regard**ons regard**ant** looking	**finiss**ons finiss**ant** finishing	**vend**ons vend**ant** selling	**buv**ons buv**ant** drinking	**recev**ons recev**ant** receiving

Conseil!

This stem is the same as for the imperfect tense; look it up on pages 172–74.

There are only three verbs which don't follow this pattern:

être	→	*étant*
to be		being
avoir	→	*ayant*
to have		having
savoir	→	*sachant*
to know		knowing

Main uses

■ The present participle is used with *en*, meaning "while doing," "by doing," or "on doing":

*Je me suis cassé la jambe **en jouant** au football.*
I broke my leg **(while) playing** soccer.

*C'est **en travaillant** beaucoup que vous réussirez à vos examens.*
You'll pass your exams **by working** a lot.

***En arrivant** à la tour Eiffel, nous avons décidé d'y monter.*
(On) arriving at the Eiffel Tower, we decided to go up.

Note also:

entrer en courant	to run into
sortir en courant	to run out
monter en courant	to run up
descendre en courant	to run down

■ It may also be used as an adjective, when it has to agree like any other adjective:

*Nathalie est une fille **charmante**.*	Nathalie is a **charming** girl.
*Ces livres sont très **intéressants**.*	Those books are very **interesting**.
*C'est une pièce **passionnante**.*	It's an **exciting** play.

The past participle

Formation

You are probably familiar with a good many past participles, since they are the second component of the *passé composé* and other compound tenses. They correspond to the English "done," "spoken," "eaten," "seen," and so forth. Here are a few as a reminder:

Regular			Irregular		
regarder	*finir*	*vendre*	*boire*	*mettre*	*conduire*
regardé	*fini*	*vendu*	*bu*	*mis*	*conduit*
looked	finished	sold	drunk	put	driven

Other irregular past participles are listed on pages 181 and 182.

Uses

■ The past participle is used as the second component of the *passé composé* and other compound tenses:

*Nous avons **acheté** des cartes postales.*   We have **bought** some postcards.

This use is explained in detail in Chapters 26 and 27.

■ To form the passive, as explained fully in Chapter 36 (note that the past participle agrees with the subject):

*Cette maison a été **construite** au*   This house was **built** in the 18th century.
dix-huitième siècle.

■ As an adjective, when, of course, it has to agree:

*une fenêtre **cassée***   a **broken** window
*un pull **tricoté** à la main*   a hand-**knitted** sweater
*Notre ville est **jumelée** avec Beauvais.* Our town is **a sister city** with Beauvais.

■ For certain bodily positions, where English uses a present participle:

être assis   to be sitting
être couché   to be lying

*Catherine et Julie étaient **assises** sur* Catherine and Julie were **sitting** on the sofa.
le canapé.
*Le chien était **couché** devant elles.*   The dog was **lying** in front of them.

OJO Attention!

You should distinguish between the **actions** *s'asseoir* "to sit **down**," *se coucher* "to lie **down**," and the **positions** *être assis* "**to be sitting/ seated**," *être couché* "to be **lying**."

je m'assieds

je suis assis

Prêts?

1 Pas de chance!

Décrivez les vignettes ci-dessous en faisant des phrases sur le modèle suivant.

Describe the sketches below making up sentences based on the following model.

Exemple:

C'est **en courant** que Clément est tombé.

1. C'est _____ que Jérémie s'est cassé la jambe.

2. C'est _____ que Michèle s'est fait mal au poignet.

3. C'est _____ que Christophe s'est brûlé la main.

4. C'est _____ que Marianne s'est coupé le doigt.

5. C'est _____ que Véronique a perdu son porte-monnaie.

6. C'est _____ le café que Mme Andrieux l'a renversé sur ses invités.

7. C'est _____ que Philippe a perdu la clef de la maison.

▶2 Trouvez le paire!

Pour chacun des noms ci-dessous, vous trouverez au moins un adjectif qui correspond. Vous verrez que tous les adjectifs sont en effet des participes présents. N'oubliez pas de les faire accorder! Utilisez le dictionnaire s'il y a des mots que vous ne connaissez pas!

For each of the nouns below you will find at least one adjective in the box. You'll see that all the adjectives are in fact present participles. Don't forget to make them agree! Use a dictionary if there are words you don't know!

Exemples:

des films intéressants
une fille amusante

1. des informations _____

2. une correspondante _____

3. des voitures _____

4. des films _____

5. des livres _____

6. un garçon _____

7. une fille _____

8. une boisson _____

9. le soleil _____

10. un billet _____

11. un travail _____

12. des oiseaux _____

13. un magazine _____

14. un CD _____

15. une vidéo _____

16. un professeur _____

amusant	effrayant	levant	couchant	intéressant	émouvant
pétillant	coupant	irritant	charmant	souriant	gagnant
fatigant	ennuyant	satisfaisant	inquiétant		

✪3 Pourquoi achetez-vous ça?

Lucie va faire des courses pour la famille, et elle explique ses achats à une dame qui fait une enquête. Faites coïncider les éléments de la deuxième colonne avec ceux de la première: l'accord des participes passés vous aidera.

Lucie is going shopping for the family and is explaining her purchases to a woman who is conducting a survey. Match the items in the second column with those in the first. The agreement of the past participles will help you.

_____ **1.** des bandes

_____ **2.** du café

_____ **3.** de la soupe aux champignons

_____ **4.** des plats

_____ **5.** du lait

_____ **6.** des fleurs

_____ **7.** du jus d'oranges

_____ **8.** des disquettes

_____ **9.** du savon

_____ **10.** du pain

a. déshydratés, pour faire des repas rapides

b. coupé, pour mon père, qui n'aime pas les baguettes

c. séchées, pour ma mère

d. formatées, pour l'ordinateur

e. parfumé à la lavande, pour la salle de bains

f. concentrée, pour la nouvelle recette

g. dessinées, pour les enfants

h. écrémé, parce que c'est plus sain

i. décaféiné, pour mieux dormir

j. pressées, comme il fait chaud

Partez!

▶4 Chez le médecin

Expliquez au médecin comment vous vous êtes fait mal, en utilisant _en_ avec le participe présent.

Explain to the doctor how you hurt yourself, using _en_ and the present participle.

Exemples:

Je me suis cassé le bras **en jouant** au hockey.
C'est **en montant** dans le bus que je me suis fait mal au genou.

(Utilisez _se faire mal, se casser, se brûler, se tordre, se couper._)

_____

_____

_____

_____

▶**5** Une activité passionnante!

Prenez quelques-uns des participes présents de l'exercice 2 et trouvez d'autres noms qu'ils pourraient décrire.

Take some of the present participles from exercise 2 and find some more nouns for them to describe.

Exemples:

une **situation** effrayante
du **vin** pétillant

_____   _____

_____   _____

_____   _____

_____   _____

_____   _____

▶**6** Une activité prévue!

Essayez de trouver des noms qui conviennent aux participes passés suivants. Faites accorder les participes si c'est nécessaire.

Try to find nouns which go with the following past participles. Make the participles agree if necessary.

Exemples:

bureau fermé
agneau rôti

_____   _____

_____   _____

_____   _____

_____   _____

_____   _____

| frit | rôti | grillé | glacé | coupé | tricoté | réduit |
| enchanté | fermé | ouvert | prévu | | | |

36 What Was Done?
the passive and *on*

 *Ā vos marques!*

What is the passive?

Most sentences tell you that "Somebody does/did something," that is, the order is **subject-verb-object**: *Martin a vendu le vélo* "Martin sold the bike." In this case the verb is **active:**

Subject	Verb	Object
Martin	*a vendu*	*le vélo.*
Martin	sold	the bike.

Quite often, however, especially in English, you can turn this around and say "The bike was sold by Martin." In this case, the object becomes the subject and the person the action was done by becomes the "agent." The verb is now **passive:**

Subject	Verb	Agent
Le vélo	*a été vendu*	*par Martin.*
The bike	was sold	by Martin.

How do you form the passive?

As in English, you form a passive verb with the relevant tense of *être* "to be" + **the past participle,** which has to agree with the subject. *Par* is "by":

*La viande **a été mangée par** le chien.*   The meat **was eaten by** the dog.
*Ces glaces **sont fabriquées par** une*   These mirrors **are made by** an Italian company.
   compagnie italienne.

You don't always have a subject (that is, whom or what the action was done **by**):

*La maison **a été construite** tout récemment.*	The house **was built** quite recently.
*Les résultats **seront annoncés** à la télévision.*	The results **will be announced** on TV.
*Les règles **ont été changées**.*	The rules **have been changed.**

> **Conseil!**
>
> Because so many passive verbs are used in the *passé composé,* it's worth learning how to recognize and use this tense, particularly in the third-person forms:
>
> | | |
> |---|---|
> | *il a été vu* | he was seen |
> | *elle a été construite* | it (*la maison*) was built |
> | *ils ont été interdits* | they have been / they were prohibited |
> | *elles ont été fabriquées* | they (*les glaces*) were made |

How to avoid the passive

Now that we've shown you how to form the passive, we have to confess that it is not used as often in French as it is in English.

There is a common way of expressing the same idea in French but avoiding the passive construction: using *on* + an active verb. *On* literally means "one," and one can say things in this way if one wishes in English, but it sounds stilted. However, *on* is used quite often in French, when you don't need to say whom the action was done by:

***On a construit** cette maison tout récemment.*	This house **was built** quite recently.
***On annoncera** les résultats à la télévision.*	The results **will be announced** on television.
***On a changé** les règles.*	The rules **have been changed.**

On dit means "it is said" or "they say" or "people say":

***On dit** que le propriétaire est très riche.*	**It is said / they say** that the owner is very rich.

> **Conseil!**
>
> *On* is very useful for expressing the idea "I was told" *on m'a dit,* "we were told" *on nous a dit,* "I was given" *on m'a donné,* etc.

Prêts?

⭐ 1 L'internat Bacassuré

Voici une publicité pour l'internat Bacassuré qui est une des meilleures écoles de France. Malheureusement une erreur de la secrétaire a fait que les verbes à la forme passive ont été omis. Remettez-les en place.

Here is an ad for the Bacassuré Boarding School, which is one of the best schools in France. Unfortunately the passive verbs were accidentally omitted. Choose the correct passive verb from the box below.

A l'internat Bacassuré:

- Les élèves _____.
- Les élèves _____ à l'examen.
- Les professeurs _____ dans les meilleures universités.
- Le matériel _____.
- Les décisions _____ en accord avec les familles.
- Des cours particuliers _____ en cas de besoin.
- Les repas _____ comme à la maison.
- Les sorties _____ entre 17h et 18h et le dimanche.
- Le succès au bac _____.

---

sont autorisées	sont cuisinés	sont donnés	sont motivés	est assuré
est spécialisé	sont prises	sont formés	sont préparés	

⭐2 Le bilan

Maurice est producteur de fruits dans le Roussillon, dans le sud de France. C'est l'été au soir d'une journée de travail, et il fait le bilan avec son épouse Marie-Claude. Faites coïncider les éléments de la colonne A et ceux de la colonne B.

Maurice is a fruit farmer in Roussillon, in the south of France. It's a summer evening, and after a day's work, he and his wife Marie-Claude are taking inventory. Match the parts of sentences in column A with those in column B.

	A		**B**
_____	**1.** On a donné	**a.**	500 kilos de melons.
_____	**2.** On a exporté	**b.**	400 clients pour les nectarines.
_____	**3.** On a jeté	**c.**	deux camions d'abricots au marché de Rungis, près de Paris.
_____	**4.** On a stocké	**d.**	50 kilos de pêches et 50 kilos d'abricots aux enfants de la colonie de vacances.
_____	**5.** On a cueilli	**e.**	100 kilos de melons parce qu'ils étaient abîmes (*spoiled, ruined*).
_____	**6.** On a envoyé	**f.**	trois camions de pêches en Allemagne.
_____	**7.** On a contacté	**g.**	100 kilos de citrons dans les frigidaires.

⭐3 Marie-Claude revoit les chiffres

Marie-Claude est seule. Elle relit les chiffres de l'exercice 2. Mettez les réponses de l'exercice 2 à la forme passive. Tous les participes passés sont au masculin pluriel.

Marie-Claude is alone, rereading the figures in exercise 2. Put the answers to exercise 2 into the passive. All past participles are masculine plural.

Exemple:

1. Cinquante kilos de pêches et 50 kilos d'abricots **ont été donnés** aux enfants de la colonie de vacances.

2. _____

3. _____

4. _____

5. _____

6. _____

7. _____

✪4 La vie à l'internat Bacassuré

Expliquez ce que l'on fait dans cet internat en utilisant *on*.

Explain what is done at this boarding school using *on*.

Exemple:

6h30   lever
On se lève à 6h30.

1.	7h	petit déjeuner
2.	7h30	étude
3.	8h	début des cours
4.	10h	récréation
5.	12h	déjeuner
6.	13h30	reprise (*resuming*) des cours
7.	16h30	football ou tennis
8.	19h30	dîner
9.	21h30	coucher

Partez!

✪5 Un nouveau bâtiment

Décrivez la construction d'un nouveau bâtiment—une maison, une école, un club des jeunes, un magasin—ce que vous voulez. Faites la description d'abord à la forme passive, puis en utilisant *on*.

Describe the construction of a new building—a house, a school, a youth organization, a store—whatever you like. Do the description first in the passive, then using *on*.

Exemple:

Le club a été commencé en 1997. D'abord le terrain a été acheté et préparé, puis . . .
On a commencé le club en 1997. D'abord on a acheté et préparé le terrain, puis . . .

(construire les murs, mettre les fenêtres et les portes, terminer le toit, peindre l'intérieur, installer la cuisine, couvrir le plancher, acheter les rideaux, installer des douches, etc.)

_____

_____

_____

_____

_____

_____

_____

_____

⭐**6** Qu'est-ce qu'on fait à votre collège?

Décrivez ce qu'on fait chaque jour à votre collège ou lycée, un peu comme dans l'exercice 3, en utilisant *on*.

Describe what is done every day in your junior high or high school, a bit like in exercise 3, using *on*.

Exemple:

On arrive à 8h45 . . .

_____

_____

_____

_____

_____

_____

37 I'm Cold Because It's Cold
climate, *avoir* expressions, and impersonal expressions

À vos marques!

This chapter deals with expressions that use "to be" in English but a different verb in French and with impersonal expressions beginning with *il* "it" + the third-person singular of the verb.

Talking about the weather

Many weather expressions are "impersonal" expressions. When talking about the weather in French, you **don't** usually begin, *"Le temps . . ."*

■ Quite a lot of weather expressions begin with *il fait:*

Quel temps fait-il?	What's the weather like?
Il fait beau (temps).	The weather's nice.
Il fait mauvais (temps).	The weather's bad.
Il fait froid.	It's cold.
Il fait chaud.	It's hot.
Il fait doux.	It's mild.
Il fait du soleil.	It's sunny.
Il fait du vent.	It's windy.
Il fait du tonnerre.	It's stormy. (*tonnerre* = thunder)
Il fait du brouillard.	It's foggy.
Il fait nuit.	It's dark.
Il fait jour.	It's daylight.

■ Others are verbs in their own right:

Il pleut.	It rains / it's raining.
Il neige.	It snows / it's snowing.
Il gèle.	It freezes / it's freezing.
Il grêle.	It hails / it's hailing.

■ Sometimes you use *il y a* "there is" (see also the section on *il y a* below):

Il y a du verglas sur les routes.	There's black ice (invisible ice) on the roads.

Conseil!

It is worth knowing how to use these expressions in the imperfect and *passé composé* because you may need to describe what the weather was doing or did yesterday, or while you were on vacation:

Il faisait beau temps et très chaud quand nous étions en vacances.
It was nice and very warm when we were on vacation.

Il pleuvait quand nous sommes partis hier.
It was raining when we left yesterday.

Il y a eu un orage hier soir.
There was a thunderstorm last night.

You also need to know the infinitives in order to talk about what the weather is going to do:

Est-ce qu'il va pleuvoir cet après-midi?
Is it going to rain this afternoon?

Saying you're hot or cold and other *avoir* expressions

■ When you are talking about people being hot or cold, you use *avoir: avoir chaud, avoir froid,* and so forth. No agreement is needed:

*Est-ce que **tu as froid**?*	**Are you cold?**
*Non, **j'ai assez chaud**!*	No, **I'm quite hot**!

■ Other common expressions with *avoir* are:

avoir raison	to be right
avoir tort	to be wrong
avoir faim	to be hungry
avoir soif	to be thirsty
avoir honte (de)	to be ashamed (of)
avoir peur (de)	to be afraid (of)
avoir sommeil	to be sleepy
avoir de la chance	to be lucky

*Oui, **vous avez raison**!*	Yes, **you're right**!
*Maman, **j'ai très faim**!*	Mom, **I'm very hungry**!
*Quand j'étais petit **j'avais peur des** chiens.*	When I was little **I was afraid of** dogs.

Saying things are hot or cold

In this case you do use *être,* and you make the adjective agree:

*L'eau **est très froide**!*	The water **is very cold**!

Il y a

Il y a means "there is," "there are." It is worthwhile to learn the main tenses because it is such a common expression:

Present	*il y a*	there is/are
Imperfect	*il y avait*	there was/were (descriptive)
Passé composé	*il y a eu*	there has/have been, there was/were (on one occasion)
Future	*il y aura*	there will be
Future with *aller*	*il va y avoir*	there's going to be
Conditional	*il y aurait*	there would be

Il y avait une piscine derrière l'hôtel.	**There was** a pool behind the hotel.
Il y a eu un accident.	**There's been / there was** an accident.
Il y aura un accident!	**There'll be** an accident!
Il va y avoir un accident!	**There's going to be** an accident!

ojo Attention!

Voilà also means "there is/are," but you use it when you are pointing something out:

Ah! Voilà mes lunettes, sur le buffet!
Ah! There are my glasses, on the buffet table!

Prêts?

▶**1** **Quel temps fait-il?**

Décrivez le temps qu'il fait selon les images.

Describe the weather according to the pictures.

1.

2.

3.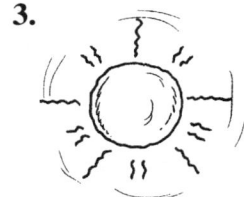

4.

5.

6.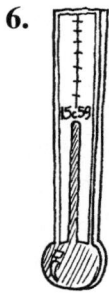

7.

8.

1. _____

2. _____

3. _____

4. _____

5. _____

6. _____

7. _____

8. _____

▶2 J'ai raison!

Dites comment vous vous sentez, selon les images.

Say how you feel, according to the pictures.

Exemple:

J'ai froid.

1.

2.

3.

4.

5.

6.

1. _____

2. _____

3. _____

4. _____

5. _____

6. _____

⭐3 Les vacances dans les Alpes

Pierre-Henri est allé en vacances dans les Alpes. Il veut écrire une lettre à sa petite amie. Combinez les expressions des trois colonnes pour faire autant de phrases que possible qui aient du sens.

Pierre-Henri is vacationing in the Alps. He wants to write a letter to his girlfriend. Combine the expressions in the three columns to form as many sentences as possible that make sense.

Le jour	il y avait	très chaud.
L'eau des torrents	il faisait	des torrents, des fleurs sauvages.
Hier soir	il y a eu	très froide.
Dans les vallées	était	très chaud, car nous marchions beaucoup.
À cause du tonnerre	j'avais	très soif, car il faisait chaud.
	il y a	un orage.
		du tonnerre.
		très peur dans mon lit.

_____

_____

_____

_____

_____

_____

_____

_____

Partez!

▶4 Le temps qu'il fait

Vous mimez vos actions ou réactions au temps qu'il fait. Par exemple, si vous vous essuyez le front, les autres élèves disent: "Il fait chaud!"

You mime your actions or reactions according to the weather, which the other students have to guess. For example, if you wipe your brow, they say, *"Il fait chaud!"*

▶**5** Dites pourquoi!

En utilisant chacune des expressions avec *avoir* de la liste à la page 257, essayez de trouver des raisons pour lesquelles vous éprouvez telle ou telle chose.

Using each of the expressions with *avoir* from the list on page 257, try to find reasons to explain why you feel like that.

Exemple:

—Tu as honte!
—Oui, c'est parce que je viens de voler une bouteille de lait.
—Oui, c'est parce que j'ai frappé mon petit frère.

_____

_____

_____

_____

_____

_____

_____

_____

⭐**6** Regardez autour de vous!

Décrivez, en utilisant tous les temps de *il y a,* ce qui se passe autour de vous.

Describe, using all the tenses of *il y a,* what happens around you.

Exemples:

Il y a un cours de français aujourd'hui.
Hier, il y a eu un orage.
Il n'y avait pas beaucoup de monde en ville hier soir.
Ce week-end il y aura un concert en plein air (*outdoor*).

_____

_____

_____

_____

_____

No! Nothing! Never!

negatives

38

À vos marques!

What is a negative?

Negatives are words such as "no," "not," "never," "no one," "nothing," "nowhere." Sometimes in English they are expressed as "not ever," "not anyone," etc.

French negatives

non	no
ne . . . pas	not
ne . . . jamais	never, not ever
ne . . . personne	no one, not anyone / nobody, not anybody
ne . . . rien	nothing, not anything
ne . . . plus	no longer, not any longer
ne . . . pas non plus	neither, not either
ne . . . ni . . . ni . . .	neither . . . nor . . .
ne . . . que	only
ne . . . nulle part	nowhere, not anywhere
ne . . . aucun(e)	no (in the sense of "not any")

How to use negative words

■ All involve using *ne* when there is a verb, and in most cases "wrapping" *ne* and a negative word around it:

*Je **ne** mange **pas** de viande.*	I **don't** eat meat.
*Je **ne** mange **jamais** de pommes de terre.*	I **never** eat potatoes.
*Nous **ne** reconnaissons **personne** ici.*	We **don't** recognize **anyone** here.
*Tu **ne** sais **rien!***	You know **nothing** / you **don't** know **anything**!

*Nous **n'**y allons **plus.***	We **don't** go there **anymore.**
*Les maths? Moi, je **ne** les aime **pas non plus**!*	Math? I **don't** like it **either**!
*En fait, je **n'**aime **ni** les maths **ni** les sciences.*	In fact, I **don't** like **either** math **or** science. (I like **neither** math **nor** science.)
*Moi je **n'**aime **que** le français!*	I **only** like French!
*Je **ne** trouve **nulle part** mes lunettes.*	I **can't** find my glasses **anywhere.**
*Mon frère **n'**a pu trouver **aucun** travail.*	My brother has **not** been able to find **any** work.

■ Some negative words can be the subject, and these come before *ne:*

***Personne ne** veut m'aider.*	**Nobody** wants to help me.
***Ni** mon frère **ni** ma sœur **ne** veut m'aider.*	**Neither** my brother **nor** my sister wants to help me.

ʘjʘ Attention!

1. In the *passé composé* and other compound tenses, *pas, rien, jamais* come before the past participle:

*Nous **n'**avons **pas** vu le château.*	We **haven't** seen the castle.
*Nous **n'**avons **jamais** vu le château.*	We **have never** seen the castle.
*Nous **n'**avons **rien** vu.*	We **haven't** seen **anything.**

They are used together before an infinitive:

*Prière de **ne pas** fumer.*	Please **do not smoke.**
***Ne rien** jeter dans l'eau.*	**Do not throw anything** into the water.

2. The other negative words are placed where they are needed:

*Je **ne** bois **ni** bière **ni** vin.*	I drink **neither** beer **nor** wine.
*Nous **n'**avons vu **que** l'extérieur du château.*	We saw **only** the outside of the castle.

3. When two negatives are used together, the order is *ne* + any two of the following words: *plus, jamais, rien:*

*Nous **ne** le ferons **plus jamais**.*	We'll **never** do it **again.**
*Nous **n'**y avons **jamais rien** trouvé.*	We've **never** found **anything** there.

4. When there is no verb, *ne* is not used:

*Qui as-tu vu? **Personne.***	Who did you see? **No one.**
*Qu'avez-vous acheté? **Rien.***	What did you buy? **Nothing.**
***Aucun** problème!*	**No** problem!
*Moi **non plus**!*	Me **neither**!

Si for "yes"

To reply "yes" to a negative question, you say *si*, not *oui*:

***Tu n'aimes pas** le poulet rôti? Mais **si,** je l'aime bien!*
You don't like roast chicken? Oh, **yes,** I like it!

Sans ("without") + infinitive + negative

Ne is not needed when *sans* is used with an infinitive and a negative:

sans rien dire   without saying anything
sans voir personne   without seeing anybody

Prêts?

▶1 Louisette ne veut rien faire

Vous vous arrêtez au camping de Beauvais et vous rencontrez Louisette, qui est de mauvaise humeur et qui répond négativement à toutes vos suggestions. Choisissez dans la case le mot négatif qui convient.

You are staying at the campsite in Beauvais, where you meet Louisette, who is in a bad mood and who replies in the negative to all your suggestions. Choose the appropriate negative word from the box.

1. Je ne mange _____ de viande.

2. Je n'aime _____ les glaces.

3. Je ne veux _____ manger _____ boire.

4. Je ne connais _____ ici.

5. Je ne veux _____ visiter.

6. Je ne veux aller _____ demain.

7. Je ne veux pas aller à Disneyland _____.

8. Je n'ai _____ de voiture depuis mon accident.

9. Non, je n'ai _____ problème.

10. _____ ne peut m'aider.

plus	aucun	rien	jamais	ni . . . ni . . .	personne
non	plus	personne	pas	nulle part	

▶**2** Une visite décevante

Vous êtes allé(e) seul(e) à Paris, mais vous n'avez pas fait beaucoup car vous avez perdu beaucoup de temps à faire la queue pour monter en haut de la tour Eiffel. À votre retour, Louisette vous interroge. Voici vos réponses, mais vous êtes fatigué(e) et vous mélangez les négatifs. Il faut les remettre à leur place!

You went to Paris by yourself, but you didn't do a great deal, because you wasted a lot of time standing in line to go to the top of the Eiffel Tower. When you get back, Louisette asks you questions. Here are your answers, but you are tired and mix up your negatives. Replace each negative in italics with the correct negative from another sentence.

1. —As-tu visité beaucoup de choses?

   —Non, je n'ai visité *aucune* _____ la tour Eiffel.

2. —As-tu vu le Louvre?

   —Non, je n'ai *non plus* _____ vu le Louvre.

3. —As-tu parlé avec les Parisiens?

   —Non, je n'ai parlé avec *que* _____.

4. —As-tu déjà visité le musée Picasso?

   —Non, je ne l'ai *nulle part* _____ visité.

5. —As-tu regardé le centre Pompidou?

   —Non, je ne l'ai pas regardé *rien* _____.

6. —As-tu acheté quelque chose dans les magasins?

   —J'ai regardé des magasins mais je n'ai *jamais* _____ acheté.

7. —Et tu as visité d'autres choses?

   —Non, je n'ai visité *personne* _____ autre chose.

8. —Tu t'es assis(e) quelque part pour prendre un café?

   —Non, je ne me suis assis(e) *pas* _____.

▶3 Mais si!

En France, on vous pose à vous et à votre famille des questions au négatif, ce qui vous surprend. Répondez à l'affirmatif!

In France, you and your family are asked some questions in the negative, which surprises you. Answer in the affirmative!

Exemple:

—Tu n'aimes pas le steak-frites?
—Mais si, je l'aime bien!

1. —Tu n'aimes pas les glaces?

   _____

2. —Tu ne veux pas aller à la piscine?

   _____

3. —Tu ne parles pas français?

   _____

4. —Vous n'avez pas tous visité le Parc Astérix?

   _____

5. —Votre père ne sait pas rouler à droite?

   _____

6. —Les enfants ne jouent pas avec les autres enfants au camping?

   _____

Partez!

▶4 Jamais!

Faites une liste de cinq choses que vous ne faites jamais, en donnant les raisons, si vous le souhaitez.

Make a list of five things you never do, with reasons if you wish.

Exemple:

Je ne mange jamais de fromage (parce que je ne l'aime pas).

_____

_____

→

_____

_____

_____

▶5 Personne ne le fait chez vous

Trouvez cinq choses que personne ne fait chez vous, en donnant les raisons, si vous le souhaitez.

Find five things nobody does at your house, giving reasons if you wish.

Exemple:

Personne ne fume, (parce que ça pollue l'air / sent mauvais).

_____

_____

_____

_____

_____

▶6 Soyons tous négatifs!

La classe se divise en deux équipes. La première équipe donne un mot négatif de la liste à la page 263, et l'autre équipe doit faire une phrase correcte avec ce mot. Faites les phrases à tour de rôle.

The class divides into two teams. The first team gives a negative word from the list on page 263, and the other team has to make a correct sentence with it. Each team takes turns.

Exemple:

—Aucun
—Nous n'avons aucun problème avec ce mot!

I Want You to Do It!
You Must Do It!

the present subjunctive

39

À vos marques!

What is the subjunctive?

The subjunctive is a special form of the verb which you have to use in special circumstances instead of the "ordinary," or "indicative," form. The subjunctive is often called a *mood*. It often expresses the subject's *opinion*—it can be a hope, a wish, or a doubt.

Conseil!

The **meaning** of the present subjunctive is nothing to worry about. In most cases it is no different from that of the present tense, the indicative.

How do you form the present subjunctive?

Regular verbs

The stem is based on the third-person plural of the present indicative. Add the following endings: *-e, -es, -e, -ions, -iez, -ent:*

regarder "to look" *ils **regard**ent*	*finir* "to finish" *ils **finiss**ent*	*vendre* "to sell" *ils **vend**ent*
je regarde	*je finisse*	*je vende*
tu regardes	*tu finisses*	*tu vendes*
il/elle regarde	*il/elle finisse*	*il/elle vende*
nous regardions	*nous finissions*	*nous vendions*
vous regardiez	*vous finissiez*	*vous vendiez*
ils/elles regardent	*ils/elles finissent*	*ils/elles vendent*

ojo Attention!

> Verbs such as *jeter, appeler, lever, espérer, employer* have the same
> spelling changes in the subjunctive that they have in the present indicative.
> See Chapter 20.

Irregular verbs

In most cases, the subjunctive endings for irregular verbs are the same as those for regular verbs: only the stem is irregular, and again this is usually formed, as for regular verbs, from the *ils/elles* forms of the present indicative. Here are some examples:

écrire "to write" *ils* **écriv**ent	*mettre* "to put" *ils* **mett**ent	*suivre* "to follow" *ils* **suiv**ent	*partir* "to leave" *ils* **part**ent
j'écrive	*je mette*	*je suive*	*je parte*
tu écrives	*tu mettes*	*je suives*	*tu partes*
il/elle écrive	*il/elle mette*	*il/elle suive*	*il/elle parte*
nous écrivions	*nous mettions*	*nous suivions*	*nous partions*
vous écriviez	*vous mettiez*	*vous suiviez*	*vous partiez*
ils/elles écrivent	*ils/elles mettent*	*ils/elles suivent*	*ils/elles partent*

The same is true for the following verbs and verbs based on them or verbs that are conjugated like them:

Infinitive		Present indicative		Present subjunctive
s'asseoir	to sit down	*ils s'***assey**ent	→	*je m'asseye*
conduire	to drive	*ils* **conduis**ent	→	*je conduise*
connaître	to know	*ils* **connaiss**ent	→	*je connaisse*
coudre	to sew	*ils* **cous**ent	→	*je couse*
dire	to say/tell	*ils* **dis**ent	→	*je dise*
falloir	to be necessary, must	—		*il faille*
ouvrir	to open	*ils* **ouvr**ent	→	*j'ouvre*
peindre	to paint	*ils* **peign**ent	→	*je peigne*
pleuvoir	to rain	—		*il pleuve*
rire	to laugh	*ils* **ri**ent	→	*je rie*
sortir	to go out	*ils* **sort**ent	→	*je sorte*
vivre	to live	*ils* **viv**ent	→	*je vive*

■ The following have an irregular stem but follow the usual pattern:

Infinitive		Present indicative	Present subjunctive
faire	to do/make	*ils font*	*je fasse*
savoir	to know	*ils savent*	*je sache*

■ There are some verbs which have a 1-2-3-6, or "boot," pattern and revert to the indicative stem in the *nous* and *vous* forms:

Infinitive

boire "to drink"

je boive	*nous buvions*
tu boives	*vous buviez*
il/elle boive	*ils/elles boivent*

Remember that *tu, il/elle* follow the *je* stem, and *vous* follows the *nous* stem in the following verbs as well:

croire	to believe	*je croie, nous croyions, ils croient*
devoir	must, to have to	*je doive, nous devions, ils doivent*
mourir	to die	*je meure, nous mourions, ils meurent*
prendre	to take	*je prenne, nous prenions, ils prennent*
recevoir	to receive	*je reçoive, nous recevions, ils reçoivent*
venir	to come	*je vienne, nous venions, ils viennent*
voir	to see	*je voie, nous voyions, ils voient*

■ These verbs follow the above pattern but don't get their stems from the *ils* form:

aller	to go	*j'aille, nous allions, ils aillent*
vouloir	to want	*je veuille, nous voulions, ils veuillent*

■ The following are totally irregular:

avoir	to have	*j'aie, tu aies, il/elle ait, nous ayons, vous ayez, ils/elles aient*
être	to be	*je sois, tu sois, il/elle soit, nous soyons, vous soyez, ils/elles soient*

How do you use the subjunctive?

Wanting somebody else to do something

You need the subjunctive after *que* when the wanting, preferring, liking (or not) involves another person. Compare these pairs of examples:

Je veux aller au supermarché.	**I want to go** to the supermarket. (**I** both want and go—infinitive, not subjunctive)
Je veux que tu ailles au supermarché.	**I want you to go** to the supermarket. (**I** want, **you** go)

*Alors, **vous préférez rester** ici?*	So, **you prefer to remain** here? (**you** both prefer and remain)
*Alors, **vous préférez que nous restions** ici?*	So, **you prefer us to remain** here? (**you** prefer, **we** remain)
*Ma mère **préfère nettoyer** ma chambre.*	My mother **prefers to clean** my room. (**mother** both prefers and cleans)
*Ma mère **préfère que je nettoie** ma chambre.*	My mother **prefers me to clean** my room. (**mother** prefers, **I** clean)

After *il faut que* for "must"

One way of using *il faut*—with the infinitive—is fully explained in Chapter 32, but it is also often used with the subjunctive, especially when you want to express without doubt **who** must do the action.

Compare these pairs of examples:

*Il **faut prendre** le train de huit heures.*	I/we/you/one must catch the 8 o'clock train. (no particular emphasis on who has to catch it)
*Il **faut que vous preniez** le train de huit heures.*	**You must catch** the 8 o'clock train (no doubt: it's **you** who must catch it)
*Il **faut faire** attention!*	**You/we/I must pay** attention!
*Michel, il **faut que tu fasses** attention!*	Michel, **you must pay** attention! (**you,** Michel)

After . . .

il est possible que . . .	it's possible that . . .
il se peut que . . .	it's possible that . . .
il est impossible que . . .	it's impossible that . . .
il est peu probable que . . .	it's improbable/unlikely that . . .
Il est possible que nous arrivions en retard.	It's possible we may arrive late.
Il est peu probable que vous gagniez le prix.	It's unlikely you'll win the prize.

Conseil!

There are quite a number of other ways to use the subjunctive.
Most subjunctives you come across you will simply need to recognize
as such, even if they are used in ways not touched on in this chapter.
Don't worry: it means the same as the "ordinary" present indicative!

Prêts?

⭐1 Difficile de se décider!

Ellie, une jeune américaine, est en vacances chez son amie Catherine à Berck-sur-Mer. Un matin, elles font des projets pour la journée. Choisissez la forme convenable du présent du subjonctif.

Ellie, an American girl, is on vacation at her friend Catherine's house in Berck-sur-Mer. One morning they are making plans for the day. Choose the correct form of the present subjunctive. Bagatelle is a big amusement park near Berck-sur-Mer.

Catherine: J'ai envie d'aller à Bagatelle. Je voudrais que tu (viens/vienne/viennes)

(1) _____ avec moi.

Ellie: Non, je préfère rester ici. Je suis fatiguée.

Catherine: Alors il faut que tu (vas/ailles/aillent) (2) _____ te baigner.

La plage est à deux pas.

Ellie: Oh non! Je ne connais personne. Ce n'est pas amusant.

Catherine: Tu ne vas pas rester toute seule toute la journée!

Ellie: Pourquoi pas? Il est possible que je (fasse/font/fais) (3) _____

une promenade jusqu'au phare (*lighthouse*) ou que je (visite/visitent/visites)

(4) _____ le musée. Il paraît qu'il est très intéressant.

Catherine: Laisse ça pour un autre jour! Je veux que tu (t'amuse/t'amuses/t'amusent)

(5) _____ en France, pas que tu (passent/passe/passes)

(6) _____ ton temps dans les musées!

Ellie: D'accord! je t'accompagne, mais il ne faut pas que tu (veux/veuilles/veulent)

(7) _____ m'emmener sur la grande roue. J'ai très peur!

⭐2 L'école primaire vue par un enfant de dix ans

On a demandé aux enfants de l'école primaire de St-Valéry-sur-Somme d'écrire une rédaction sur les améliorations qu'ils voudraient apporter à leur école. Voici la rédaction de Mohamed, 10 ans. Il a de bonnes idées mais il n'est pas sûr de ses verbes. Aidez-le à choisir le bon verbe dans la case.

The children at St-Valéry-sur-Somme grade school have been asked to write an essay on the improvements that they would like to see made to their school. Here's the essay of Mohamed, 10 years old. He's got some good ideas, but he's not too sure of his verbs. Help him to choose the right verb from the box.

> Je voudrais que les maîtres **(1)** _____ moins sévères et
>
> que l'on **(2)** _____ plus de desserts à la cantine. J'aimerais que
>
> l'on **(3)** _____ l'anglais depuis l'école maternelle et que l'on
>
> **(4)** _____ des maîtres qui parlent bien l'anglais. Je voudrais que l'on
>
> **(5)** _____ du sport tous les jours et que l'on **(6)** _____
>
> en excursion tous les mois. J'aimerais qu' **(7)** _____ des cours
>
> spéciaux pour les enfants qui ne comprennent pas. Il faudrait que l'on
>
> **(8)** _____ des films vidéo sur les pays étrangers et que l'on nous
>
> **(9)** _____ à jouer d'un instrument de musique. Je préférerais que nous
>
> **(10)** _____ plus tôt le matin et que nous **(11)** _____
>
> de bonne heure le midi.

ait	aille	commencions	soient	il y ait	fasse
terminions	apprenne	voie	enseigne	serve	

⭐3 Projets de vacances

Claire et Alain Leclerc partent généralement en vacances avec leurs parents. C'est le mois de mai, et l'été arrive. Ils imaginent ce qu'ils vont faire au mois d'août. Mettez les verbes qui sont entre parenthèses au subjonctif.

Claire and Alain Leclerc usually go on vacation with their parents. It's May, and summer is coming. They are imagining what they are going to do in August. Put the verbs in parentheses into the present subjunctive.

—Qu'allons-nous faire de nos vacances?

—Il se peut que nous (aller) **(1)** _____ en Alsace comme d'habitude.

—Mais non, ce n'est pas possible que nous (loger) **(2)** _____ chez tante Yvonne, elle reçoit ses amis allemands.

—C'est vrai. Dans ce cas, il est possible que nous (rester) **(3)** _____ à la maison.

—Je pense que non. Il se peut que l'on (être) **(4)** _____ invité par mamy pour passer le mois d'août dans sa villa de St-Tropez. Ce serait chouette (*great! super!*)! Alors il est possible que l'on (se baigner) **(5)** _____ dans la Méditerranée, et que l'on (bronzer) **(6)** _____ et que l'on (voir) **(7)** _____ des personnes célèbres. Super!

—Attends un peu. Il est peu probable que papa et maman (être) **(8)** _____ d'accord pour aller dans un endroit à la mode. Alors il se peut qu'ils (décider) **(9)** _____ de rester à la maison et qu'ils nous (envoyer) **(10)** _____ par le train. Ce serait vraiment extra!

Partez!

⭐4 Que faut-il que nous fassions?

Voici quelques situations. Pensez à toutes les choses qu'il faut que vous fassiez!

Here are some situations. Think of all the things you must do!

Vous partez demain en vacances.
Vous cuisinez un gâteau.
Vous faites du babysitting chez des amis.
Vous avez un examen de français bientôt.

Exemples:

Il faut que nous fassions les valises.
Il faut que j'achète de la farine et du sucre.
Il faut que je m'occupe des deux enfants.
Il faut que j'apprenne bien les verbes!

_____

_____

_____

_____

_____

_____

⭐5 Quel frère!

Imaginez que le petit frère de votre correspondant(e) est un peu sauvage et qu'il y a un tas de choses que vous n'aimez pas qu'il fasse. Pensez à des choses que vous n'aimez pas et dites-le-lui!

Imagine that your pen pal's young brother is a bit wild and that there are lots of things that you don't like him doing. Tell him the things you don't like him to do.

Exemples:

Colin, je n'aime pas que tu mettes les pieds sur les fauteuils!
Colin, je voudrais que tu manges avec une fourchette et pas avec tes doigts!
Colin, je préfère que tu t'essuies la bouche avec ta serviette!

_____

_____

_____

_____

_____

⭐6 Dans la boule de cristal

Pour votre semaine de formation professionnelle en France, on vous a placé(e) chez une diseuse de bonne aventure. Elle vous laisse prédire le futur, mais vous en êtes moins sûr(e) qu'elle. Alors, vous qualifiez vos prédictions avec *il est possible que, il se peut que, il est peu probable que.* Inventez cinq prédictions pour votre camarade de classe.

For your week's work experience in France, you have been placed with a fortune teller. She lets you predict the future, but you are less confident than she is, so you qualify your predictions using *il est possible que, il se peut que, il est peu probable que.* Invent five predictions for your classmate.

Exemples:

Il est possible que tu voies une personnalité importante cette semaine.
Il est peu probable qu'elle vienne chez toi prendre un café.

_____

_____

_____

_____

_____

Verb Charts

40

1. The three conjugations (groups or "families") of regular verbs are listed with all their tense endings in full.

2. For all other verbs, the tenses which have standard endings for all forms (future and conditional, imperfect, *passé composé*) are simply given in the first-person singular (*je*) form.

3. The main irregularities which should be noted are highlighted in **bold print.**

4. Numbers in parentheses in the tense column headings refer to the chapter(s) in which that tense is explained in detail.

5. The infinitive, which is given in the shaded bar, is explained in detail in Chapter 31.

Regular verbs

	Present indicative (20)	Imperative (22)	Present participle (35)	Future (23)
-er verbs: *regarder* to look (at)				
je	regarde		regardant	regarderai
tu	regardes	regarde		regarderas
il/elle	regarde			regardera
nous	regardons	regardons		regarderons
vous	regardez	regardez		regarderez
ils/elles	regardent			regarderont
-ir verbs: *finir* to finish				
je	finis		finissant	finirai
tu	finis	finis		finiras
il/elle	finit			finira
nous	finissons	finissons		finirons
vous	finissez	finissez		finirez
ils/elles	finissent			finiront
-re verbs: *vendre* to sell				
je	vends		vendant	vendrai
tu	vends	vends		vendras
il/elle	vend			vendra
nous	vendons	vendons		vendrons
vous	vendez	vendez		vendrez
ils/elles	vendent			vendront

Otherwise regular -er verbs with spelling adjustments. **Only** the tenses to which the adjustments apply are listed. All other tenses are totally regular.

acheter *to buy*				
je	achète			achèterai
tu	achètes	achète		achèteras
il/elle	achète			achètera
nous	achetons	achetons		achèterons
vous	achetez	achetez		achèterez
ils/elles	achètent			achèteront

Also: amener, emmener, mener, (se) lever, se promener, peser.

Conditional (24)	**Imperfect** (25)	*Passé composé* (26, 27, 35)	*Passé simple* (29)	**Present subjunctive** (39)
regarderais	regardais	ai regardé	regardai	regarde
regarderais	regardais	as regardé	regardas	regardes
regarderait	regardait	a regardé	regarda	regarde
regarderions	regardions	avons regardé	regardâmes	regardions
regarderiez	regardiez	avez regardé	regardâtes	regardiez
regarderaient	regardaient	ont regardé	regardèrent	regardent
finirais	finissais	ai fini	finis	finisse
finirais	finissais	as fini	finis	finisses
finirait	finissait	a fini	finit	finisse
finirions	finissions	avons fini	finîmes	finissions
finiriez	finissiez	avez fini	finîtes	finissiez
finiraient	finissaient	ont fini	finirent	finissent
vendrais	vendais	ai vendu	vendis	vende
vendrais	vendais	as vendu	vendis	vendes
vendrait	vendait	a vendu	vendit	vende
vendrions	vendions	avons vendu	vendîmes	vendions
vendriez	vendiez	avez vendu	vendîtes	vendiez
vendraient	vendaient	ont vendu	vendirent	vendent
achèterais				
achèterais				
achèterait				
achèterions				
achèteriez				
achèteraient				

	Present indicative (20)	Imperative (22)	Present participle (35)	Future (23)
espérer *to hope*				
je	espère			
tu	espères	espère		
il/elle	espère			
nous	espérons	espérons		
vous	espérez	espérez		
ils/elles	espèrent			

Also: s'inquiéter, préférer, protéger, répéter, (se) sécher.

	Present indicative (20)	Imperative (22)	Present participle (35)	Future (23)
employer *to use*				
je	emploie			emploierai
tu	emploies	emploie		emploieras
il/elle	emploie			emploiera
nous	employons	employons		emploierons
vous	employez	employez		emploierez
ils/elles	emploient			emploieront

Also: appuyer, envoyer (*irregular future, see below*), essuyer, nettoyer, se noyer. *In verbs with* -ay- *the change to* -ai- *is optional:* essayer, payer, *etc.*

	Present indicative (20)	Imperative (22)	Present participle (35)	Future (23)
appeler *to call*				
je	appelle			appellerai
tu	appelles	appelle		appelleras
il/elle	appelle			appellera
nous	appelons	appelons		appellerons
vous	appelez	appelez		appellerez
ils/elles	appellent			appelleront

	Present indicative (20)	Imperative (22)	Present participle (35)	Future (23)
jeter *to throw*				
je	jette			jetterai
tu	jettes	jette		jetteras
il/elle	jette			jettera
nous	jetons	jetons		jetterons
vous	jetez	jetez		jetterez
ils/elles	jettent			jetteront

Conditional (24)	Imperfect (25)	*Passé composé* (26, 27, 35)	*Passé simple* (29)	Present subjunctive (39)
emploierais				emploie
emploierais				emploies
emploierait				emploie
emploierons				employions
emploieriez				employiez
emploieraient				emploient
appellerais				appelle
appellerais				appelles
appellerait				appelle
appellerions				appelions
appelleriez				appeliez
appelleraient				appellent
jetterais				jette
jetterais				jettes
jetterait				jette
jetterions				jetions
jetteriez				jetiez
jetteraient				jettent

	Present indicative (20)	Imperative (22)	Present participle (35)	Future (23)
manger to eat				
je	mange		mangeant	
tu	manges	mange		
il/elle	mange			
nous	mangeons	mangeons		
vous	mangez	mangez		
ils/elles	mangent			

Also: All -er verbs with stem ending in -g-.

lancer to throw				
je	lance		lançant	
tu	lances	lance		
il/elle	lance			
nous	lançons	lançons		
vous	lancez	lancez		
ils/elles	lancent			

Also: All -er verbs with stem ending in -c-.

Irregular verbs (groups of verbs)

ouvrir to open				
je	**ouvre**		**ouvrant**	
tu	**ouvres**	**ouvre**		
il/elle	**ouvre**			
nous	**ouvrons**	**ouvrons**		
vous	**ouvrez**	**ouvrez**		
ils/elles	**ouvrent**			

Also: accueillir, couvrir, découvrir, offrir, souffrir.

sortir to go out				
je	**sors**		**sortant**	
tu	**sors**	**sors**		
il/elle	**sort**			
nous	**sortons**	**sortons**		
vous	**sortez**	**sortez**		
ils/elles	**sortent**			

Also: courir, dormir, s'endormir, mentir, partir, sentir, servir.

Conditional (24)	Imperfect (25)	Passé composé (26, 27, 35)	Passé simple (29)	Present subjunctive (39)
	mangeais		mangeai	
	mangeais		mangeas	
	mangeait		mangea	
	mangions		mangeâmes	
	mangiez		mangeâtes	
	mangeaient		mangèrent	
	lançais		lançai	
	lançais		lanças	
	lançait		lança	
	lancions		lançâmes	
	lanciez		lançâtes	
	lançaient		lancèrent	

		ai **ouvert**	ouvris	**ouvre**
				ouvres
				ouvre
				ouvrions
				ouvriez
				ouvrent
		suis sorti(e)*		**sorte**
				sortes
				sorte
				sortions
				sortiez
				sortent

*Sortir, partir, s'endormir *take* être, *the others* avoir.

	Present indicative (20)	Imperative (22)	Present participle (35)	Future (23)
peindre to paint				
je	**peins**		**peignant**	
tu	**peins**	**peins**		
il/elle	**peint**			
nous	**peignons**	**peignons**		
vous	**peignez**	**peignez**		
ils/elles	**peignent**			
Also: craindre, éteindre, joindre.				
conduire to drive				
je	**conduis**		**conduisant**	
tu	**conduis**	**conduis**		
il/elle	**conduit**			
nous	**conduisons**	**conduisons**		
vous	**conduisez**	**conduisez**		
ils/elles	**conduisent**			
Also: traduire, produire, détruire.				

Individual irregular verbs

aller to go				
je	**vais**		allant	**irai**
tu	**vas**	**va** (*but* **vas-y**)		
il/elle	**va**			
nous	**allons**	**allons**		
vous	**allez**	**allez**		
ils/elles	**vont**			
s'asseoir to sit down				
je	**m'assieds**		**s'asseyant**	**m'assiérai**
tu	**t'assieds**	**assieds-toi**		
il/elle	**s'assied**			
nous	**nous asseyons**	**asseyons-nous**		
vous	**vous asseyez**	**asseyez-vous**		
ils/elles	**s'asseyent**			

Conditional (24)	Imperfect (25)	*Passé composé* (26, 27, 35)	*Passé simple* (29)	Present subjunctive (39)
	peignais	ai **peint**	**peignis**	**peigne** **peignes** **peigne** **peignions** **peigniez** **peignent**
	conduisais	ai **conduit**	**conduisis**	**conduise** **conduises** **conduise** **conduisions** **conduisiez** **conduisent**

irais	allais	suis allé(e)	allai (*as reg.* -er)	**aille** **ailles** **aille** **allions** **alliez** **aillent**
m'assiérais	**m'asseyais**	me suis **assis(e)**	**m'assis**	**m'asseye** **t'asseyes** **s'asseye** **nous asseyions** **vous asseyiez** **s'asseyent**

	Present indicative (20)	Imperative (22)	Present participle (35)	Future (23)
***avoir** to have*				
je	ai		ayant	aurai
tu	as	aie		
il/elle	a			
nous	avons	ayons		
vous	avez	ayez		
ils/elles	ont			
***boire** to drink*				
je	bois		buvant	boirai
tu	bois	bois		
il/elle	boit			
nous	buvons	buvons		
vous	buvez	buvez		
ils/elles	boivent			
***connaître** to know*				
je	connais		connaissant	connaîtrai
tu	connais	connais		
il/elle	connaît			
nous	connaissons	connaissons		
vous	connaissez	connaissez		
ils/elles	connaissent			

Also: reconnaître, paraître, apparaître.

	Present indicative (20)	Imperative (22)	Present participle (35)	Future (23)
***coudre** to sew*				
je	couds		cousant	coudrai
tu	couds	couds		
il/elle	coud			
nous	cousons	cousons		
vous	cousez	cousez		
ils/elles	cousent			
***courir** to run*				
je	cours		courant	courrai
tu	cours	cours		
il/elle	court			
nous	courons	courons		
vous	courez	courez		
ils/elles	courent			

Conditional (24)	Imperfect (25)	*Passé composé* (26, 27, 35)	*Passé simple* (29)	Present subjunctive (39)
aurais	avais	ai **eu**	**eus**	**aie** **aies** **ait** **ayons** **ayez** **aient**
boirais	**buvais**	ai **bu**	**bus**	**boive** **boives** **boive** **buvions** **buviez** **boivent**
connaîtrais	**connaissais**	ai **connu**	**connus**	**connaisse** **connaisses** **connaisse** **connaissions** **connaissiez** **connaissent**
coudrais	**cousais**	ai **cousu**	**cousis**	**couse** **couses** **couse** **cousions** **cousiez** **cousent**
courrais	**courais**	ai **couru**	**courus**	**coure** **coures** **coure** **courions** **couriez** **courent**

	Present indicative (20)	Imperative (22)	Present participle (35)	Future (23)
croire to think, believe				
je	**crois**		**croyant**	croirai
tu	**crois**	**crois**		
il/elle	**croit**			
nous	**croyons**	**croyons**		
vous	**croyez**	**croyez**		
ils/elles	**croient**			
devoir to have to, must, ought; owe				
je	**dois**		**devant**	**devrai**
tu	**dois**	**dois**		
il/elle	**doit**			
nous	**devons**	**devons**		
vous	**devez**	**devez**		
ils/elles	**doivent**			
dire to say, tell				
je	**dis**		**disant**	dirai
tu	**dis**	**dis**		
il/elle	**dit**			
nous	**disons**	**disons**		
vous	**dites**	**dites**		
ils/elles	**disent**			
écrire to write				
je	**écris**		**écrivant**	écrirai
tu	**écris**	**écris**		
il/elle	**écrit**			
nous	**écrivons**	**écrivons**		
vous	**écrivez**	**écrivez**		
ils/elles	**écrivent**			
envoyer to send				
je	**envoie**		envoyant	**enverrai**
tu	**envoies**	**envoie**		
il/elle	**envoie**			
nous	envoyons	envoyons		
vous	envoyez	envoyez		
ils/elles	**envoient**			

Conditional (24)	Imperfect (25)	*Passé composé* (26, 27, 35)	*Passé simple* (29)	Present subjunctive (39)
croirais	**croyais**	ai **cru**	**crus**	**croie** **croies** **croie** **croyions** **croyiez** **croient**
devrais	**devais**	ai **dû**	**dus**	**doive** **doives** **doive** **devions** **deviez** **doivent**
dirais	**disais**	ai **dit**	**dis**	**dise** **dises** **dise** **disions** **disiez** **disent**
écrirais	**écrivais**	ai **écrit**	**écrivis**	**écrive** **écrives** **écrive** **écrivions** **écriviez** **écrivent**
enverrais	envoyais	ai envoyé	envoyai (*as reg.* -er)	**envoie** **envoies** **envoie** envoyions envoyiez **envoient**

	Present indicative (20)	Imperative (22)	Present participle (35)	Future (23)
être *to be*				
je	**suis**		**étant**	**serai**
tu	**es**	**sois**		
il/elle	**est**			
nous	**sommes**	**soyons**		
vous	**êtes**	**soyez**		
ils/elles	**sont**			
faire *to do, make*				
je	**fais**		**faisant**	**ferai**
tu	**fais**	**fais**		
il/elle	**fait**			
nous	**faisons**	**faisons**		
vous	**faites**	**faites**		
ils/elles	**font**			
falloir *to be necessary*				
il	**faut**			**faudra**
	(*third-person singular only*)			
lire *to read*				
je	**lis**		**lisant**	lirai
tu	**lis**	**lis**		
il/elle	**lit**			
nous	**lisons**	**lisons**		
vous	**lisez**	**lisez**		
ils/elles	**lisent**			
mettre *to put*				
je	**mets**		mettant	mettrai
tu	**mets**	**mets**		
il/elle	**met**			
nous	**mettons**	**mettons**		
vous	**mettez**	**mettez**		
ils/elles	**mettent**			
Also: promettre, remettre.				

Conditional (24)	**Imperfect** (25)	*Passé composé* (26, 27, 35)	*Passé simple* (29)	**Present subjunctive** (39)
serais	**étais**	ai **été**	**fus**	**sois** **sois** **soit** **soyons** **soyez** **soient**
ferais	**faisais**	ai **fait**	**fis**	**fasse** **fasses** **fasse** **fassions** **fassiez** **fassent**
faudrait	**fallait**	a **fallu**	**fallut**	**faille**
lirais	**lisais**	ai **lu**	**lus**	**lise** **lises** **lise** **lisions** **lisiez** **lisent**
mettrais	mettais	ai **mis**	**mis**	**mette** **mettes** **mette** **mettions** **mettiez** **mettent**

	Present indicative (20)	Imperative (22)	Present participle (35)	Future (23)
***mourir** to die*				
je	**meurs**		**mourant**	**mourrai**
tu	**meurs**	**meurs**		
il/elle	**meurt**			
nous	**mourons**	**mourons**		
vous	**mourez**	**mourez**		
ils/elles	**meurent**			
***naître** to be born*				
je	**nais**		naissant	naîtrai
tu	**nais**	(*no imperative*)		
il/elle	**naît**			
nous	**naissons**			
vous	**naissez**			
ils/elles	**naissent**			
***pleuvoir** to rain*				
il	**pleut**		**pleuvant**	**pleuvra**
	(*third-person singular only*)			
***pouvoir** to be able, can*				
je	**peux** (*but* **puis-je?**)		pouvant	**pourrai**
tu	**peux**	(*no imperative*)		
il/elle	**peut**			
nous	**pouvons**			
vous	**pouvez**			
ils/elles	**peuvent**			
***prendre** to take*				
je	prends		**prenant**	prendrai
tu	prends	prends		
il/elle	prend			
nous	**prenons**	**prenons**		
vous	**prenez**	**prenez**		
ils/elles	**prennent**			

Also: apprendre, comprendre, reprendre.

Conditional (24)	Imperfect (25)	*Passé composé* (26, 27, 35)	*Passé simple* (29)	Present subjunctive (39)
mourrais	**mourais**	suis **mort(e)**	**mourus**	**meure** **meures** **meure** **mourions** **mouriez** **meurent**
naîtrais	**naissais**	suis **né(e)**	**naquis**	**naisse** **naisses** **naisse** **naissions** **naissiez** **naissent**
pleuvrait	**pleuvait**	a **plu**	**plut**	**pleuve**
pourrais	**pouvais**	ai **pu**	**pus**	**puisse** **puisses** **puisse** **puissions** **puissiez** **puissent**
prendrais	**prenais**	ai **pris**	**pris**	**prenne** **prennes** **prenne** **prenions** **preniez** **prennent**

	Present indicative (20)	Imperative (22)	Present participle (35)	Future (23)
recevoir *to receive*				
je	**reçois**		**recevant**	**recevrai**
tu	**reçois**	**reçois**		
il/elle	**reçoit**			
nous	**recevons**	**recevons**		
vous	**recevez**	**recevez**		
ils/elles	**reçoivent**			
Also: apercevoir, s'apercevoir, décevoir.				
rire *to laugh*				
je	**ris**		**riant**	rirai
tu	**ris**	**ris**		
il/elle	**rit**			
nous	**rions**	**rions**		
vous	**riez**	**riez**		
ils/elles	**rient**			
Also: sourire.				
savoir *to know*				
je	**sais**		**sachant**	**saurai**
tu	**sais**	**sache**		
il/elle	**sait**			
nous	**savons**	**sachons**		
vous	**savez**	**sachez**		
ils/elles	**savent**			
suivre *to follow*				
je	**suis**		suivant	suivrai
tu	**suis**	**suis**		
il/elle	**suit**			
nous	suivons	suivons		
vous	suivez	suivez		
ils/elles	suivent			
Also: poursuivre.				

Conditional (24)	Imperfect (25)	*Passé composé* (26, 27, 35)	*Passé simple* (29)	Present subjunctive (39)
recevrais	**recevais**	ai **reçu**	**reçus**	**reçoive** **reçoives** **reçoive** **recevions** **receviez** **reçoivent**
rirais	**riais**	ai **ri**	ris	**rie** **ries** **rie** **riions** **riiez** **rient**
saurais	**savais**	ai **su**	sus	**sache** **saches** **sache** **sachions** **sachiez** **sachent**
suivrais	suivais	ai **suivi**	suivis	suive suives suive suivions suiviez suivent

	Present indicative (20)	Imperative (22)	Present participle (35)	Future (23)
tenir to hold				
je	**tiens**		**tenant**	**tiendrai**
tu	**tiens**	**tiens**		
il/elle	**tient**			
nous	**tenons**	**tenons**		
vous	**tenez**	**tenez**		
ils/elles	**tiennent**			

Also: contenir, retenir.

venir to come				
je	**viens**		**venant**	**viendrai**
tu	**viens**	**viens**		
il/elle	**vient**			
nous	**venons**	**venons**		
vous	**venez**	**venez**		
ils/elles	**viennent**			

Also: devenir, revenir, se souvenir.

vivre to live				
je	**vis**		vivant	vivrai
tu	**vis**	**vis**		
il/elle	**vit**			
nous	vivons	vivons		
vous	vivez	vivez		
ils/elles	vivent			

voir to see				
je	**vois**		**voyant**	**verrai**
tu	**vois**	**vois**		
il/elle	**voit**			
nous	**voyons**	**voyons**		
vous	**voyez**	**voyez**		
ils/elles	**voient**			

vouloir to want, wish				
je	**veux**		voulant	**voudrai**
tu	**veux**			
il/elle	**veut**			
nous	**voulons**			
vous	**voulez**	**veuillez***		
ils/elles	**veulent**			

*There is normally no imperative, but veuillez + *infinitive is used in the sense of "be kind enough to . . .":* Veuillez répondre tout de suite. *Please reply immediately.*

Conditional (24)	Imperfect (25)	*Passé composé* (26, 27, 35)	*Passé simple* (29)	Present subjunctive (39)
tiendrais	**tenais**	ai **tenu**	**tins**	**tienne** **tiennes** **tienne** **tenions** **teniez** **tiennent**
viendrais	**venais**	suis **venu(e)**	**vins**	**vienne** **viennes** **vienne** **venions** **veniez** **viennent**
vivrais	vivais	ai **vécu**	**vécus**	vive vives vive vivions viviez vivent
verrais	**voyais**	ai **vu**	**vis**	**voie** **voies** **voie** **voyions** **voyiez** **voient**
voudrais	**voulais**	ai **voulu**	**voulus**	**veuille** **veuilles** **veuille** **voulions** **vouliez** **veuillent**